Interrogating the Relations between Migration and Education in the South

Migrating Americas

Adopting a uniquely critical lens, this volume analyzes the relationship between forced migration, the migrations of people, and subsequent impacts on education. In doing so, it challenges Euro-modern and colonial notions of what it means to move across 'borders.'

Using Abiayala and its diasporas as theory and context, this volume critiques dominant colonial attitudes and discourses towards migration and education and suggests alternatives for understanding how culturally grounded pedagogies and curricula can support migrating youth and society more broadly. Chapters use case studies and first-hand accounts such as testimonios from a variety of countries in the South, and discuss the lived experiences of Afro-Colombian, Haitian, and Indigenous youth, among others, to challenge the rigid disciplinary borders upheld by Euro-modern epistemologies.

This text will benefit researchers, academics, and educators with an interest in international and comparative education, multicultural education, and Latin American and Caribbean studies more broadly. Those specifically interested in anticolonial education, diaspora studies, and educational policy and politics will also benefit from this book.

Ligia (Licho) López López is Senior Lecturer at Melbourne Graduate School of Education, University of Melbourne Australia.

Ivón Cepeda-Mayorga is Senior Researcher and Lecturer at the School of Humanities and Education at the Tecnológico de Monterrey, Mexico.

María Emilia Tijoux is a sociologist, professor, and researcher from the Department of Sociology in the Faculty of Social Sciences at the Universidad de Chile, Chile.

Routledge Research in Decolonizing Education

The *Routledge Research in Decolonizing Education* series aims to enhance our understanding and facilitate ongoing debates, research, and theory relating to decolonization, decolonizing education and the curriculum, and postcolonialism in education. The series is international in scope and is aimed at upper-level and post-graduate students, researchers, and research students, as well as academics and scholars.

Books in the series include:

Decolonizing Transcultural Teacher Education through Participatory Action Research
Dialogue, Culture, and Identity
Jean Kirshner and George Kamberelis

Global South Scholars in the Western Academy
Harnessing Unique Experiences, Knowledges, and Positionality in the Third Space
Edited by Staci B. Martin and Deepra Dandekar

Interrogating the Relations between Migration and Education in the South
Migrating Americas
Edited by Ligia (Licho) López López, Ivón Cepeda-Mayorga, and María Emilia Tijoux

For more information about the series, please visit www.routledge.com/Routledge-Research-in-Decolonizing-Education/book-series/RRDE

Interrogating the Relations between Migration and Education in the South

Migrating Americas

Edited by Ligia (Licho) López López, Ivón Cepeda-Mayorga, and María Emilia Tijoux

NEW YORK AND LONDON

First published 2022
by Routledge
605 Third Avenue, New York, NY 10158

and by Routledge
2 Park Square, Milton Park, Abingdon, Oxon, OX14 4RN

Routledge is an imprint of the Taylor & Francis Group, an informa business

© 2022 selection and editorial matter, Ligia (Licho) López López, Ivón Cepeda-Mayorga, and María Emilia Tijoux; individual chapters, the contributors

The right of Ligia (Licho) López López, Ivón Cepeda-Mayorga, and María Emilia Tijoux to be identified as the authors of the editorial material, and of the authors for their individual chapters, has been asserted in accordance with sections 77 and 78 of the Copyright, Designs and Patents Act 1988.

All rights reserved. No part of this book may be reprinted or reproduced or utilised in any form or by any electronic, mechanical, or other means, now known or hereafter invented, including photocopying and recording, or in any information storage or retrieval system, without permission in writing from the publishers.

Trademark notice: Product or corporate names may be trademarks or registered trademarks, and are used only for identification and explanation without intent to infringe.

Library of Congress Cataloging-in-Publication Data
A catalog record for this title has been requested

ISBN: 9780367547578 (hbk)
ISBN: 9781032147598 (pbk)
ISBN: 9781003090519 (ebk)

DOI: 10.4324/9781003090519

Typeset in Sabon
by KnowledgeWorks Global Ltd.

For all fellow peoples of Abiayala,
who are crossing borders today

searching for a habitable place
in this ever-hostile world

Ligia, Ivón, and María Emilia

Contents

List of Figures ix
About the Editors and Contributors x
Acknowledgements xiii

The Beautiful Black Girl: Abiayala, Young People, and Movement 1
LIGIA (LICHO) LÓPEZ LÓPEZ AND MARÍA EMILIA TIJOUX

1 Exploring Afro Colombian English Learners' Identities through a Critical Intercultural Approach: Transforming Journeys 17
MAURE AGUIRRE ORTEGA

2 The New 'Others' in Schools and the Regimes that Order Them: Re-production of Institutionalized School Practices in Chile in the 21st Century 36
CLAUDIA CARRILLO-SÁNCHEZ

3 Indigenous Mexican Migrant Youth School Testimonios in the Florida Heartland: Farmwork, Migration, Language, Discrimination, and Extracurricular Activities 59
YENNY SALDAÑA, MARIANA SANTIAGO, ANA GUEVARA, LILIANA MATA, EDUARDO MORALES, BRIANA SALAZAR, CRISTINA SALDAÑA, ADOLFO SALDAÑA, AND REBECCA CAMPBELL-MONTALVO

4 Migration, Betterment, and Modernity: Encounters and Un-Encounters Between Mobility and Access to Education as Life Projects in Three Generations of Migrants from Loja, Ecuador 79
MARÍA MERCEDES EGUIGUREN

5 Indigenous Women of Chiapas Migrating: Transformation and Education 98
IRASEMA VILLANUEVA AND MARÍA ELENA TOVAR

6 Forced Migration, Violence, Education, and Testimony: For a Place in the World 117
MIGUEL ANGEL MARTÍNEZ MARTÍNEZ

Conclusion. The Relevance of the Body and Emotions in the Care for Migrating People: Experiences of Abiayala 136
IVÓN CEPEDA-MAYORGA AND MARÍA EMILIA TIJOUX

Index 158

Figures

2.1 Take a stand against racism 47
2.2 Two-handed performance 48
2.3 Empowerment and appropriation of Afro-Black aesthetics 49

About the Editors and Contributors

Maure Aguirre is a foreign language teacher, educator and researcher at *Grupo de Investigación Acción y Evaluación en Lenguas Extranjeras GIAE*, School of Languages, Universidad de Antioquia, in Medellín-Colombia. She is currently working on different projects within Critical Language Education. Her academic interests include identity of language learners, critical interculturality, teacher education, and critical perspectives on language and culture.

Rebecca Campbell-Montalvo holds a Ph.D. in Applied Anthropology and is a Postdoctoral Research Associate in the Department of Curriculum and Instruction in the Neag School of Education at the University of Connecticut. She researches K-12 resource access for linguistic, racial, ethnic, and migrant groups, as well as STEM equity for undergraduate women, underrepresented groups, and sexual and gender minority students.

Claudia Carrillo-Sánchez holds a Ph.D. in Social Sciences. Her lines of research include human migrations, racism, racialization-sexualization, socio-educational inequalities, bodies, and emotions. She has served as a researcher on numerous projects including ECOS-CONICYT 170030 (2021–2018), housed at University of Chile and the Institut Interdisciplinaire d'anthropologie du Contemporain, EHESS Cnrs Paris/France and the INCASI Project in the H2020-MSCA-RISE-2015 Program.

Ivón Cepeda-Mayorga holds a Ph.D. in Humanistic Studies with an emphasis on ethics. She is a senior researcher and lecturer at the School of Humanities and Education at the Tecnologico de Monterrey in Mexico City. Her research addresses questions of dignity, violence, peace studies and the philosophy of limits.

María Mercedes Eguiguren holds a Ph.D. in Political and Social Sciences and is an Associate Professor at the Central University of Ecuador. She works in the field of migration studies, with a focus on the relationships between mobility, socio-spatial inequalities, and the subjective experience of migration.

Ana Guevara lives in Florida and is a sales associate in the retail industry. She works full-time and is studying part-time at her local community college.

Ligia (Licho) López is Caribbean, Queer, and of Abiayala. She lives as an uninvited person on Wurundjeri-Woiwurung Countries. She is the author of *The making of Indigeneity, curriculum history, and the limits of diversity* (Routledge, 2018), and *Indigenous futures and learnings taking place* (with G. Coello. Routledge, 2021). Her work has also appeared in the *The British Journal of Sociology*, *Race ethnicity and Education*, and *Curriculum Inquiry* among others.

Miguel Angel Martínez Martínez holds a Ph.D. in Philosophy from Universidad Nacional de Mexico (UNAM). He is a professor at Tecnológico de Monterrey Campus Puebla, Mexico and a member of the National System of Researchers. His research addresses serious human rights violations.

Liliana Mata migrates with her family each year for farmwork. She is a 2021 high school graduate, despite all the obstacles COVID-19 put in her way.

Eduardo Morales grew up helping his family with farmwork to help them financially. He loves to cook and is currently working at a Mexican store as a butcher.

Briana Salazar was born in the US and is a first-generation child to immigrant parents. She feels they are the reason she will succeed in life.

Adolfo Saldaña is a full-time high school student in Florida. He enjoys reading, especially the works of Rick Riordan.

Cristina Saldaña will be a high school senior in the 2021–2022 school year. She spends her free time reading and painting.

Yenny Saldaña was born in México and was raised in the US and has first-hand experience with the treatment of immigrants and their children. She works full-time as a Packing Specialist for a pharmaceutical manufacturing company.

Mariana Santiago was born in the US into a wonderful family. As a child of an immigrant, she always dreamed of making her parents proud and continues to strive for success.

María Emilia Tijoux holds a Ph.D. in Sociology from Paris VIII. She is a professor of sociology at *Universidad de Chile* where she coordinates the Center for Racism and Contemporary Migration. Her research engages with the everyday life of migrants in Chile and the difficulties they face when they arrive in the country.

María Elena Tovar Gonzalez holds a Ph.D. in Latin American Studies from the Universidad Nacional de Mexico (UNAM). She was the Rector of *Universidad de Ciencias y Artes de Chiapas* (UNICACH) from 2002 to 2006. Dr. Tovar Gonzalez is a History professor at UNICACH and the Tecnológico de Monterrey. Her books include: Inquisitorial judgments in the XVIII century, 1988; The political-social structure of Mexico in the XIX century, 1990; Farmers foreigners in the Soconusco, 2006; Chiapas in the Constitutional Congress in 1917, 2018.

Irasema Villanueva holds a Master degree in Human Rights Defense from Universidad Autónoma de Chiapas, Mexico, where she leads workshops on gender equity in Mexico. Her latest publication *Los derechos de las niñas, niños y adolescentes en el marco constitucional de Chiapas* [The children's rights in the Chiapas Constitutional Framework] appeared in *El constitucionalismo chiapaneco* [Chiapanec constitutionalism], Porrúa, Mexico, 2018.

Acknowledgements

What is movement without *la tierra* (the Earth)? Earth is where we begin the wonderous journeys in this edited collection. We acknowledge the Lands *of* which we are and which make our work possible: Abiayala, the Wallmapu, the Tlali Nantli, the Pachamama Nepantla, Xihmai, the Sinú, its riverbanks and the Caribbean coast. Wurunjeri-Woiwurrung Countries and their elders have been looking after the lands from which Ligia writes in collaboration with María Emilia, Ivón and the contributors to this volume. The contributors, their labor, their relations with other people in migration and schooling contexts, their relations with other beings, human and more-than-human, take place in Abiayala, Turtle Island, and in movement. The lives of the peoples storied in this collection of chapters begins, in many cases, centuries back in Africa via the Atlantic, and in Abiayala itself, in places known by other names. These lands are storied geographies replete with tales of Earth sounds. The collective of stories, systematically registered here as research, is indebted to the narrative composition of the continent. The work in this volume is part of that composition and without it, it would simply be inexistent. Our most sincere gratitude to our ancestors for rebelling and defending the Land and its futures. In their rebellion is where this work emerges as a contribution to the continuous *lucha*.

We acknowledge the lives and journeys of survival of the many young people whose accounts make these chapters and the volume. Their participation in the research inquiries documented here are possibilities for forming societies more attuned to life flourishing through migration and movement in and through education. They gave us profound insights of the unresolved challenges of the Abiayala, but they also compel us to look for alternative paths for the recognition and engagement of migrating peoples, and other ways to consider educational practices under multiple contextual pressures. We acknowledge them and their passage through these pages. We recognize that while acknowledgement may be significant, it remains insufficient to the life struggles that exceed these pages.

Writing in these pandemic times has often meant isolation, desolation, and indignation. We would like to express our sincere gratitude and recognition to all the contributors in this volume, and those who engaged with it and are not here. We thank them for their companionship, their persistent commitment, their *fuerza de hechar pa' adelante* even when the virus relentlessly devastated their/our communities. Their patience and dedication despite the uncertainty of these times and the multiple pauses and restarts is unmatched. Their work has given us, as we hope is the case for many, the opportunity to consider *and be with* migrating peoples, and their struggles in educational contexts. Their writings offer us an invaluable opportunity to learn and reflect upon words and thoughts raised by the voices of Abiayala. Attempting to shift the geography of reason in an ever-colonizing academia, to think with concepts of Abiayala, and to do so in translation from vernacular linguistic forms to the English language, was an arduous and time-soaking task. Thank you for remaining part of it every step of the way.

And now to their families. Even when writing appears as though it were a solitary task, we understand that the work on these pages is also possible due to the support and accompaniment of the people and families around each author. Our gratitude also goes to those beloved ones who supported and sustained each author during this writing labor.

The learning process in producing this volume would be incomplete without the dedication of the various reviewers across the world who by saying yes, entered the conversations the book hopes to initiate. Mil gracias a Armando Muyolema, Claudia Zapata, Luz Graciela Castillo, Pedro Lebrón Ortíz, David Barillas, Adela Cedillo, Alberto Ortíz, Freyca Calderon, Julia Suarez-Krabb, María Concepción Castillo González, Itzel Barrera de Diego, Esther Ohito, Daniel Friedrich, Samuel Rocha, and Sarah Truman. Your insightful, generous, and kind readings, a rarity and an extraordinary gift, enriched the work in each chapter and us all in the process. Working with multiple languages and in translation required the tactful craft that the many translators and thinkers of language gifted this project. We thank all the translators who worked with each author to ensure that their ideas were expressed in the best possible way: David Korfhagen, Ana Luisa Sánchez Hernández, Karina Bailey, Miriam González Villanueva, Madeleine Arenivar, Jonathan Alexander Sierra Sánchez, and Andrés Augusto Ibarra Montenegro.

Finally and firstly, we thank our families and beloved ones for the patience and limitless support in this editorial and writing process. Ivon: Thanks to Dante who is always supporting me with love and care, and thank you Ivón and Pepe, who have always believed in my dreams. Your words inspire those dreams. Living and working in diaspora and under further foreclosed borders in the pandemic has meant that family had to work twice as hard to be there for us, virtually, intensely. Ligia: *Gracias* to María (Ciro), Francisco, Marcelino, Leandro, and Leonardo for all the care, shared virtual meals, storytelling, and belly-laughter. I thank abuelas Josefa and Basilia the most, for their way making and ancestral guidance. Their legacy of movement in making Abiayala is the bloodline of this work.

The Beautiful Black Girl
Abiayala, Young People, and Movement

Ligia (Licho) López López and María Emilia Tijoux

La Niña negra y el espejo/Black girl and the mirror

Vestida toda de azul[1]
aguarda una niña hermosa
que llegue el bus del colegio
y la lleve a la escuela.

Espera pacientemente
luego se pone de pie,
camina por el pasillo
de aquella casa tan fría
que hoy es nueva para ella.

A pocos pasos se encuentra
con un espejo colgado
que tiene un marco dorado.
Lo observa de arriba a abajo,
con toda curiosidad
se va acercando, despacio...
y va descubriendo en él,
la magia que este produce.

¡Abre sus ojos, sonríe!
y complacida descubre
su imagen de niña negra,
reflejada en el espejo.

Alza sus ojos al cielo feliz de reconocerse.
Arrugando su nariz hace un par de muecas más,

A beautiful girl
dressed all in blue waits
for the school bus to arrive
and take her to school.

She waits patiently
then stands up,
walks through the hallway
of that such cold house
that today is new to her.

A few steps away
she stumbles upon a hanging mirror
with a golden frame.
She analyzes it bottom to top,
with utmost curiosity.
she approaches it, slowly...
and starts discovering in it,
the magic it produces.

She opens her eyes, she smiles!
Pleased, she discovers
her image of a Black girl
reflected in the mirror.

She looks to the heavens happy to
recognize herself.
Wrinkling her nose she makes a
couple more faces,

y vuelve y se reconoce como una niña negra. Luego, pasa sus manos, y se toma la cabeza, tocándose su peinado, contemplándose sus trenzas, que van marcando caminos por todita su cabeza.	and returns to see herself as a Black girl. Then she runs her hands over her head, touching her hair, contemplating her braids that make little paths all over her head.
Se mira y se mira como para constatar que la imagen de aquel espejo es de ella de una niña hermosa una niña negra una pequeña guerrera con rasgos de una princesa.[2]	She looks at herself, and she looks at herself to confirm that the image on that mirror is hers of a beautiful girl a Black girl a young warrioress with traits of a princess.
Una voz fuerte la saca de la imagen del espejo, había llegado el bus para irse al colegio.	A loud voice takes her out of the image in the mirror, the bus had arrived to take her to school.
Caminó con rapidez, se sentó, cerró sus ojos, y comenzó a recordar la imagen de aquel espejo. Cuando llegó al colegio y se dirigió al salón, se dio cuenta que no había ninguna otra niña negra que fuera igual, como ella, y eso la entristeció.	She walked quickly, sat, closed her eyes, and began remembering the image in the mirror. When she arrived at school and headed to her classroom, she realized there were no other Black girls like her and that saddened her.
Las otras niñas la miran con mucha curiosidad, no faltó la que dijera, que era una niña rara, que era de otro color, que no era igual a ellas. Se revistió de poder y con voz firme les dijo: no soy niña de color. Yo soy una niña negra.	The other girls observe her with much curiosity; there was always the one to tell her she was a weird girl, that she was of a different color, that she was different from them. She gathered strength and in a firm voice she told them: I am not a colored girl. I am a Black girl.

De sol, luna, ríos, mar, manglares y esteros, nací en el litoral, me recibió una partera, y me han alimentado con lo que se da en mi tierra[3] me chumbaron[4] de bebe, y cada que me enfermaba me curaban mis abuelas con plantas medicinales que todavía conservan.	Of the sun, moon, rivers, sea, mangroves, and estuaries, I was born in the littoral, welcomed by a midwife, and I have been nourished with what my Land produces, I was swaddled as a baby, each time I was ill my grandmothers healed me with medicinal plants they still safeguard.
No soy niña de color. Yo, soy una niña negra, que hoy está en la capital desplazada por la guerra, que llegó a mi territorio y lo inundó de violencia, desplazándonos de todo, dispersando nuestra herencia que aún sigue resistiendo, los embates de esta guerra.	I am not a colored girl, I am a Black girl, that today is in the capital displaced by the war that arrived in my Land and flooded it with violence, stripping us of everything, dispersing our legacy, that continues to resist the blows of this war.

This poem is data, theory, philosophy, history, and Afrofuturism (Womack, 2013) constructed in a transborder collective. The poem is also so much more than this flat text can register. The words are a creation of Jenny Tenorio Caicedo (2020), an Afro-Colombian writer from Tumaco, Nariño, a town on the Pacific Coast of what is known today with the colonial name of Colombia (Tenorio Caicedo, 2019). The poem is lifted off the page across the Colombia-Ecuador border by Afrodiasporic young influencers @HermanosGonzalezHurtado Yakira & Kiano (on Facebook and YouTube). Their performance of the poem had 22,000 views on Facebook within a week of being posted. Yakira and Kiano make culture in and from Esmeraldas, a province on the Pacific coast of a place named, after European imaginary lines, Ecuador (López López & Coello, 2021). The character that emerges from Jenny's ink and Yakira and Kiano's voices is a 'beautiful Black girl' who, from her forced migratory lived experience, invokes the Ancestors to enact Black existentialism in school (Gordon, 1996). Jenny, Yakira, Kiano, the beautiful Black girl, and the Ancestors come together to produce theory of Abiayala (Wagua, 2007). In other words, this collective labor and phenomenological intelligence (Irobi, 2006) inscribed in the *Black girl and the mirror* poem is the theory that will guide this introduction to *Interrogating the Relations between Migration and Education in the South: Migrating Americas*. Poetry is theory. That is, theory as the modes of interpretation and meaning making (Gordon & Gordon, 2005) articulated in sound, words, words strung together, and in movement. The patterned and sound(less) rhythms engineered by maroons in flight produced interpretation, meaning, and the poetry of scape toward Black dignity. The accents that project the words into the cyber space, the rhythmic sounds of the words as they are strung together, the movement of the bodies in and through the *Black girl in the mirror* poem, although unregistered by the flatness of this written text, are constitutive of the poetry and the theory that ground this work. We begin with the poem to foreground Black epistemologies born in Abiayala. We begin with the poem to foreground Black culture makers, youth, and relationality with place to institute the political act within which this work is located.

This is a book about migrations of people and their (the people and the migrations) relationships with education. The orientation of this work by design defies familiar points of departure to invite the readers to think migration and education from other angles. This introduction is an attempt to forge less-familiar perspectives. Three elements make up this introductory work. In each of them, we present a sustaining element of the book—Land, youth, and movement. Combined, these three elements articulate a political project to the study of people migration and socialities of migration in Abiayala (the Lands from which the book and its chapters emerge) and its diasporas. In section one of this introductory chapter, we speak against the very title of the book and its coloniality in order to make room for Abiayala. We understand *Abiayala as theory* and what takes place in it as *theories of Abiayala*. This section, beyond a Land acknowledgement, is a situating of this work *in place*, and writing place into the multidisciplinary academic work that attempts to understand the phenomena of people migrating in relation to education. Instead of centering the discussion of education reinscribing coloniality as schooling, in section two we invoke the presence and importance of young people and their socialization through migration. We do so understanding young people as another key relational element in migration dynamics with social implications in the region. Section three is devoted to the movement of people as migration across space, time, and *sentimientos*. Without discounting the baring of geopolitical borders (within and outside of Nation States) on the educational lives of people, this section interrogates the taken-for-granted histories constitutive of Abiayala that far exceed border formations in recent history. A conceptual contribution of this section that returns to Abiayala as theory is *pueblear* as an act of people, in movement with one another, forming *pueblo*.

Abiayala as Theory, Theories of Abiayala

Abiayala: Abonosad Yala. Saved territory, preferred territory by Baba and Nana, and in an extended way can also mean mature land, land of blood. It refers to the American continent.

(Wagua, 2007, p. 165)

We have previously referred to the place colonially called 'Latin America' as Abiayala (Muyolema, 2001). Abiayala is *an* Indigenous way of understanding and naming the Lands from which the writings in this book emerge. The above definition appears in Guna historian Aiban Wagua's 2007 book *Así lo vi, así me lo contaron: Datos de la Revolución Guna de 1925, versión del Sagladummad Inakeliginya y de gunas que vivieron la revolución de 1925* [That's how I saw it, thus they told me: Data from the Guna revolution of 1925, a version from Sagladummad Inakeliginya and from Gunas that lived through the 1925 revolution]. As the title indicates, the book *is* and *makes* history of one of countless Indigenous struggles in the region. Chapter 5 invites us to connect with the rebellious struggles of Zoques, Tsotsil, and Tseltal Peoples for the protection of territories and lives against colonial forces. Struggles for the protection of Land against appropriation, extraction, and exploitation is foundational to Abiayala theories and Abiayala as theory.

This name of the Lands (Abiayala) is also born (in the wider public consciousness) out of struggle. In the late 1970s, one of the struggles the Guna[5] faced was against US business person Thomas M. Moodie's aggressive tourism campaign in Pidertupi Island, Guna territory (Keme & Coon, 2018). Besides halting Moody's neo-colonial project in defense of their territory and victoriously ousting him from Guna Yala, another important outcome was the defense of the continent in the act of renaming it as Abiayala. The Guna collaborated with Aymara leader Takir Mamani (Lima, 2015), entrusting them[6] with a part of their cosmogony such that the naming of the region was rectified. In meeting with other Indigenous peoples on the continent, Mamani started spreading the word from the late 1970s. Various Indigenous Peoples in the North and South of Abiayala have to date welcomed and adopted the name. In the process, otherwise ways of relating to the Land and place went beyond the use of an imposed colonial name (Latin America) derived from an Indo-European language (Latin) and a colonizer's name (Americo Vespucci). This epistemological shift proposed by the Guna and taken up by other Peoples of Abiayala dislodges what in Armando Muyolema's analysis (2001) is the always supposed colonial policy of naming. For Muyolema (p. 328) '*nombrar es luchar*' [naming is struggling], and naming as an act of restoring place beyond taking by humans is constitutive of Abiayala theories and Abiayala as theory.

While Abiayala has been known to many of us as such for over four decades now, for the Guna, Abiayala *has existed* for longer than can be told in colonial chronological time. Importantly, Abiayala is but one way of naming/understanding this Land. While various Indigenous Peoples of this region employ Abiayala to name the continent, there are infinite Indigenous ways of understanding and naming the place *of* which one is. As an anticolonial struggle of the Peoples of these Lands, Abiayala is an opening to connect with the multiplicity of the region without blending, against all assimilation, the multiple histories inhabiting the Lands, waters, and skies of the region. Being of place, of Land, of *pueblo* is Abiayala theory in the nonseparation of Land from people. That separation is one of many failed colonial attempts to take place in the lives of the peoples of Abiayala. As with the poem of the beautiful Black girl, Abiayala is a collective trans-border creation against all border impositions, it is one made in movement across time and borderlines, by people carrying a message, a name, a cosmogony. Abiayala is a transborder creation infused, enriched, and co-designed (to use a common term of these days), with the memories, knowledges, and philosophies of African diasporic peoples. Black Afro-descendants imbue Abiayala with meaning, spirituality, and rich and complex modes of being that configure the very life of the continent.

In Guna cosmogony, as it is available at the current moment and as we are able to register it at present, there are four moments in the history of Earth. Gwalagunyala is a first moment of creation after which the Earth is hit by cyclones. Dagargunyala is a moment of chaos, disease, and fear that culminates in darkness. Dinguayala is a moment where Earth is swept by fire. Abiayala *is the moment of mature land, land of blood, saved land, land loved and preferred by Baba and Nana* (Keme & Coon, 2018). As mature Land and Land saved, Abiayala defies the scientific colonial logic of development and the salvific discourses orienting the gaze over the region (Escobar, 2008, 2011). This defiance deems developmentalism (*el desarrollismo*) and salvation superfluous in Abiayala. The people and the more-than-people beings in the continent are already mature and saved. They/we have been mature and saved outside Euro-defined timelines, where 1492 only marks the discovery of European ignorance of mature worlds of incalculable magnitude. In Guna cosmogony, *we have reached full maturity*. As Land already saved, *we are not in need of salvation by other people's gods*. We are already preferred, loved, and looked after by Baba and Nana, the creators of Abiayala, our creators.

Baba and Nana care for us as the grandmothers look after the beautiful Black girl in the poem, as the midwife ensures her Black existence when the Black girl comes into the world. That care for and continuation of Black lives is Abiayala theory. The maturity of the continent is written in the Black girl's relationality with the sea, river, mangroves, sun, and estuaries in how those elements are not external to the Black girl but are in entanglement with the girl. The maturity of the continent is evident in the beautiful Black girl's food literacy and affirmed knowledge of how the girl is sustained with what Earth births in the Land of which the Black girl is. The maturity of the continent is registered in the beautiful Black girls' medicinal knowledge and on the preservation by the grandmothers of the lives of the medicinal plants that in turn preserve people's lives. That is the saved phenomenology of Abiayala. The saved territory that speaks in the firm voice of a proud Black girl who rejects the naming of others and reclaims the naming of her collective self as a Black girl—*Yo soy una niña negra*. Against the logics of displacement, the beautiful Black girl owns the geography of herself, of the coast that birthed her, the Pacific coast. The beautiful Black girl has a lucid recent-history understanding of conflict and is a knower of the push factors conditioning her 'rural' to 'urban' migration. This sharp perception, from the first arrival of the invasive and the later enslaving ships, is the maturity of a people in a saved territory that looks after all Black lives, and all forcefully displaced lives, all war-torn lives, and all terrorized lives from the Venezuelan families crossing over the Simon Bolivar International Bridge into Colombia, to the Haitian youth seeking refuge in Chile, to the unaccompanied minors fleeing the Guatemalan layered war against Indigenous people looking to Mexico for shelter, and beyond.

Chapter 1 is an account of how curricula produced in Abiayala looks after Afro-Colombian youth lives while resisting white American cultural imperialism. Chapter 2 lifts the practices of Haitian youth and other 'condemned of the earth' in which they look after each other's lives by deploying Abiayala imaginations, creating curricula against the order(s) of the Chilean nation state. In Chapter 6, the workshops are communal practices of Abiayala to sustain the lives of youth and peoples in movement through Mexico. In Chapter 5, the formation of social movements and translinguistic collectives centered on Indigenous women are Abiayala forms of care and protection for lives under various genocidal threats in recent history (past 528 years). Finally, Chapters 4 and 3 account for the educational paths that Indigenous and rural youth from Ecuador and Mexico take and negotiate throughout the continent in order to look after place and family.

This book has been an attempt to be with Abiayala theories and to produce Abiayala as theory through the phenomenological lives spoken and written by thinkers and participants of research in and of the region. Returning to Abiayala, the name and the epistemological shift in naming, for the Guna and other Indigenous Peoples 'you cannot inhabit a Land with dignity if you don't give it a dignified name' (Echazú & Gomes dos Santos, 2020). This sentiment is echoed by Mamani who argues that 'placing foreign names on our villages, our cities, and our continents is equivalent to subjecting our identities to the will of our invaders and their heirs' (Quillaguamán Sánchez in Keme & Coon, 2018 p. 42). In this vein you cannot write (of) a Land with dignity if you do not have a dignified name. As editors we do not. This *Migrating Americas* book indignantly retains the colonizer's name. The removal of 'Latin,' from 'Latin America,' displaces just one colonial holder over the Land and, in Mamani's words, continues to subject the continent to the invaders. The plural, Americas, is but one small anticolonial gesture to restore the multiple and complex ways of being and affecting worlds that colonial processes have attempted to eliminate by simplification and regulation from Columbus, to indigenists, to interculturalists, and inclusive and diverse educationists today.

To state the obvious, a dignified way to title this work would be to call the Land and its migrations Abiayala. This would be an entry point into returning to the multiple ways of naming place and life in the continent by the multiple origin stories that live in the region. Against its title, the book is rooted in Abiayala, in the phenomenologies of us as a region beyond the salvific imaginary (of the) 'North.' The chapters are vivid proof of what it may mean to wrestle to turn to us, our autochthonous epistemologies (Espinosa Miñoso, 2017), modes of question asking, of theorizing, of collective forming, and mobilizing that give meaning and imaginings to our social lives. As you read through the book and encounter familiar ideas, theorists, and even the heirs of the invaders, to borrow Mamani's compounding words, you may conclude that we have failed. In this mature Land, failure is a foreign concept. In the Land of blood, we speak of persistence, survival, restoration, and understanding, and that is what the chapters strive to do about human migration and emerging socialities. In that sense, the chapters do Abiayala theories. The workshop in the migrant shelters as a space of resistance in the face of neglect and the inadequacy of Euro-modern philosophy (Chapter 5) and the emergence of new Black socialities of multi-layered diaspora-ing against imperial English-language education (Chapter 1) are examples of how this work navigates the liminal space between the pull of Euro-modern modes of thinking and theorizing life and the fugitivity from those *to be with* and grow Abiayala (as) theory.

Young people/Juventud

On the particular focus of education in this volume, we propose prioritizing young people. We do so shifting from education as institutionalized practices to young people as producers of the complex forms of existence encompassing education. This shift is significant for two key reasons: (1) It unsettles the dominance of institutional and institutionalized analysis of migration/migrants/migrant youth. Often the study of people's migration, and in particular forms of forced migration (labor, environmental, resulting from conflict, etc.), is undertaken through the prism of institutions. By institutions, we are referring to clearly (although not exclusively) defined facilities or establishments (e.g., ministries, clinics, schools, etc.) exercising governance through Euro-modern logics. The production of institutional and institutionalized analysis of migration is understandable given that migration, in this context, is often the outcome of systemic institutionalized processes (racism, environmental devastation, systemic inequalities, forced removals, impoverishment, food injustices, etc.). Though necessary, these institutional sociological analyses often reproduce dominating views where the people participating in migration processes are straightjacketed as objects, even if cast as subjects, of the institutions that seek to govern their lives and destinations. Centering institutions, even if accentuating the lives of people, is another form of deprioritizing the phenomenological intelligence people produce and enact in excess of institutions. Such deprioritizing re-centers Europe and its mechanisms of control as neo-colonial forms of domination from well-intentioned sociological analysis. This becomes pronouncedly damaging in the context of young people as coloniality gets rearticulated via its development mechanism. (2) It de-naturalizes the common sense that automatically assumes young people through Lockean and Darwinian analysis as *tabulae rasae* installed in an evolutionary scale of development. As such, young people are no other than the given object of institutional governance whose malleability is at the disposal of adult desires for control. This relational dysfunction is out of place in Abiayala cosmogony where young people—as Abiayala—are mature Land and saved territory. Young people—made up as 'immigrants' (López López, 2019)—in and of Abiayala, acted upon as objects of development for the Americas/any nation state, is unquestionably a colonial act foreign to Abiayala. To practice Abiayala as theory means to suspend this colonial logic that subjects youth to the cages of development and our histories to unsuitable invasive logics. Hence, throughout the book, we understand youth beyond a specified developmental stage demarcated by 'adults' as a kind of (less-developed) human in need of full human control/guidance/help by 'adults.'

Let us return to the poem of the beautiful Black girl, and to how she produces complex forms of existence that encompass education. Upon entering the school for the first time, the beautiful Black girl is faced with centuries of antiblack racism in Abiayala (Gordon, 1995). Abiayala is in fact occupied as a breeding ground for antiblackness. The arrival of the beautiful Black girl to this school exposes the presumed lack of racial segregation in Abiayala (Espinosa Miñoso, 2017). The absence of Black people in the school that the Black girl enters speaks loudly of the quiet racial segregation in Abiayala where Black, Brown, deeply or middle-melanated bodies have been *made other ('otra') and foreign ('extraña')* in the very Land that birthed them, in the very Land that they have custodially cared for for centuries. Stepping into the school for the first time and interrupting the lack of *negritud* (Césaire, 1939/1994) of the school, the Black girl begins to create a pedagogy of Black presence in spaces of Black absence. This presence defies the multiple figures of the Black in schools and societies from decorative to heroic and beyond (Ocoró Loango, 2011; Ocoró Loango, 2020). This pedagogy is an educational invitation for schools to be responsive to the actual realities of Abiayala, a place of Black existence, of diasporas that resemble the multiplicities that have always made this Land mature. Through the movement of her Black body on her way to the classroom, the Black girl begins to produce pedagogies of anti-racism (Wade et al., 2019), opening up the school to the movement of previously inexistent Black bodies in this space. The school building as a pedagogical space is given an opportunity to begin a transformation in attending to corporalities and histories it is unaccustomed to and in doing so is exhorted to produce previously unconceived visualities and imaginations. When the Black girl encounters othering in the sustained 'curious' gaze of the non-Black girls in the school, the Black girl launches a defense against that common antiblack act and its protracted history in schools. As a defense, the beautiful Black girl articulates a pedagogical lesson that teaches the school curriculum (enacted by the other girls) to suspend exclusion in favor of widening the scope of who and how young lives can show up at the school doors to learn.

Similarly, the two young Afro-Ecuadorian youth Yakira and Kiano in reciting or spitting (as they say in spoken word cultures) the poem are creating new soundscapes. In doing so, they are enacting what Irobi (2006) terms 'philosophy of the sea.' This philosophy is underpinned by the African continent where 'life, or 'being' is a performed and collective activity,' where 'thought is validated in action,' and where 'the regulation of feelings and the perceptions that people have of themselves, their universe and their sense of community are formulated into oral and performative structures [...] through dance, song, mime, movement, processions, spectacle and drama' (p. 4). As school-age youth and translocated African cultural intelligence (Irobi, 2006) *of* the Abiayala, their cultural production is more than the poem; it is what Irobi (2006) calls 'transcendental phenomenology in action' (p. 5). It is a remapping of the visibilities of Abiayala that re-narrate the region as African and other diasporas, of forced migration, interrogating the commonsense sediment that holds us hostage to institutional norms invented with somebody else's fantasies in mind. The philosophies, pedagogies, and lessons the beautiful Black girl and Yakira and Kiano insert into the school are just an example of what young people have to offer in any context of migration—internal or otherwise—throughout Abiayala. What declarative interruptions to the *modus operandi* of schools are they enacting that elude the attention of schools preoccupied with doing business as usual? What are schools, and the educational imagination more broadly, missing out on through their inattention to the instituting acts young people perform everyday as existential struggle *vis-à-vis* education? How else might we, who share an interest in education and schooling in migration contexts, come to the encounter with young people to learn with them about survival, resilience, movement, and the forging of modes of existence more attuned to Abiayala?

Throughout this collection, you will encounter youth as producers of complex forms of existence encompassing education, whether it is through the testimonies of Indigenous Mexican youth in Florida and Michigan (Chapter 3), or the youth from the south of the Ecuadorian Andes mapping human geographies of movement across time and education (Chapter 4). Further up on the Andes in the Aburra Valley, Afro-Colombian youth invite us into the territory of contestation of family history in relation to place and language (Chapter 1). Returning to the Southern Cone, Afro-Abiayala youth photographed in the primary classrooms in La Chimba, at the other side of the Mapocho River, register in the map of normative education, a defiant aesthetic that, in their own words, 'give life' (Chapter 2).

Movement of Peoples

Giving life and keeping (a)live turns into movement, the movement of people across space, time, and *sentimientos*. We call this movement *pueblear*, the act of people, in movement with one another, forming *pueblo*. To that we dedicate the last section of this text as added conceptual elements funding the work in all the chapters of this collection. We experience the term 'migration' as one that arrived with the boats both figuratively and factually speaking. The term, the imposition, derived from arbitrary lines forming Nation States, yields new kinds of peoples and human genres (migrants, immigrants, aliens, illegal people, undocumented people, etc.) ripe for administration and commodification (López López, 2018). Thus, we challenge that heritage and begin to do so turning to the current movement of movements from the South up. Instead of migrations, we focus here on movement. Movement is a term, a concept more attuned to Abiayala realities, to Abiayala as theory. As Afrodiasporic historian Evelyne Laurent-Perrault puts it, 'the world in which Africans and people of African descent lived during the eighteenth and nineteenth centuries, particularly in the Caribbean, was defined by transshipment, movement, travel, displacement, and dislocation' (Laurent-Perrault 2020, p. 134). Prior to the eighteenth century, movement characterized peoples of Abiayala in the formation of geographies where multiple (what we now call) cultures converged, built, produced frictions, epic encounters, and complex modes of worlding life that extended to transoceanic travels from (what is now known as) Peru to the Pacific (Armitage & Bashford, 2013). Movement, as collective practice, became maroonage (Vergara Figueroa & Cosme Puntiel, 2018), the intellectually orchestrated and philosophically articulated departure towards dignified Indigenous and Black existence against colonization and plantations in the Caribbean and the Americas. Extensions of that characterize movements for more habitable geographies throughout Abiayala today.

As we write these pages, multiple movements are taking place throughout the continent, among them is the one taking place in Chile. This October (2020), more than one million people of all ages, genders, and multiple walks of life took to the streets to protest, demanding adequate health care, education, income, and a new constitution (CIPER Chile, 2019; BBC News, 2019; Diario Concepción, 2019; Le Monde Diplomatique, 2019). The friction of people's bodies entering the marching flow of the streets generated a certain emancipatory heat while 'physically distancing' against the 'social distancing' mandate of the COVID-19 pandemic. The feeling and being of a people in massive social contact is expressed sensorially, affectively, through embraces, looks, and complicities afforded in the movement of the streets. Approaching one another's presence dancing and bouncing, it seems as though life flowered, as if it were reborn. 'The people united will never be defeated,' that cry that resounded throughout Abiayala's recent history, has twisted these times, turning them into another iteration of Allende's 1970s and the revolutionary struggles that Abiayala has always known (Illanes, 2012; Modak, 2008; Power, 2008; Valdivia, 2003). The flashing colors of the air read poetry, painted drawings, flagged posters of *…por ti abuela, para que tengas una pension digna* [for you grandma, for a dignified pension], *por mis hijxs y mis nietxs* [for my children and grandchildren], *por mi población y por mi gente* [for my population, my people].

In this collective formation of resistances, the individual vanishes among the people to make a People, a *pueblo* in movement. The faces of social warriors fade, as do the national flags stained with so much blood, after so much death, after countless disappearances. The faces fade to forge new struggles spearheaded by women who denounce the 'rapist state,' and by young people reclaiming rights leading the way. The streets are no longer the same. They are rivers in which the labor of Indigenous peoples, workers, students, retirees, and children flow. The streets are moved by the peoples that will tell this history. On the back of *this* October revolution, reverberations travelling across geopolitical borders are heard in Peru as the *pueblo* struggles for legitimate democracy and freedom (I'm so Tired of This, 2020; Peru's Week of Protests in Pictures, 2020), and in Guatemala's cry for adequate health care and education (Abbott, 2020; Associated Press, 2020). The People have come out as one body with all *sentimientos* to brighten the lifeless existence in which fascism's dictatorships have attempted to bury Abiayala. Out also comes the beauty of Jenny Tenorio's poem to demonstrate what it means to be young and resist one's school's antiblack history, while also claiming that *Black is beautiful*, that being girl/woman is power-ful.

The same spirt that charges these movements of the streets, moves through the feet of people that walk jungles in caravans, the arms that swim rivers, and the legs that step on buses and trains fleeing violence and misery with the conviction that they will arrive at Abiayala saved/safe. To move is to engender change in the search for the otherwise outside of fear. To move as a social movement is to seek collective action in order to survive massacres engineered with racism, femicide, militarism, forced removals, and all the other diseases plaguing Abiayala. Inequality is the premier social quality of the continent delivered by the few hands that hoard the continent's resources while permanently impoverishing peoples, stealing the Lands *of* which they are and which guarantee their livelihoods, stealing their wages, and threatening their very lives. The people in movement search for a hopeful 'North' in any direction where Abiayala, a saved and mature Land, can look after them and their offspring (Marsh, 2019; Pedemonte & Vicuña, 2020). Crossing arbitrarily demarcated and invented borders, and upon arrival, if arrival is granted, historically sedimented white supremacy, nationalism, and xenoantagonisms disregard their existence. They are cast as predators, invaders, infected, super spreaders, rapists, and in that the people in movement summon the principles of freedom and equality meant to serve as the moral compass of the modern Nation States that disregards their very lives. Their fugitive departures and the moral challenge are now ancestral practices of Abiayala instituted and rehearsed by *cimarrones*—Indigenous and later African—over five hundred years ago (Ortiz, 2021; Vergara Figueroa & Cosme Puntiel, 2018). Returning to Tenorio's writing, the beautiful Black girl comes out of the poem in the voices of Yakira and Kiano to denounce before the world the conditions that Afro-Colombians flee when they move, for instance, from the Pacific to other places and cities in the country. The audacity of the Black girl's caregivers to uproot her from the Land, the medicinal plants, the rivers, sea, mangroves, and estuaries to raise her elsewhere is an existential and visionary labor despite all the threat the city can be to their modes of being. The move to create these practices *in movement*, to generate self-sustaining forms of existence in movement, are acts of making *pueblo*, of *pueblear*, because of and despite all risks and threats.

Pueblear is the practice of being Abiayala and of Abiayala. As a noun, *pueblo* often denotes a despicable place of backwardness and lack of rationality inhabited by 'Indians' and 'Blacks.' *Pueblear* also means a continuous movement between localities. *Pueblear* is a constant back and forth between traditions, art, flavors, and memories that inhabit *pueblos*. It is recognizing the value of feelings emergent out of captivating magic that fills every look, every breath. *Pueblear* is a means to resist the instrumentalizing impulse to commodify these magical and colorful ways of being *pueblo*. To resist here means to break with commodifying agendas in order to propose a discovery of re-cognition through emotions and feelings of the traditions that give meaning to the particular ways of being of each locality. From the Black and Indigenous geography of an already-mature Land, for us *pueblear* means to resist while being rooted and in movement, no matter what it takes to defend life. In *pueblo*, the Land and the people are one. *Pueblo* is one who takes to the streets to protest and to flee. *Pueblos* are formed out of the life-threatening realities and in movement against the current. The dignity that *pueblos* build today emerges out of the desire for freedom, informed by the maroon ancestors, envisioned in collective practices on the margins of state abandonment and societal indifference. *Pueblear* implies working with *pueblos* to devise new ways of fighting for life outside dominating forces. *Pueblear* means to dignify that which is without, changing what is within through a critical examination that begins to disarm that which has impeded movement. *Pueblear* with dignity means communal strength, collective labor, the conquest of rights denied, liberating horizons, the outcome of debate and collective meditation that enable nourishment, shelter, study, and work among all and for all. Individually and collectively, the chapters in this volume are a *pueblo* and an effort towards *pueblear* futures in education that are more habitable for Abiayala, in Abiayala's terms, for its peoples, and in movement.

Author note: The writing labor in this chapter and the editorial work of this volume were made possible by Wurundjeri and Woiwurrung Countries and Wallmapu. We pay our respects to the elders who have been custodians of life for millennia in these geographies. Our scholarship is indebted to their custodianship and strives to learn to continue caring for Country and Land. The pages that come are an attempt to do just that.

Notes

1 Reprinted with permission from Jenny Tenorio. The translation was made by Ligia with the helpful assistance of Dr. María del Carmen De Avila, Dr. José Bañuelos Montes, and Emma Smith. All other translations are by Ligia unless otherwise noted.
2 This stanza, performed by Yakira and Kiano, does not appear in the printed poem. Yakira and Kiano's video appeared on their Facebook wall in the second half of 2020.
3 This stanza, performed by Yakira and Kiano, does not appear in the printed poem.
4. In the Pacific region of Colombia *chumbar* (the verb in the infinitive form), according to Jenny Tenorio, 'is (or was, as it is rare nowadays) a type of ritual practiced by the elders on newborn babies when putting them to sleep. In addition to lulling them, they straightened the baby's legs and arms, and wrapped them with a large cloth. Then they tied them from top to bottom with a strip of cloth (*faja*) to restrict the baby's movement for comfort. That practice helped babies sleep peacefully and long enough to allow the mother to calmly carry out impending tasks. The community sustained the belief that this practice would help children grow' (personal communication, April 9, 2021).
5 Here a digital site that may be helpful in expanding one's knowledge is https://www.gunayala.org.pa/index.htm.
6 Throughout this chapter, 'them' operates as the default pronoun for all peoples we refer to. This is an added effort to queer ways of engaging with others and weakening the strong colonial grip held over Abiayala, our ways of being us/our ways of being with people and with more-than-people beings.

References

Abbott, J. (2020, November 28). 'We are fed up': Guatemalans continue anti-government protests. *Aljazeera*. Available at: https://www.aljazeera.com/news/2020/11/28/guatemalans-return-to-protest-as-anger-at-government-persists.

Armitage, D., & Bashford, A. (2013). *Pacific Histories: Ocean, Land, People*. New York: Springer.

BBC News. (2019). https://www.bbc.com/mundo/noticias-america-latina-50115798.

Césaire, A. (1994). *Cahier D'un Retour Au Pays Natal* [Journal of a homecoming]. Ibadan: New Horn Press.

CIPER Chile. (2019). https://www.ciperchile.cl/2019/10/27/el-reventon-social-en-chile-una-mirada-historica/.

Diario Concepción. (2019). https://www.diarioconcepcion.cl/cultura/2020/10/18/las-reacciones-artisticas-que-dejo-el-18-de-octubre-de-2019.html.

Echazú, G., & Gomes dos Santos, L. (2020, September 2). How Indigenous & Black People are Fighting Colonialism in the Academy. *Chacruna*. Available at: https://chacruna.net/indigenous-black-academics-decolonization/.

Escobar, A. (2008). *Territories of Difference: Place, Movements, Life, Redes*. Durham: Duke University Press.

Escobar, A. (2011). *Encountering Development: The Making and Unmaking of the Third World* (Revised edition). Princeton: Princeton University Press.

Espinosa Miñoso, Y. (2017). Hacia la construcción de la historia de un (des)encuentro: La razón feminista en la agenda antiracista y decolonial en Abya Yala [Towards the construction of history of (un)encounter: Feminist reason in anti-racist and decolonial agendas in Abya Yala]. *Praxis: revista del Departamento de Filosofía, 76*, 1–14.

Gordon, L. (1995). *Bad Faith and Antiblack Racism*. New York: Humanity Books.

Gordon, L. (Ed.). (1996). *Existence in Black: An Anthology of Black Existential Philosophy* (1st edition). New York: Routledge.

Gordon, L. R., & Gordon, J. A. (Eds.). (2005). *Not Only the Master's Tools: African American Studies in Theory and Practice*. New York: Routledge.

I'm so tired of this: Peru youth vow to remain on the streets. (2020, November 14). https://www.aljazeera.com/news/2020/11/14/im-so-tired-of-this-peru-youth-vow-to-remain-on-the-streets.

Illanes, M. A. (2012). *Nuestra historia violeta. Feminismo social y vida de mujeres en el siglo XX* [Our violet history: Social feminism and the life of women in the 20th century]. Santiago: Editorial LOM.

Irobi, E. (2006). The Philosophy of the Sea. *Worlds & Knowledges Otherwise, 1*(3), 1–14.

Keme, E., & Coon, A. (2018). *Native American and Indigenous Studies, 5*(1), 42–68.

Laurent-Perrault, E. (2020). Arturo Alfonso Schomburg, the Quintessential Maroon: Toward an African Diasporic Epistemology. *Small Axe: A Caribbean Journal of Criticism, 24*(1[61]), 132–141. https://doi.org/10.1215/07990537-8190674.

Le Monde Diplomatique. (2019). https://www.lemondediplomatique.cl/chile-la-nueva-revolucion-de-octubre-1-por-juan-pablo-pallamar.html.

Lima, Constantino—Orígenes del Indianismo. (2015, May 22). https://www.youtube.com/watch?v=eYv9oXItAII.

López López, L. (2019). Refusing Making. *Journal of Curriculum and Pedagogy*, 161–174. https://doi.org/10.1080/15505170.2018.1541828.

López López, L., & Coello, G. (Eds.). (2020). *Indigenous Futures and Learnings Taking Place*. New York: Routledge.

Marsh, K. (2019) *Un lugar en el mundo* [In a place in the world]. Madrid: Planeta.

Modak, F. (Ed.). (2008). *Salvador Allende. Pensamiento y acción* [*Salvador Allende. Thought and action*]. Buenos Aires: Lumen FLACSO Brasil CLACSO.

Muyolema, A. (2001). De la "cuestión indígena" a lo "indígena" como cuestionamiento. Hacia una crítica del latinoamericanismo, el indigenismo y el mestiz(o)aje [From the "Indian question" to the "Indian" as a questioning. Towards a critique of Latin Americanism, Indianism, and mestiz(o)aje]. In Rodríguez, I. (Ed.), *Convergencia de tiempos: Estudios subalternos/contextos latinoamericanos estado, cultura, subalternidad*. Amsterdam: Rodopi. pp. 314–327.

Ocoró Loango, A. (2011). La emergencia del negro en los actos escolares del 25 de mayo en la Argentina:del negro heroico al decorativo y esteriotipado [The emergence of Black in school events of May 25 in Argentina: From the heroic Black to the decorative and stereotypical Black]. *Pedagogía y Saberes*, *34*, 33.50. https://doi.org/10.17227/01212494.34pys33.50.

Ocoró Loango, A. (2020, May 24). *Revisitando la negritud en los actos escolares del 25 de mayo* [Revisiting *negritud* in May 25 school celebrations]. Ecys. Available at: https://www.ecys.flacso.org.ar/post/revisitando-la-negritud-en-los-actos-escolares-del-25-de-mayo.

Ortiz, P. L. (2021). *Filosofía del cimarronaje* [Philosophy of marronage]. Toa Baja: Editora Educación Emergente.

Pedemonte, N., & Vicuña, J. (Eds.). (2020). *Migración en Chile* [Migration in Chile]. Santiago: Editorial LOM.

Peru's week of protests in pictures. (2020, November 17). *The Guardian*. Available at: https://www.theguardian.com/world/gallery/2020/nov/17/peru-week-of-protests-in-pictures.

Power, M. (2008). *La mujer de derecha, el poder femenino y la lucha contra Salvador Allende. 1964-1973* [The woman of the right, feminine power, and the struggle against Salvador Allende. 1964-1973]. Santiago: Centro de Investigaciones Diego Barros Arana.

Associated Press. (2020, November 22). *Guatemala protesters set congress on fire during budget protests*. The Guardian. Available at: http://www.theguardian.com/world/2020/nov/22/guatemala-protesters-set-congress-on-fire-during-budget-protests.

Tenorio Caicedo, J. (2019). *Entre el olvido y la esperanza* [Between oblivion and hope]. Cali: Editorial Grainart.

Tenorio Caicedo, J. (2020). *El retrato de mi casa* [The portrait of my home]. Cali: Editorial Grainart.

Valdivia, V. (2003). *El golpe después del golpe: Leigh vs Pinochet. Chile 1960-1980* [The coup after the coup: Leigh vs Pinochet. Chile 1960-1980]. Santiago: Editorial LOM.

Vergara Figueroa, A., & Cosme Puntiel, C. L. (2018). *Demando mi libertad: Mujeres negras y sus estrategias de resistencia en la Nueva Granada, Venezuela y Cuba, 1700-1800* [I reclaim my freedom: Black women and their resistance strategies in New Granada, Venezuela, and Cuba, 1700-1800]. Cali: Universidad ICESI.

Wade, P., Scorer, J., & Aguiló, I. (Eds.). (2019). *Cultures of Anti-Racism in Latin America and the Caribbean*. London: University of London Press.

Wagua, A. (2007). *Así lo vi y así me lo contaron: Datos de la Revolución Guna. Version del sagladummad Inakeliginya y de gunas que vivieron la Revolución de 1925.* [That is what I saw that is how they told me: Accounts of the Guna revolution. Version by *sagladummad Inakeliginya* and the Gunas who lived the 1925 revolution] Nan Garburba Odeloged Igar.

Womack, Y. L. (2013). *Afrofuturism: The World of Black Sci-Fi and Fantasy Culture*. Chicago: Chicago Review Press.

Chapter 1

Exploring Afro Colombian English Learners' Identities through a Critical Intercultural Approach

Transforming Journeys

Maure Aguirre Ortega

The stories described in this chapter intend to make visible the tensions that occur when exploring Afro Colombian young learners' identities as they are exposed to a critical intercultural pedagogical unit, a proposal understood as a way to resist and deconstruct dominant and colonizing discourses of English. This chapter first presents an overview of the context, the statement of the problem, and the participants of the research project that I conducted in 2018 in Medellín, Colombia, within the framework of my master's thesis. Then, this text elaborates on the conceptual elements that guided the pedagogical engagement in this research, and students' responses to the unit are shown as a prelude to reflections and proposals for future work.

Language education in Colombia has been shaped by the establishment of language policies that deny the linguistic, cultural, social, and epistemological richness of the country (Ortiz et al., 2019). These policies set unreasonable goals for those communities that have been historically unprivileged, thus causing the enlargement of economic, social, professional, and academic gaps among social groups. The Colombian Ministry of Education established the National Bilingual Plan 2004–2019 (Ministerio de Educación Nacional, 2005), which stipulates English as the official foreign language of the country and determined that students have to learn English for communicative, educational, and productive purposes; those who learn it are promised easier access to higher education and better work opportunities (Ministerio de Educación Nacional, 2005.). These ideas confirm the utilitarian view that the Colombian government has on English which is referred by Usma (2009a) as 'economic, practical, industrial, and military' (p. 133). As a consequence, Colombian bilingual education leaves aside the socio-cultural elements inserted in language learning and teaching and perpetuates the imperialist and colonial character of English language learning in the country.

Despite the efforts of different movements led by Afro and Indigenous communities to be recognized by the state and its system of rights and democracy, according to Pinzón (2009), only until the 1991 constitution,

DOI: 10.4324/9781003090519-2

they were acknowledged as members of a multicultural and multi-ethnic country. Besides limited access to the health system and precarious living conditions, Colombian Afro descendants lack formal government schooling, which adds more inequities between this social group and the rest of the country's population (Departamento Administrativo Nacional de Estadística, 2019; Ministerio de Cultura, 2010). Another factor that affects these populations' educational development is internal migration. Afro descendants have historically been displaced by armed groups that have violated their rights, forcing them to leave their territories; in many cases, this kind of migration happens from rural to urban areas (García Sánchez & Montoya Arango, 2010; Martinez, 2016). This often means that persons within these communities have to drop out of school, start labor life at a very young age, have poor health conditions, live in places where basic public services are scarce, and only a few restart educational processes (Martinez, 2014). Regarding language education, Afro communities have less access to learning English, which positions them to deal with the consequences of not being considered as 'competitive' in the labor market.

The social order established in Colombia positions 'mestizos,' an expression commonly used to refer to the mix between its different peoples, but actually used to privilege whiteness and European descent (Wade, 2003), on the highest scale of the hierarchy, which has given them more social opportunities than Afro Colombians (Guerrero Arias, 2016). As a consequence, these latter perceive English as a tool to have access to better life opportunities and as a platform to eradicate the feeling of inferiority they have experienced for years (Guerrero Arias, 2016). Colombians believe that a high level of English proficiency guarantees better jobs, social status, and further academic development (British Council, 2015). Therefore, English is seen as their opportunity to overcome national educational and marketing standards and fulfill societal expectations that respond to a systemic and hierarchical oppression of the most vulnerable people.

The Colombian Government, in association with the US Embassy, has launched several initiatives that aim at providing unprivileged groups with English, leadership, and academic programs to potentiate their access to higher education as a guarantee of better quality of life. Furthermore, these programs aim to reinforce the ethnic and racial identity of their beneficiaries; identity that is predisposed to meet the historical canons of what it means to be Black. Based on my experience as coordinator and teacher in one of these programs, students of these scholarships lead their identity construction process towards the 'English native speaker ideal' (González, 2010) and adopt behaviors, ideologies, and even linguistic patterns from the USA (following monolingual Anglo linguistic normative codes), as the target society, without critically analyzing and deconstructing them. As a consequence, they keep reproducing dominant discourses of English, a language that according to Escobar Alméciga (2013) has become the path for being a successful citizen and not a resource for individual and social identity construction; this situation exemplifies the potential loss of the historical and cultural memory of Afro Colombian communities and the omission of who they are. Moreover, participants must demonstrate their ethnic origin, their low socio-economic status, and their academic background to have access to complementary education in English, which clearly perpetuates the stratification process that accompany the language policies in Colombia (Usma, 2009a). That is why, addressing unbalanced power relationships through English learning might allow these students to regain their cultural and social identity and to acknowledge that assuming international, national, and governmental discourses of English ignores and downplays their identities.

As the teacher-researcher in this project, I would like to share our journey of transformation. After being discriminated by our ethnic identity, and even overcoming the idea that English is the solution to our social, economic, and educational issues, my students and I continue struggling to find our place in a country so diverse that might still not be prepared to understand its linguistic, cultural, and social richness. This chapter aims at sharing a critical intercultural pedagogical experience in an English course in Medellín, Colombia, which intended to allow young Afro Colombian descendants to explore their identities through language, and in this way, tackle questions of power and unequal relationships embedded in their everyday interactions and their process of learning English. This is the story of five of them and it is also my story.

The English Scholarship Program

The program was sponsored by the US Embassy in Colombia and implemented by different language centers in the country, in charge of the execution, follow up, and evaluation of the academic and economic aspects of it (Programa de inglés para estudiantes, s.f.). In 2017, a cohort of this program was constituted in Medellín, Colombia. To be eligible, students had to be 15 years or younger, they had to come from low-income families, registered in a public school, and they had to show good grades. The call was opened and only twenty-two students were selected. Throughout the selection process, participants were interviewed and questions related to family, academic, and social background were asked. As a reminder of who they were, the most important and crucial question was related to their affiliation to being Black.

This two-year English program aimed at developing leadership skills to inspire Afro Colombian teenagers to become active leaders in their communities. Students attended a ten-hour-per-week English course and several leadership workshops. The institution where this program took place offers classes for adolescents that come from medium-high income families, and most of them study at private schools. The syllabus covered in the English courses given to such population was the same curriculum assigned to the courses young Afro fellows were exposed to. As a consequence of this, classes and therefore teachers ignored the needs, the cultural background, and the previous academic experiences that participants of the scholarship program had gone through. That was one of the reasons why a significant number of students did not achieve the linguistic goals of the program; 14% of them dropped out due to economic and family issues, and the fact that they were not achieving the language objectives set by the program, and 5% withdrew because of their low performance given the said goals. A couple of teachers and I reported this situation, but adapting or even thinking about creating a new syllabus was not on the institution's agenda because it demanded time and effort from their academic department, which represented more investment in the program.

In terms of the social component, students attended leadership workshops given in English, which intended to encourage students to become community leaders. These were the only extra class events they were required to attend; the topics covered in these sessions were related to the commemoration of dates such as American Independence Day and the US elections. Besides, these workshops aimed at showing students how the monocultural Christian American family is like, the traditions they have when celebrating Christmas and Easter, and the different representations of what the coordination of the program called 'the American culture,' which followed stereotypical ideas of the communities that inhabit the country and only addressed the cultural practices of those at the top of the social hierarchy. Therefore, by reproducing the dominant white-supremacist self-portrayal of the US, the leadership workshops portrayed the stereotypical American lifestyle that Colombian society dreams of rather than encouraging fellows to explore their potential to become social leaders. This approach to English language left aside students' cultural backgrounds despite being one of the pillars of this program. Neither the classes nor the leadership component was intended to preserve the students' cultural and ethnic identity. As a result, instead of valuing their diversity and projecting themselves as active leaders in their communities, students started to adopt dominant discourses of English as their life philosophy and aspirations that pretended to deny their roots by shaping their subjectivity into something that they can never become: white.

When the program started, I recognized its potential to impact young Afro learners' realities, but with time, I understood that behind the intention of teaching English and inspiring them to become leaders of their communities, the way in which English was positioned into their lives only intended to perpetuate the social order that has already been established in our country; a system in which Black people, in order to be considered part of the society, needed to forget who they were (Vergara-Figueroa, 2018). For instance, students had economic, social, and family issues that started to permeate the development of the English classes, and even when these situations were reported, there were no strategies implemented to tackle such issues. So, the question relies on what was really important, to show Afro teenagers that they could become professional and successful individuals that might conquer the United States, or to support the Black struggles by providing spaces for self-recognition and for strengthening a community historically disregarded and deprioritized.

The Theoretical Foundations of the Pedagogical Intervention

The US Embassy in Colombia has supported the national government in search of racial and ethnic equality to tackle the discrimination and marginalization that Afro and Indigenous communities experience (Sánchez-Garzoli, 2013). With this objective in mind and considering the academic and social issues presented in the previous section, I knew the scholarship program was not reaching its potential; if the main objective was to encourage Afro teenagers to become leaders who challenge gender, labor, and ethnic discriminatory practices in their closest communities, and to strengthen their cultural and ethnic identity through learning English, the program needed improvement. Thus, I designed a critical intercultural curricular unit with the intention of encouraging the participants to deconstruct the discourses they had adopted from dominant cultures and to redefine the construction process of their identities within a more equitable English learning environment. For this reason, I will elaborate on the notions of identity and critical interculturality that guided such an initiative and I will reflect on such definitions.

On the one hand, identity is defined by Norton (2013) as the relationship individuals construct, over time and space, with the world. Consequently, identity construction is permeated by history, context, and language, which makes it dynamic and visible through social and linguistic practices (Weedon as cited in Norton, 2013, p. 4; 7). On the other hand, for Fanon (2009, as cited in Oto, 2018), the notion of identity goes beyond the person and their relationship with the other; in fact, identity refers to the interaction between subjectivity and social contexts from which the dominant and colonizing practices on being and knowing emerge. Following the latter idea, the transformation of identities comes from the socio-cultural situations that people experience, which influence the positions they assume in society. It is important to question to what extent Colombian Afro descendants' identity has been socially defined, especially in a country where for decades such community has been silenced and dehumanized, taking them to a position in which they try to be what they cannot: white. As Wynter (1999) states, in one sense, Black communities have been conditioned to recognize themselves as nothing and Colombian Afro descendants are not an exception.

In addition, according to Weedon (2004), to understand someone's identity construction process, it is crucial to see language as the meaning making factor and the means that allow them to analyze and question the assumptions made about their identities. Furthermore, Norton (2013) explains that the positions individuals intend to embrace in the near future, which she calls imagined identities, define the relationships they hope to have with other people and communities. However, such imagined identities are predefined by dominant cultural and social groups to the extent that Afro descendants are placed to deny their subjectivity in order to fit in, to survive the educational, social, academic, and economic standards of current society.

This pedagogical intervention was guided by the notion of critical interculturality proposed by Walsh (2005). This idea involves the construction of equitable interactions and relationships among cultures where conditions of equality are crucial, and respectful and inclusive interactions intend to deal with issues of discrimination and racism. Therefore, interculturality seeks to counteract the hegemony of dominant social groups by fostering respect and legitimacy in society. In fact, critical interculturality intends to value different ways of knowledge that have been historically underestimated. This proposal aims at unveiling, analyzing, and questioning what and how forms of control and power are perpetuated in society, allowing individuals to redefine and reformulate different ways of behaving, thinking, and living (Walsh, 2010).

For Tubino (2004), critical interculturality cannot be understood as a mere theory; it is actually a way of being and an essential attitude to understand and face the society we live in and all the interactions and positionalities that dominate our relationships with others and with the world. It is clear that critical interculturality looks for the eradication of unequal power relationships that do not allow cultural groups to respectfully and fairly engage in dialogue. Furthermore, this approach also demands individuals to take actions and transform their realities, impacting their communities, and hence, constructing a fairer society.

Critical interculturality opens a door to explore students' diversity at different levels, allowing them to problematize concepts of sexuality, race, ethnicity, and language, and also to create horizontal interactions that contribute to the deconstruction of the social and hierarchical order. I acknowledge now that considering the huge impact students' racial identity had on the exploration of their identities, it would have been even more powerful to also discuss these ideas under the concept of antiblackness

(Wynter, 1999). Exploring in depth the foundations of oppression and anti-Black racism as a pre-stage of this research might have provided us with more elements to deconstruct the dominant and colonizing ideas embedded in our English teaching and learning experience. Nevertheless, this first step mapped a path of possibilities in language education for Afro Colombians.

Participants of This Journey

A journey cannot start without defining the travelers: five students from the scholarship program and myself. Ana, the tallest one, had to grow up fast babysitting her sister while her mom worked at a restaurant. Ana considered herself a 'paisa' (the name given to people from Medellín, Colombia). In identifying as paisa, she saw herself as part of a community in Colombia typically associated with hard-working, cunning, open-minded mestizo people who have a spirit of merchant, negotiator, and businessmen. This imaginary around the paisa is part of their historical position as one of the most important and dominating social groups in the country (Posada, 2003; Londoño Vega, 2006). She talked about Afro Colombian people with a feeling of rejection and did not feel confident identifying herself as an Afro descendant. She always said she did not want to be like them, like those 'noisy and disrespectful Afro people' that lived in her neighborhood. Ana was a clear example of a Black kid that in order to immerse herself in a very competitive society denies her roots.

Deisy was born and raised in Quibdó, Colombia, a mining region, historically constituted mostly by formerly African enslaved peoples and their descendants, and a territory rich in natural resources exploited by dominant social groups; as claimed by Vergara-Figueroa (2018), this is due not only to the intentions to displace these communities, but also to the purposes of appropriation of the land, of dispossession of the community territory, and the eradication of the community in general (Wade, 1990). When she turned 14, her family moved to Medellín. She felt proud of her roots and enjoyed celebrating the ancestral festivals from her community. When Deisy came to Medellín, things were not easy. Her classmates called her names, criticized her braided hairstyle, discriminated her by her skin color and how she spoke, and made her feel inferior.

Another member of this group was Jefferson. He practiced track racing and wanted to become the best at it. He had studied at different schools due to economic issues, a situation that always made him feel left behind. Jefferson was born in Quibdó but was raised by his mom and step-father in Medellín. Jefferson was curious about his Afro roots, but like Ana, he self-identified as paisa. He never had a relationship with his dad, whom he last saw at the age of three. When he talked about his dad, he seemed nostalgic but at the same time apathetic.

Daniel was the only one in the group who lived with both parents. His parents, both teachers at a public school, were born in Quibdó; they lived in a rural area until illegal armed groups displaced them and forced them to move to Medellín. There was something Daniel never openly talked about; he felt he was never good enough for his father, which made their relationship really complex. Although Daniel lived his first year in Quibdó, he was not aware of his roots and cultural identity, but he was curious about what other classmates knew about his ethnic community. Daniel had a dream, to show the world that 'Afro people could also be scientists and not just construction workers.'

Bruno's mom fled Quibdó due to economic and safety issues when she was expecting him. He is a sweet and optimistic young man. His parents had a violent relationship with one another; Bruno always tried to protect his mom but also wanted to have a relationship with his dad; Bruno's dad was his role model because he was the only one in his family who had a degree as an English teacher and was in charge of supporting the household economy. The most important person in Bruno's life was his grandfather, who lived in Quibdó and embodied his Afro roots.

Ana, Deisy, Jefferson, Daniel, and Bruno originally come from an African diaspora set in Quibdó, which means they carry the historical background of being internal migrants and descendants of enslaved peoples as it has been associated with the region of Chocó. Some of them migrated and settled in a new territory where their cultural and social practices have been influenced not only by the interaction in their new communities, but also by their original diaspora that challenges the positions they assume as members of it (Contreras, 2005; Rotimi et al., 2016), and which adds complexity to the socialization processes they face.

As the teacher-researcher, I am the last passenger on this journey. I came to Medellín when I was fifteen. I am from Montería, a small town and capital of the department of Córdoba located in the Caribbean region of Colombia, where Indigenous and Afro communities interact all the time. However, I am not Afro, neither do I belong to one of the Indigenous communities established in this territory such as Zenú or Embera Katío (Equipo Humanitario Colombia, 2016). I moved to Medellín to study where I started to feel intimidated by the way people behaved and communicated. At the university, my classmates laughed at my accent and at the words I used to name things. Social interaction was difficult; I did not trust anybody, and I isolated myself. I started to miss home, doing the things I used to do, eating the food I grew up with, knowing where to go and feeling socially accepted. I struggled to adapt and becoming part of a new community took time. Medellín pushed me to grow even faster, to understand and experience my diversity and to think about life differently. I have changed a lot; although once I felt ashamed of who I was and where I came from, I am now proud of all the layers of my identity. I have come to realize I am not from a place, I am in motion.

The Critical Intercultural Pedagogical Unit

As part of a research project carried out in 2018 during my master's studies, I designed a critical intercultural curricular unit with the objective of creating spaces to deconstruct the dominant discourses that students had adopted and encourage them to explore their identities within a more equitable environment in an English class. This research engagement lasted sixty-four hours of direct instruction and provided tasks that allowed learners to explore different ways of being, knowing and living, question power relationships, and propose actions that might contribute to the construction of a fairer society. The activities developed within this unit were adapted and created by me. I modified some activities suggested by Janks et al., (2013), some of the exercises proposed by the textbook of the institution, and created some activities based on purposes and objectives of critical interculturality suggested by Walsh (2010) and Tubino (2004), which I adopted as the principles and objectives of this unit:

1 Critical interculturality allows to re-conceptualize and re-found ways of thinking, acting, and living.
2 Critical interculturality promotes the understanding and construction of knowledge and problematizes power relationships.
3 Critical interculturality promotes the transformation of power relationships.
4 Critical interculturality builds intercultural citizens committed to democracy and inclusion.
5 Critical interculturality promotes the critical reading of the world to understand, re-learn, and act in the present.
6 Critical interculturality promotes the dialogue between differences.

In this research, I used audio-visual input material, images, reading handouts and identity videos. These resources incorporated information in English and Spanish about different cultural practices, ideas of knowledge, ways of communicating within communities, perspectives on life, diversity, and resistance. For example, some videos presented Indigenous teenagers from Leticia, the capital city of the Amazon region in Colombia, who had migrated from rural areas, and even the jungle, to the urban zone looking for better economic and educational opportunities. These teenagers elaborated on ideas about their sense of belonging to their communities, what the concept of knowledge and territory meant for them, and they shared their affiliations to an Indigenous community now located in the metropolitan spheres. Similarly, there was a video in which an Afro Colombian young woman talked about the same notions mentioned above but portraying the life and struggles of the Afro community in Quibdó, Chocó; she had migrated from another town in the same department due to violence in the area. Additionally, images and articles used always represented problematic situations in communities that have historically been privileged and others that have been discriminated. For the identity videos, students were asked to create short films to talk about themselves and the communities they identify with.

For data collection, I interviewed the five participants of this research project before and after the implementation of the unit. I video recorded the total hours of instruction and collected students' journals and work. After triangulating data, the following four categories, which I will elaborate on in the next section, emerged: first, the identity construction in relation to pre-established identities, which elaborates on the students affiliations to certain cultural groups and on the ideas they had about themselves before the implementation of the unit; second, the identities as English learners as they state students' perceptions towards English and the positions they assume as speakers of this language; third, the identity construction in relation to imagined identities and societal expectations, notions that portray students' aspirations and dreams of who they want to become; and fourth, the deconstruction of unequal relations of power and students' reactions to them, which are related to the exploration of the different representations about ideas of race, gender, language, and cultural practices in society.

Responses to the Critical Intercultural Pedagogical Unit

Daniel and Ana initially recognized themselves for what they were good at, what other people thought about them, how members of their community referred to them and the roles they assumed in the social groups they belonged to. Daniel and Ana let others define them; their identity construction process was permeated by how their families, their school community, and their groups of friends saw them:

> 'Let's see, in my family, I'm like, I mean I have the role of the older sister; if my mom has to go to work and she has no one to leave my sisters with, literally the two smallest ones, it is my responsibility to stay with them, yes, to make them food, I must be super attentive and avoid that something happens to them.' (Initial interview, Ana, April 10).

Ana and Daniel referred to themselves by highlighting the positive features of the roles they assume in their community. On the contrary, Bruno saw the duality present in the way others perceive him affecting what he thought about himself. Bruno mentioned contradictory ideas of how people defined him. He knew that some people positioned him as a model to follow because of his strong academic skills but when they thought about social and personal aspects, people discriminated him because of his weight and skin color as it can be seen in the following testimony:

> 'You're so smart Fat Black. I am scared of telling people that: tell about sex Tell about weapons, smoking and wars Tell about negative things.' (Excerpts taken from the journal entry 1, Bruno, April 26).

Bruno knew he was a smart kid but that was overshadowed by his racial identity, which is why he allowed others to label him as the 'fat guy.' For Bruno, other people determined who he was and created the necessity to fulfill their expectations; however, for Daniel and Ana, their identities were defined by what they thought about themselves. Unfortunately, this does not necessarily correspond to a subjective process, Ana and Daniel's have already been predisposed to identify themselves as Black people as the dominant society understands blackness, that is, they identified as black from an anti-Black stance. This carries the heavy load that this racial concept implies.

From another perspective, students were not totally aware of how their identities interacted and overlapped; this meant students thought their identity was static, that it was only defined from one perspective, and they did not conceive that who they were was permeated by different layers of their subjectivity, mixed and complemented by the social, personal, and cultural circumstances they experience. Before the implementation of the unit, Jefferson, Daniel, Deisy and Ana only affiliated themselves to the Afro community. In fact, Deisy was the only one who by the end of this research, continued associating who she was merely to her ethnic identity; the other participants understood that what defined them was not just the ethnicity they belonged to but the interaction among features such as their sexual orientation, cultural practices, race, their linguistic repertoire, and their ways of thinking and understanding the world.

Additionally, they explored their identities as English learners. The ideas about what being an English speaker represented for them and how it permeated who they were and wanted to be were transformed throughout the implementation of the critical intercultural unit. Deisy, Ana, Bruno, Jefferson, and Daniel thought that by learning English, they were going to have economic benefits, better job opportunities, access to knowledge, and purchasing power. Similarly, when I was a pre-service teacher, I saw the profession as an opportunity to progress economically and improve social status. We all thought that English was going to provide us with opportunities abroad and with a privileged social condition. For instance, Ana reproduced the discourses about gains and privileges that were associated with speaking English and Daniel was aware of the superior status given by society to English and he saw the communicative purposes that learning it could bring.

> '[...] English is such an important and recognized language and used ahhh it is something that will open many doors for me and will allow me to communicate with others and learn things that I may not know [...].' (Initial interview, Daniel, April 3, my translation).

Students went from seeing English as a tool for positive gains at economic, social, academic, and personal level to considering English as a determinant factor that positioned them in advantaged or disadvantaged situations according to the community they interacted with. Thinking about what speaking English made them feel, Ana, Deisy, Bruno, Jefferson, and Daniel recognized that depending on the place and community they were in and interacted with, they felt powerful or powerless:

> 'When I am in English class, I am TOPDOG, I have more knowledge that some of the other students, however, in other aspects I am a UNDERDOG like the participation.' (Excerpt taken from the journal entry 4, Daniel, June 14).

Jefferson, Ana, Deisy, and Daniel recognized that their ideas about English changed thanks to the spaces given in class to explore, understand, and discuss topics related to their cultural practices, their identities, and the relations of power and domination embedded in society. For example, Daniel expressed that this experience encouraged him to go beyond the process of learning English and to start thinking about himself as an agent of transformation:

> '[...] Well, not really, because the most important thing is not really the grammar or things like that, but knowing how to express yourself to the world and knowing what it is happening and about everyday situations and know what you can do to help, Do you get me?; because one knows that the world has its problems and one, as a young person, has to find a way of expressing positive things to the world and obviously also helping.' (Final interview, Daniel, June 19, my transcription).

Furthermore, students moved from seeing English as a job and travelling opportunity to using it as a means of communication, as the chance to learn about others and contribute to the solution of their community problems. Most of them understood that speaking English nowadays is not a guarantee of a promising future. They learned that English does not always grant them privileges; it also brings unequal power relationships, perpetuating discrimination and domination. Nevertheless, not all participants lived the same transformation. For Bruno, the most significant gain in this process was his language proficiency improvement. He continued seeing English as merely language structures:

> 'Oh in English, not some mistakes, well, I saw those letters that I wrote in English in the first two years and I was like oh seriously those mistakes, really? And I looked at my notebook and I, seriously and I am like uhh I had those basic mistakes, the teacher told me you have some basic mistakes and it was truth, I used to say she has 23 and I ahh she is she is, I do not know, and now I am more perfectionist.' (Final interview, Bruno, June 23, my transcription).

Personally, I had questioned myself many times about the reasons why I felt proud of speaking English, but it was during this experience that I reflected on how I position myself as an English speaker. This journey influenced the way I communicate, the language choices I make, and the topics I discuss. Now I prioritize reflection, interpretation, and analysis of our contexts and our identities over language features. It is essential to problematize the fact that language teaching in Colombia and in the world is still dominated by instrumentalist ideas about English bringing a huge challenge for teachers that want to open spaces in class to contribute to the construction of a fair society in which horizontal relationships are constructed and diversity is valued. English continues being a threat to local and ancestral knowledge and languages, and an obstacle to exploring different ways of communicating, interacting, and thinking.

Regarding imagined identities, Ana, Daniel, Bruno, Deisy, and Jefferson initially defined them based on the professions they wanted, on the roles they expected to assume in society and the position of community leaders they hoped to assume. For instance, Bruno considered getting a job and studying at the university as being successful. Nevertheless, other students like Jefferson wanted to participate more in his community and develop leadership skills to contribute to the construction of a fairer society:

> '[...] I hope I can be a better leader, develop myself better in group activities, with other people, develop more socially because I know more people and are people of my same ethnicity, of my same age [...].' (Initial interview, Jefferson, April 10, my transcription).

Students' future identities became more socially oriented not because of the English learning but because of the critical and intercultural approach that guided the discussions and topics developed in the curricular unit; they recognized themselves as agents of social change who needed to adopt more critical and active roles within their communities.

> 'Well I think my mentality has changed too much because before I was not interested in social issues, I did not watch the news, I did not care about those things, but now I think my mind has gone from being something indifferent to like wanting to do something for society [...] I can also help others because not everyone has the same capabilities or the same conditions, because I am not so wealthy but I have what it is necessary and there are other people that they do not have that, so I realized that I can also help with minimal things even if I am young. I felt like very, like someone that can contribute.' (Final interview, Daniel, June 19, my translation).

Besides that, using English as a means of discussion, students deconstructed and reacted to unequal relations of power. First, this process started by raising awareness about cultural differences and diversity. Students named stereotypes, defined prejudices towards cultural groups, and learned about different cultural practices and diverse definitions of knowledge, communication, and science. Second, students identified and unveiled patterns of power and domination in relation to culture. They questioned why the voices of certain communities were silenced and why others were privileged.

> 'TEACHER: Why are Indigenous languages are not spoken by many people? [...]
> BRUNO: Because they are not globalized
> JEFFERSON: Because you have not real, the same opportunities than when learning another language. You don't have the same opportunities learning French than learning an Amazonian language
> TEACHER: [...] You have more opportunities for what?
> STUDENTS: For work, for meet new people
> TEACHER: Why do we have fewer opportunities with Indigenous languages?
> STUDENTS: Because there is not companies that need persons that know indigenous languages and because the indigenous languages is less spoken around the world, so it is harder you communicate with other persons [...]
> JEFFERSON: I say that they are not valued because at the time, other more powerful civilizations repressed those cultures and all those beliefs, so that's why there are very few people who still have them because people from other nations came to colonize us and they imposed another culture and others customs. For us, it is weird but because we were raised with different beliefs and cultures [...].' (Excerpts taken from class transcription, May 8).

Finally, students problematized the relationships of inferiority and superiority embedded in our everyday interactions and in society. To address this issue, students presented ideas about respect and recognition of diversity, proposed strategies to acknowledge and value differences and shared actions to construct a more equitable, democratic, and fair world.

> '[...] you aren't only teaching how to do something, you are teaching traditions and sense of belonging for something because the world isn't about science, the world is about experiences, traditions, histories, knowledges, voices and the most important PEOPLE [...].' (Excerpt taken from Bruno's letter, May 31).
>
> '[...] generate spaces for sharing of different cultures in our cities, for example, fairs, recreative activities, concerts, camps, and more [...].' (Excerpt taken from Daniel's work, June 7).

Daniel confessed he doubted about his sexual orientation and that he was extremely afraid to discuss it and recognized that the LGTBI community was undervalued and discriminated. It was evident that he did not want his family to realize how he felt towards this topic because in his opinion, homosexual people were not considered important in society.

Jefferson faced a difficult moment when he recognized that the Afro community he identified with was marginalized by other social groups. Similarly, Bruno reflected on how people were discriminated because of their skin color and their physical appearance. Students understood their community had been historically overshadowed by dominant groups.

> 'Afro-descendants are less privileged because they are rejected for the appearance and skin color also is so strange see news about Chocó and other cultures.' (Excerpt taken from Bruno's work, June 7).

In my case, I realized that I had never felt brave enough to express my opinions because I believed my ideas were not important, so I always let others speak. I realized that people I love and even myself had perpetuated stereotypes about women and their role in society. I did not challenge others and myself to deconstruct relations of power and dominance. Only until I understood the complexity of who I was and embraced my identity construction process, I started to feel important in society, to make my voice heard, and to act as an agent of transformation.

We had all explored our identity before the implementation of this project, but it was probably the first time in which doing it became a conscious process full of recognition, interpretation, analysis, deconstruction, and action. We had not reflected about our roles and positions in society and much less about how diverse we were. When this implementation was over, we had more questions than answers about our identity construction process.

Learnings and Dreams for the Future

We opened our hearts to talk about being bullied, discriminated, abandoned, and being afraid of what we felt. Going beyond their skin color was new for Bruno, Ana, Jefferson, Deisy, and Daniel. How they initially defined themselves was permeated by what society, especially dominant groups, had inserted in their minds about who they were. Their desire of fitting in and being visible for other communities influenced their dreams and future life expectations, pushing them to follow the pattern established by the social order.

Only until 1991, the Colombian government officially recognized that Afro communities had the same rights that had been attributed to the rest of the population (Pinzón, 2009); this does not indicate that discrimination towards them stopped. In Colombia, citizens adopted the discourse and the superiority complex of those in power; Colombian society has allowed the national governments to determine its past, present, and future. One of their weapons has been English learning, a process that continues to position the United States at the top of our aspirations as a nation (Usma, 2009b). In Colombia, Afro descendants are expected to defend and fight for their rights, to preserve their cultural identity, and to contribute to the development of society. However, policies of inclusion and equity established to achieve the ideal of a multicultural society keep perpetuating discourses of non-identification process and privileging certain dominant ethnic groups (Mosquera, 2007).

Bruno, Deisy, Ana, Jefferson, and Daniel intended to challenge Colombian society and its history. On the one hand, they dreamed about going to university and fulfilling their academic expectations, which clearly goes against the official reports which state that a low percentage of Afro descendants achieve professional success. On the other hand, according to a report by the Colombian Ministry of Culture in 2010, Afro communities are expected to have better labor and academic opportunities to participate more in political and social movements, have access to housing and health aid, and contribute less with illicit activities. Nevertheless, these expectations only depend on the Colombian government and the reality is that Afro communities are still the deprioritized.

Throughout this experience, we understood that who we are is not just related to where we come from, our phenotype, or our accent. We understood that our identities come from a constant social construction which exemplifies the complexity in defining the concept of identity as it was stated in the theoretical section of this chapter; it was challenging to acknowledge that our ideas about who we are have been influenced by dominant, discriminatory, and colonizing perspectives. The social, cultural, and geographical circumstances have molded and guided the positions we assume in the different contexts in which we interact and the relationships we develop with the communities we are affiliated with.

Bruno and Daniel had bought the Colombian government discourse about English learning. They thought that by speaking this language, they were going to be accepted as members of dominant groups of society. Even though Bruno did not change his mind after this experience, Daniel saw English as a means for contributing to social transformation. In addition, students recognized that speaking English benefits them in some situations and marginalizes them in others. However, learning English continues representing a life-changing experience, as we get to be more conscious of its implications.

English programs offered to Afro communities are not usually adapted neither designed based on their needs, which does not contribute to their educational success. The pedagogical proposal presented in this chapter met the objective of providing spaces that allowed participants to explore the complexities of their identities through a critical intercultural focus on English teaching; this permitted the deconstruction and problematization of unbalanced and unfair relations among communities. With this, it is evident that English teaching and learning, instead of perpetuating ideologies from dominant social groups, can promote equitable interactions and intercultural dialogue among communities as a way to contribute to the construction of an inclusive, democratic, and fair society.

Even though the theoretical foundations of this project could also have been nurtured by other postures in regard to racial issues, this initiative responded to a call made by the field of foreign languages in Colombia to work towards the construction of a fairer and more inclusive education. This research also aimed at opening paths for the deconstruction and co-construction of the English curricula to which Afro language learners are exposed to. Future projects like this need to be transversal to all areas of education in Colombia, and they will demand the continuity of research on identity. Colombia needs more democratic and inclusive laws and policies at all levels and more critical teachers, students, and citizens in general who dream of a fair country; therefore, this cannot be achieved if we allow our fights to be silenced.

References

British Council. (2015). *El inglés en Colombia: Estudio de políticas, percepciones y factores influyentes* [English in Colombia: Study of policies, perceptions and influencing factors].

Contreras, Y. (2005). Diaspora a new possibility in a country of displaced people [Lecture]. Asociación de Colombianistas. Retrieved from: https://colombianistas.org/. [2020].

Departamento Administrativo Nacional de Estadística [DANE]. (2019). Población Negra, Afrocolombiana, Raizaly Palenquera [Resultados del Censo Nacional de poblaciónу Vivienda 2018]. DANE Información para todos. Retrieve from: shorturl.at/hCMV1 [20220].

Programa de inglés para estudiantes. (s.f.). Embajada de EE.UU en Colombia. Retrieved from: https://co.usembassy.gov/es/ [2020].

Equipo Humanitario Colombia (2016). *Informe final MIRA* [Final report MIRA].
Escobar Alméciga, W. Y. (2013). Identity-forming discourses: a critical discourse analysis on policy making processes concerning English language teaching in Colombia. *Profile Issues in Teachers' Professional Development*, 15(1), 45–60.
García Sánchez, A. & Montoya Arango, V. (2010). *Afrodescendientes en la ciudad de Medellín: aprendizajes para una interculturalidad equitativa. ¡Eyy pille!... Aquí estamos ¡somos afro!* jóvenes afrocolombianos en la ciudad de Medellín: identidades, representaciones y territorialidades [Afro-descent People in the city of Medellín: learning for an equitable interculturality. Eyy pille!... Here we are, we are Afro! Afro-Colombian youth in the city of Medellín: identities, representations and territorialities]. Medellín: Alcaldía de Medellín. Secretaría de Cultura Ciudadana.
González, A. (2010). English and English teaching in Colombia: tensions and possibilities in the expanding circle. In *The Routledge Handbook of World Englishes*. Routledge. pp. 354–374.
Guerrero Arias, B. E. (2016). *Literacies and racial ideology: a black Colombian young male's learning and participation in an urban school* (Doctoral dissertation). University of Illinois, United States.
Janks, H., Newfield, D., Dixon, K., Ferreira, A., & Granville, S. (2013). *Doing critical literacy: texts and activities for students and teachers*. New York, United States: Routledge.
Londoño Vega, P. (2006). La identidad regional de los antioqueños: un mito que se renueva [The Regional Identity of the People of Antioquia: A Myth That Renews]. In Carrera Damas G., Leal Curiel C., Lomne G., & Martinez F. (eds.) *Mitos políticos en las sociedades andinas. Orígenes, invenciones, ficciones*. Caracas: Travaux IFEA. pp. 203–230.
Martinez, S. (2014). "El sol no siempre brilla para todos": estrategias de inserción de los jóvenes afrocolombianos a la ciudad de Pereira ["The sun does not always shine for everyone": strategies of insertion of Afro-Colombian youth to the city of Pereira]. *REMHU: Revista Interdisciplinar da Mobilidade Humana*, 22(43), 251–274.
Martinez, S. (2016). La migración de afrocolombianos hacia las ciudades: dinámicas de movilidad, redes étnicas y procesos de ocupación espacial [The migration of Afro-Colombians to the cities: dynamics of mobility, ethnic networks and processes of spatial occupation]. In *Territórios de gente negra. Processos, transformacoes e adaptacoes. Ensaios sobre Colombia e Brasil*. Brasil: Universidade Federal Do Recôncavo Da Bahia. pp. 115–124.
Ministerio de Cultura. (2010). República de Colombia. Afrocolombianos, Población con Huellas de Africanía. Retrieved from: shorturl.at/qBKLS [2020]. [Republic of Colombia. Afro-Colombians, African Footprint Population].
Ministerio de Educación Nacional, [MEN]. (2005). Programa Nacional de Bilingüismo, Colombia 2004–2019 [Presentation]. Retrieved from: https://www.mineducacion.gov.co/1621/articles-132560_recurso_pdf_programa_nacional_bilinguismo.pdf [2020]. [National Bilingual Program, Colombia 2004–2019].
Mosquera, C. (2007). Reparaciones para negros, afrocolombianos y raizales [Repairs for blacks, Afro-Colombians and Raizals.]. In C. Mosquera & L. Barcelos (Eds.). *Afro-reparaciones: Memorias de la Esclavitud y Justicia Reparativa para Negros, Afrocolombianos y Raizales*. Bogotá: Universidad Nacional de Colombia. pp. 213–276.
Norton, B. (2013). *Identity and language learning: extending the conversation* (2nd ed.). Bristol, UK: Multilingual Matters.

Ortiz, J. M., Usma, J. A., & Gutiérrez, C. P. (2019). Critical intercultural dialogue opening new paths to internationalization in HE: repositioning local languages and cultures in foreign language policies 1. In *Educational approaches to internationalization through intercultural dialogue*. Routledge. pp. 71–85.

Oto, A. D. (2018). A propósito de Frantz Fanon. Cuerpos coloniales y representación [About Frantz Fanon. Colonial bodies and representation]. *Pléyade Santiago*, (21), 73–91.

Pinzón, O. A. H. (2009). Las minorías étnicas colombianas en la constitución política de 1991 [Colombian ethnic minorities in the political constitution of 1991]. *Prolegómenos. Derechos y Valores*, 12(24). 189–212.

Posada, C. (2003). La raza negra en Colombia: antioqueños y chocoanos [The Black Race in Colombia: Antioquians and Chocoans]. *Estudios de literatura colombiana*, (12), 105–109.

Rotimi, C. N., Tekola-Ayele, F., Baker, J. L., & Shriner, D. (2016). The African diaspora: history, adaptation and health. Current Opinion in Genetics & Development, 41, 77–84.

Sánchez-Garzoli, G. (2013). *Apoyo de EE.UU. a afrocolombianos tomando pasos en buena dirección* [U.S. Support to Afro-Colombians Taking Steps in Good Direction]. WOLA, Incidencia a Favor de los Derechos Humanos en las Américas.

Tubino, F. (2004). Del interculturalismo funcional al interculturalismo crítico [From functional interculturalism to critical interculturalism]. In Samaniego, M. & Garbarini, C. G. (comps) *Rostros y Fronteras de la Identidad*. Chile: Universidad Católica de Temuco. pp. 151–164.

Usma, J. (2009a). Education and language policy in Colombia: exploring processes of inclusion, exclusion, and stratification in times of global reform. *Profile Issues in Teachers' Professional Development*, 11, 123–141.

Usma, J. (2009b). Globalization and language and education reform in Colombia: a critical outlook. *Íkala, Revista de Lenguaje y Cultura*, 14(22), 19–42.

Vergara-Figueroa, A. (2018). *Afrodescendant resistance to deracination in Colombia*. Cham, CH: Palgrave Macmillan.

Wade, P. (1990). El Chocó: una región negra [The Chocó: a black region]. *Boletín Museo del Oro*, (29), 121–149.

Wade, P. (2003). Repensando el mestizaje [Rethinking the mixture]. *Revista Colombiana de Antropología*, 39, 273–296.

Walsh, C. (2005). *La Interculturalidad en la Educación* [Interculturalism in Education]. Peru: Ministerio de Educación, Dirección Nacional de Educación Blingüe Intercultural.

Walsh, C. (2010). Interculturalidad crítica y educación intercultural [Critical interculturality and intercultural education]. In Viñada, J., Tapia, L. & Walsh, C. (Eds.) *Construyendo interculturalidad*. Bolivia: Instituto Internacional de Integración del Convenio Andres Bello. pp. 75–96.

Weedon, C. (2004). *Identity and culture: Narratives of difference and belonging*. United Kingdom: McGraw-Hill, Education.

Wynter, S. (1999). Towards the sociogenic principle: Fanon, the puzzle of conscious experience, of "identity" and what it's like to be "Black". In M. Durán-Cogan & A. Gómez-Moriana (Eds.) *National identities and sociopolitical changes in Latin America between marginizalization and integration*. United States: University of Minnesota.

Chapter 2

The New 'Others' in Schools and the Regimes that Order Them: Re-production of Institutionalized School Practices in Chile in the 21st Century

Claudia Carrillo-Sánchez

Migration has been part of human history. However, its global dynamics and effects show it as a complex social phenomenon in contemporary society. The crossing of borders between states is usually seen as a problem and not as a right (Herrera & González, 2011; Fuentes & Castellanos, 2020). On the one hand, internal migration within states tends to be seen as a 'natural' or 'normal' event that is invisible. On the other hand, in the framework of international migration, more restrictive policies emerge to limit the mobility of people. This involves both the states of the countries of origin of migration and the countries of destination and therefore has political, economic, social, cultural, and demographic implications for both the sending and receiving states (Zamora, 2005; Bello, 2010).

The forms of migration constitute a systemic process that involves not only the arrival of adults in the countries of destination of migration, but also the presence of children[1] who tend to be concentrated mainly in public school institutions. In the particular case of Chile, this is exacerbated by the scarcity of migration policies[2] and, in turn, educational policies for this school population. Both issues are determining factors that re-produce deep educational inequality and social injustice.

Within the framework of the above considerations, the main objective of this chapter is to critically address the construction of the new 'others,'[3] as an individual located in the place of 'essential otherness' (Rojas & Castillo, 2005, p. 19). This is the case in public schools with high enrollment of children from international migration in Santiago de Chile, after the re-production of certain **institutionalized school practices** (an issue scarcely worked on in the Chilean context). These institutionalized school practices respond to the ideology of school control, and therefore tend to regulate, discipline, and normalize children in general. I propose the concept of **school practices of pluriverse sense-thoughts**[4] as a contrasting perspective, taking into account that sense-thoughts are processes mediated by

DOI: 10.4324/9781003090519-3

feelings and reason (Mavisoy, 2018; Green, 2006); and pluriverse, because the existential possibilities are manifold[5] (Mavisoy, 2018; Salazar, 2018; Escobar, 2014), sense-think the pluriverse (Fals Borda, 2015). School practices of pluriverse sense-thought seek to reveal the ecology of knowledge and surpass the monoculture of knowledge in schools.

The Context: The Metropolitan Region of Santiago

The Metropolitan Region of Santiago (capital city of Chile[6]) was the context for this research. Two criteria were key in selecting the context: first, the segregated city model promoted since the 19th century; and second, the concentration of the highest percentage of immigration in Chile[7]. These two criteria link the construction of otherness with immigration[8] as substantial elements of this chapter.

The historical construction of the otherness responds to the segregated city model promoted by Benjamín Vicuña Mackenna (mayor of Santiago), through an urban remodeling program between 1872 and 1875 in the city of Santiago. His objective was to enhance the face of the city and make it a reflection of cultural-economic progress, so he established a path that separated the 'Christian' city from the 'barbarian' city (Margarit & Bijit, 2014 p. 58). He built a border that separated 'civilization' from 'barbarism' in order to create his own city (Vicuña, 1872). In this way, the area called 'La Chimba' (a Quechua-derived word), in the Metropolitan Region, was historically built as the 'other side' (which in Quechua refers to the other side of the river). This area, located on the other side of the Mapocho river in Santiago de Chile, was destined to house the unwanted. This re-produced the separation of the 'white' city (seen as bright and clean), from the other city, the Indigenous and African one (seen as dark, dirty, and as synonymous with socially dangerousness) (Leyton & Huertas, 2012).

Then a social-racial hierarchy was established, and dichotomous pairs were used to classify individuals between irrational/rational, primitive/civilized, traditional/modern, etc. This constituted one of the main nuclei to conceive humanity from Eurocentric coloniality/modernity, through a gradation scale that hierarchically ranked people, as superior and inferior, according to their skin color where the 'white' individual occupied the superior place (Quijano, 2014).

The sanitary separation in the city of Santiago divided the population in two large areas: the first one reserved for people from the country's elite and the second one for the marginalized. Thus, otherness was built historically, from and for the city. This socio-spatial differentiation as a question that persists in Santiago needs to be addressed by human geography from a contemporary perspective (Santos, 2000; Montoya, 2018). This model of a segregated city established 'two cities whose business and cultural flows circulate permanently, but never merge in terms of reproductive or class relationships' (Leyton & Huertas, 2012, p. 41).

The need to research the historical construction of otherness and immigration, as historical facts of the 19th century, lies in the fact that the social-racial classification that was established in colonial times remains current in the 21st century. Historically, the abyssal lines were established on the other side of the river, to initially relocate internal migrants from the countryside, and later international immigrants (Chinese, Arabs, Peruvians, and currently other Latin American and Caribbean immigrants). At present, school enrollment of children from international migration is concentrated mainly in some public schools located on the other side of the river[9].

Although Chile has not historically been characterized as a country of immigration, during the last decade, the figures have shown a significant increase. According to Godoy (2020), for 2018, the increase was 23.2% according to records between 2014–2017, while for 2019, the increase was 19.4% compared to the previous year. According to the latest reports for 2020, this figure amounted to 1,492,522 and represents 5.02% of the total population in Chile.

Methodological Considerations: Approaches, Techniques, and Analysis Strategies

The research framework that gives rise to this chapter is derived from my doctoral thesis. The findings I document here address the following research objective: to reveal which are the institutionalized school practices that are re-produced as a function of the identity process of cultural assimilation, and therefore the explicit and implicit inculcation of the ideals about the Chilean nation (Carrillo-Sánchez, 2020). This research was carried out in public elementary schools with high enrollment of children of migrant backgrounds in the Metropolitan Region of Santiago de Chile[10].

Based on qualitative approaches, the methodological strategies I used to collect the data were: in-depth interviews with teachers, support professionals, educational assistants, and directors; on-site observations in history, geography, and social sciences classes, general training, student entrance/exit, and school recreation; group work with basic education students (through reflective work to privilege the voices and experiences of the students and focus on school practices, and organizational policies), and a review of documentary sources such as internal institutional framework of the school, community frameworks, the legal framework, the national curriculum, and the citizen training curricular plan (to develop knowledge that is fundamental for life in a society). The data analysis was conducted through qualitative analysis by theorization (Mucchielli, 2001) and discourse analysis (Van Dijk & Mendizábal, 1999).

Operationalizing Key Concepts

To define school practices, it is necessary to specify three theoretical-conceptual perspectives that would allow us to deepen the study of school practices in general: the technical-instrumental perspective, the practical-social perspective, and the critical-dialogical perspective.

Considering the technical-instrumental perspective, school practices are instrumental actions that are carried out according to objectives determined by external agents. Therefore, the practices are reduced to means and ends, that is to reach established goals. The weakness of this perspective is that its vision is reduced and simplistic, since it seeks to measure what is observable and promote the rational-objective logic of technical-instrumental practices. This perspective is also defined as instrumental action, an ideology of control, or technocratic pedagogy (Apple, 1994; Giroux, 1990).

In contrast, from a practical-social perspective, school practices are complex actions in which the subjectivity of individuals intervenes. Therefore, school actions are situated in the social context by means of a network of socially constructed meanings (oriented and determined by the symbolic constructions attributed to them) and promote comprehensive-interpretative logics. The weakness of this perspective is when school actions are not deliberate, they end up being functional to the continuity of the established social system. This practical-social perspective is also defined as practical thought, process model, reflection from action and practical deliberation (Dewey, 1967; Stenhouse, 1991; Jackson, 1992).

Finally, within the critical-dialogical perspective, school practices need to be analyzed critically and dialogically, because they respond to an established social order. Therefore, the critical-dialogical perspective promotes the power of communication and discourse argumentation to analyze school practices. This critical-dialogical perspective promotes the emancipatory-democratic logic and is also defined as liberating education and teaching as a critical-communicative activity (Freire, 2000; Stenhouse, 1991).

The operationalization of the concept of **institutionalized school practices** within the framework of this chapter refers to those planned practices that are re-produced systematically to respond to the institutional character of the school. Therefore, these practices are characterized by having patterns of order and repeated action patterns that obey the technical-instrumental logic of the ideology of control in the school. The school as an institution is one of the ideological apparatuses of the state, created to train individuals efficiently (Althusser, 2015). Through sanctions, awards, punishments, selections, and classifications, the dominant culture is re-produced. Through a technocratic pedagogy, the school as an institution promotes instrumental practices, seeks determined objectives, and displays an ideology of control. These institutionalized school practices leave out 'on the other side of the line' in abyssal thought (De Sousa Santos, 2010, p. 13), all knowledge, cultures, and practices considered 'others.' They only leave inside what is functional for the purposes of the school and its existence. Examples of institutionalized practices that are implemented to consolidate the national and symbolic identity construction of 'we' are: general (weekly) training of students to sing the Chilean national anthem and raise the flag, celebrating Chilean national holidays, and celebrating civic events. Given the specific nature and qualities of these practices, they can be differentiated from ordinary school practices since they arise at random and are not institutionalized.

The operationalization of the concept **school practices of pluriverse sense-thoughts** (a conceptual contribution of this chapter) articulates epistemes that make it possible to feel and think collectively (Mavisoy, 2018), to promote school practices from the perspective of the ecology of knowledge (De Sousa Santos, 2011) and to reestablish the balance with nature. These school practices of pluriverse sense-thinking are articulated with a dynamic-social-community and critical-dialogic-emancipating dimension because it incorporates multiple other ways of knowing. Therefore, diverse knowledge coexist when different cosmovisions (ancestral traditions, beliefs, aesthetics, etc.) are re-known and connect people with their territories of origin, their histories, and their locus of enunciation. For people, their locus of enunciation or personal history (Mignolo, 2015) are inherent to their condition of human being, and their literality and territoriality constitute forms of social meaning. Therefore, the school practices of pluriverse sense-thoughts promote cognitive justice (De Sousa Santos, 2011) and convey harmonious processes with Mother Earth to reestablish the integral balance of the human-culture-nature relationship (Mavisoy, 2018). This is so given the interrelation and complementarity that exists between human beings and the other worlds[11] that surround the human world (Escobar, 2014).

According to Escobar (2014), the practices of community, relationality, and pluriversity in Latin America continue to exist throughout the centuries. An example of this is the millenary Nasa[12] sense-thoughts when they express that 'the word without action is empty. Action without word is blind. Word and action outside the spirit of the community are death' (Escobar, 2014, p. 50). From the school practices of pluriverse sense-thoughts, word and action emerge as sentimental thinking in interrelation with the community; this implies the ecology of knowledge and the (urgent) need to exist ourselves, feel ourselves, think ourselves, and project ourselves in community, with other persons, other knowledge, and other school practices. This existence has as its central axis the sociogenic principle proposed by Wynter (2009), regarding the invention of existence, to distinguish it from the vocabulary of white European existentialism. Therefore, the invention of the experience, mainly Afro/Black and Indigenous, understood as the ability to create and the practice of freedom, to live with other people. It refers to existing oneself, because existence is constructed dialectically with the community.

Taking into account the above considerations, from the perspective of school practices of pluriverse sense-thoughts, it is appropriate to speak of educational ecosystems based on Abiayala's (educational) paradigm as a pedagogy of the senses and tenderness. From this paradigm, it will be possible to dismantle the educational colonial apparatus of the modern nation-state (Sarango, 2014), to learn everything about life, in life, with life, and for life, through horizontal interrelationships of knowledge. Dismantling the colonial educational apparatus of the modern nation-state (Sarango, 2014), implies resisting ourselves, emancipating ourselves, and constructing more humane educational systems ourselves.

Educational systems should promote more ecological, solidary, and communitarian social relations, in consistent with the belonging and relevance to the territory, in balance with Mother Earth, the Pachamama. In this sense, the school practices of pluriverse sense-thoughts are opposed to the Eurocentric hegemonic thought that proclaims unique ways of knowing the world from scientific knowledge constructed as objective, universal, even neutral. These practices correspond to alternative pedagogies, for example, the Pedagogy of Mother Earth (Green, 2011), where the plurality of knowledge interacts with the community. For example, the insubordinate pedagogies approach as an educational-political project from the geographies of 'others' seeks to build interconnections between the historical, territorial, and political to construct knowledge that makes people visible. This is necessary in order to vindicate the historical denial of Afro/Black and Indigenous peoples and also to resist the domination of imposed hegemonic knowledge (Pinheiro, 2015).

Children of Migrant Backgrounds in Chile

Hegemonic thinking and asymmetrical power relations often deny and silence children's voices and their sense-thoughts in the social, cultural, political, and school context. In the socialization of children in family and school life, children tend to be kept in the place of the infant (from the Latin infantis 'he who does not speak'). Schools in Chile are the main space for the socialization and education of children of migrant backgrounds, for three main reasons: basic and secondary education is compulsory in Chile; there is a family investment to educate their children in the receiving country; when families arrive in Chile, they seek to quickly enter the workforce and the school becomes a space of safety and protection for their children. The enrollment of children of migrant backgrounds is mainly concentrated in public school institutions (Bellei, 2013; Ministerio de Educación, Centro de Estudios, Mineduc, 2018). In the research that this chapter draws from, the three participating school had 65%, 67%, and 70% enrollment of young people with migrant backgrounds. The concentration of enrollment of migrant children in these schools deepens the gaps of educational inequality in Chile.

A pertinent issue to address in this chapter is the naming of children as 'being of migration.' Children are usually named as migrant girls or boys, when the migratory condition does not belong to them. It is the adults who make the decisions of migrating for them. The children's presence in the country is a consequence of the migratory trajectory of the adults on whom the children depend. Most of the children participating in this research indicated that adults did not ask their opinion before the embarking on the migratory journey. Some of the children said that before the trip, they were not even informed and had to suddenly leave. These children are usually named as children of immigrants, and some of them are in Chile under the responsibility of relatives who are not their parents in the traditional sense of the term. At the time of writing this chapter, there were no arrivals in Chile of migrant children who travelled alone except for those who travelled through the unaccompanied minor services offered by airlines (Cepeda, 2019). According to UNICEF reports (2020), the population of children and adolescents (between 0 and 17 years old) in Chile was 4,259,155, which is 24.2% of the total population of the country (17,574,003). Of these, 2.8% are foreigners.

Currently, these children tend to embody the category of 'new others' in the schools, given processes of racialization marked by skin tone, phenotypical characteristics, differentiated corporalities, aesthetics, tone of voice, accents, knowledge, ancestral knowledge and beliefs, etc. They represent to the 'Chilean us' a sort of threat to stability (Aninat & Vergara, 2019; Navarrete, 2019), at both the macro level (nation-state) and micro levels (school/institution). The threat to stability tends to re-produce the imaginary construction of people of migrant backgrounds and their descendants as the 'others' who are not nationals because they are of another national order (Todorov, 2010).

The National Order and the Construction of 'Others'

The increase in immigration during the last decade puts a strain on the national order in the country, which is why immigration tends to be conceived as a problem. Evidence of this is the 'Humanitarian Return Plan' promoted by the Ministry of the Interior and Public Security of Chile since 2018. The initial objective of this plan was the 'voluntary' return of Haitian immigrants back to Haiti. This 'Humanitarian Return Plan' takes a new name from the year 2020: 'Humanitarian Plan for the orderly return[13].' The plan aims to promote the general return of foreign people to their countries of origin once 'voluntarily' declaring under oath their intention to return to their country individually or in family groups[14]. This plan has as motto: 'to order the house' and promote the national feeling of protecting the space considered as own and sovereign[15]. This plan promotes not only the 'masked deportation' of adults (either individually or in groups), but also an 'ideological training' that befalls mainly on the children of migrant backgrounds who remain in Chilean schools, where the national sentiments are a vital reference for the preservation of 'Chilean identity' (Palacios, 1918; Larraín, 2014).

National sentiments appear in the historical-colonial context of Chile (1600–1810) in the creation of *Colegio de Naturales*[16] in 1697, which was reserved for educating the Mapuche children of chiefs in order to 'ideologically integrate' them to the nation. Later, the national sentiment appears in the creation of the National School in 1883 (after the Pacific War[17] ended in 1883), with the objective of integrating everyone into the Chilean nation as a political and ideological strategy of border integration through the schooling. In this context, the Tarapaquian persons of northern Chile were characterized as barbarians and, therefore, had to be saved and redeemed through education (González, 2002). In the logic of integrating everyone into the Chilean nation, the border integration schools were established to promote the exaltation of Chilean patriotic symbols, national sentiment, military bureaucratic apparatus, and the legal system (Díaz & Ruz, 2009).

The Construction of the New 'Others' in Schools: The Re-production of Institutionalized School Practices

Historically in Chile, the cultural assimilation of the 'others' was part of the civilizing view for the salvation of the 'barbarians' through education; today in Chilean schools of the 21st century, the new 'others' are the children of migrant backgrounds, mainly from Venezuela, Peru, Haiti, Colombia, Bolivia, and the Dominican Republic (Godoy, 2020).

Education, conceived as a gateway to citizenship, has been the ideal means to transform the masses into citizens (Muñoz, 2015) and where cultural assimilation is promoted through schools as educational institutions. Cultural assimilation is re-produced through institutionalized schooling practices, for example by upholding patriotic symbols in schools for national integration. According to Sagredo (2013), the patriotic symbols constitute central elements that can be conceived as conditions for national survival, and part of the Chilean heritage and identity.

National identity implies the construction of a 'we' as an identity process that is oriented towards differentiating markedly from the 'others.' Children of migrant backgrounds constructed as the 'new others' tend to be assimilated into the framework of a common national project. The purpose of this project is to instruct and demarcate what our culture, our customs and idiosyncrasies, our values, and our religion should be defined from the

'Chilean us' (Tijoux, 2014). This process of cultural assimilation appears in an explicit, crude, and manifest way through institutionalized school practices such as: forcing students to stand and line up in the school yard every Monday; singing the Chilean national anthem and hoisting the Chilean flag; dictating mandatory dancing and singing of Chilean dances and songs in national holidays celebrations, and obligatorily adopting certain corporal, verbal, and gestural behaviors that conform to 'Chilean ways.' All these appear in an implicit, subtle, and refined way through educational discourses and the teaching and learning of certain curricular contents that exclude some knowledge that are left on the 'other side of the abyssal line' (De Sousa Santos, 2010, p. 13). There lies everything that does not enter into the logic of hegemonic nationalist thought.

The public school is a strategic institution to promote nationalist purposes (Gallego, 2010); therefore, the national anthem and flag are used as patriotic rituals (Silvia & Allori, 2005). Patriotic rituals emerge in the school to create the student's national identity (López de Lara, 2017), the construction of nation, and the institutional life in the school (Sánchez, 2000; McLaren, 1995). These are collective practices that have an explicit meaning (Amuchástegui, 1995).

Institutionalized School Practices and Their Effects on People's Lives

Institutionalized school practices tend to re-produce regimes that constrain the intellect, body, and spirit of children. They do so with the purpose of homogenizing and normalizing them within the dominant culture. Cultural assimilation impacts students in general and, in particular, those who have migrated. The political[18] and educational[19] discourses are often pregnant with racist, classist and xenophobic ideologies that seek the assimilation of these students into the dominant culture. Therefore, the homogenization, normalization, and regulation of all the dimensions of the person seek to re-affirm the national sentiment and the 'Chilean identity.'[20] Cultural assimilation has negative consequences in the lives of children, their sense-thoughts, and their emotional and cognitive development because the other knowledge that they bring with them are denied and excluded (they are not part of the hegemonic thought of the Chilean nation). The other knowledge are excluded precisely because they are conceived as others and therefore are made to disappear from reality so they cease to exist. The sense-thoughts, popular knowledge, and ancestral knowledge that Afro/Black and Indigenous children bring with them to school are thus expropriated.

For De Sousa Santos (2009), the other side of the abyssal line is the realm beyond legality and illegality, but also truth and falsehood since these are forms of radical denial that translate into a radical absence as place of non-being. The place of non-being refers to the expropriation of knowledge and the expropriation of the person who carries such knowledge, non-existent and almost sub-human. Therefore, the person and their knowledge tend to be systematically dehumanized, as in the case of anti-black racism (Sexton, 2012; Gillborn, 2006; Zarate, 2017). For Grosfoguel (2011), the universalization of the dominant European episteme left out the epistemologies and cosmovisions coming from Africa and Latin America, because they were considered inferior. All the traditions of knowledge that were undervalued were denominated in the 16th century as 'barbaric,' in the 19th century as 'primitive,' in the 20th century as 'underdeveloped,' and at the beginning of the 21st century as 'antidemocratic' (p. 344).

Social Control in School and Some Practices of Resistance

The principal findings in this research point to institutionalized school practices that re-produce the normalization and body disciplining of children. The intervention on the body is deployed through different control mechanisms in the socialization process to homogenize the diversity of sense-thoughts, knowledge, and other forms of expression that children bring with them. The process of socialization in schools involves institutional power, asymmetric power relations, and control mechanisms in order to normalize and discipline daily life interactions in schools.

For Foucault (1998), the body normalization and discipline is carried out by control devices; from the findings in this research, the teachers participating in this study tend to homogenize the students and exercise a rigorous control over the expression and body movement (gestural and verbal) of children primarily those with migrant backgrounds. The normalization and corporal discipline is translated in an imprisonment of the person. This is so by means of explicit and/or implicit signals that exercise dominion on the corporal control of students, silencing and regulating mainly their varied forms of expression (connected to the territories and communities of origin). An example of this is the accent, volume (voice), linguistic rhythm (speed), and use of vernacular.

By means of corporal control, symbolic violence is exercised through mechanisms such as vigilance and punishment (Foucault, 1998). In the school institution, this is related to the rewards and punishments to students by teachers and principals based on established disciplinary behaviors. In other words, the disciplinary behavior of the students is translated into prizes or punishments depending on the case (misconduct is classified in the manual of school coexistence as: serious, less serious, and light). Through this research, we find that the control mechanisms impact students in general, but particularly those of Afro/Black and Indigenous backgrounds (Carrillo-Sánchez, 2020). During the interviews with most of the teachers and principals, there were multiple manifestations of racism (cultural, differentialist, and biological), attributing particular characteristics to Afro/Black and Indigenous children, for example: 'they scream most of the time'; 'they always laugh quite loudly and move their hands a lot'; 'they can't hardly ever stay still'; 'they have rhythm in their blood and the music in their body'; 'they are messy'; 'they wear their hair wild'; 'they wear fairly short and tight clothing.'

From the data gathered in this research, one conclusion that can be drawn is that institutional power operates permanently to act upon the students' bodies through institutionalized school practices that are concrete and impact children (with greater or lesser force), according to the color of their skin, their country of origin, their social interactions, and the power games that take place in school. The control over the bodies of the children, mainly of Afro/Black and Indigenous backgrounds, and their sense-thoughts are re-produced through institutionalized school practices to establish determined ways of being, doing, and behaving according to the school space and time.

While conducting fieldwork, practices of resistance emerged. Between classes and with no teachers or administrators in sight, a group of students from Haiti and Colombia vindicates the Afro/Black aesthetic through new performances. The vindication of Afro/Black aesthetics is necessary, in order to resist the racial stereotypes that are imposed in Chile (Rivera, 2018; De la Hoz & Rentería, 2018; Villareal, 2017; Bidaseca, 2017). The girls put naked Barbie dolls on the table and use pieces of cloth, thread, needles, and scissors to design the doll's clothes, accessories, and hairstyle. Below are some images of these resisting creations (Figure 2.1–2.3).

The three students boldly engage in the resistance practice even though they may incur a disciplinary action. Bringing Barbie dolls into the classroom is a practice forbidden by the teachers. However, the children constantly resist in and during recess, in between class periods, and while a teacher is away. The children skillfully hide the various implements and supplies so as not to be caught. They strategize hiding them in the desks in the back of the room. Below I offer an account of how I witnessed this form of resistance.

I observe that the three children of migrant backgrounds from Haiti and Colombia are engaging in a practice of resistance to reverse the power and social control of institutionalized school practices. When I approach these students, they invite me to observe, and while I observe, I ask them to tell me about what they are doing. The students explain that they are engaged in this resistance practice since the beginning of the year (it is now June). They tell me that when one of the classes was over, and shortly before the next class began, they get fabric scraps for free to dress up the dolls because they do not have their original clothes. The students buy these naked dolls at the market fair, where they can be bought at a reduced price because

The New 'Others' in Chile Schools 47

Figure 2.1 Take a stand against racism
Source: Santiago de Chile, 2019.

they are second-hand. They students also tell me that they buy the dolls because they can dress them the way women dress in Haiti and Colombia, with hairstyles, colors, and designs that give life to the spirit. When I ask what they mean by 'give life to the spirit?' They tell me, 'the colors of the clothes in Chile are very sad, opaque, they are like the colors of the dead' (Classroom observation, Grade 6).

The performances documented through the images and the fieldnotes account for the resistances to the supremacy of the imposed hegemonic aesthetic and the 'white' 'Western' canons of beauty (Martinez-Oña & Muñoz, 2015). For Prussing & Salazar (2009), the standardization of the

48 Claudia Carrillo-Sánchez

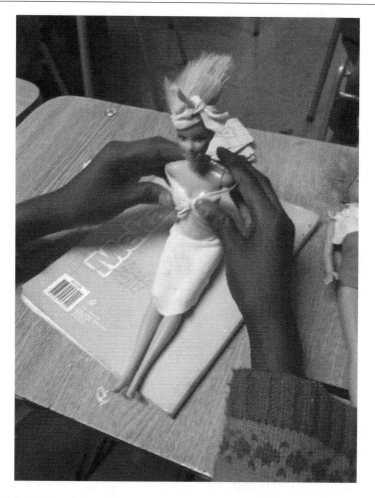

Figure 2.2 Two-handed performance
Source: Santiago de Chile, 2019.

aesthetic canons of European origin through, for instance, advertising generates in people feelings of contempt for the features of Afro/Black and Indigenous people. Therefore, some people are looking, for example: to iron and straighten their hair, to dye their hair, and to use contact lenses to lighten their eye color, and the use of facial cream to lighten or depigment the natural skin tone.

The practice of resistance expressed through the previous photos and explanation that the children provided highlights several important elements: the three children perform the three Barbie dolls aesthetics as an act of resistance to the hegemony of aesthetic canons, the three Barbie dolls

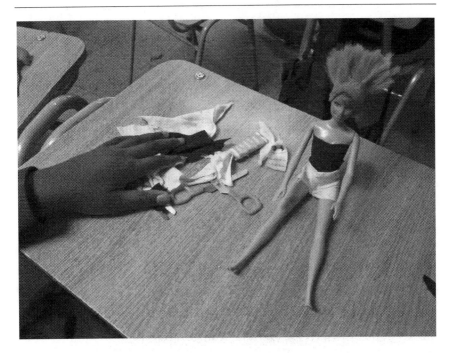

Figure 2.3 Empowerment and appropriation of Afro-Black aesthetics

Source: Santiago de Chile, 2019.

have a light skin tone that may be considered to match the 'racialized' Euro-ideal in Chile, the three children that play with these Barbie dolls are of migrant Afro/Black background. I should point out that the three dolls in the images above break the 'white' hegemonic aesthetic model imposed on Chilean society. The children intentionally modify the length of the dolls' hair and the style so it features some the Afro/Black aesthetics they know. The students perform this resistance practice in the classroom in the little school time they are afforded. Their resistance is supported by their classmates, who are also of African descent. They do so standing by the classroom door to be on guard so they can alert their peers of when the teacher or principal approaches the classroom. That way, the girls would have enough time to hide their dolls, supplies, and implements.

School Practices of Pluriverse Sense-Thoughts

The school practices of pluriverse sense-thoughts are a disruptive proposal based on the need for cognitive justice, to counteract the power-knowledge relations imposed by Eurocentric thinking (Rivera, 2018; Mavisoy, 2018; De Sousa Santos, 2010). The power-knowledge relations tend to be imposed by all those that govern world capitalism and also by the people that re-produce the hegemony of Eurocentric thought (Quijano, 2014).

The children of migrant backgrounds attending mainly public schools of Chile bring with them a set of sense-thoughts, other knowledge, and other ways of doing that are left on the other side of abyssal line (employing a logic of 'Western' hegemonic thought). The conceptual proposal of school practices of pluriverse sense-thoughts aims to contribute to the construction of a new model of society through education. This is so in order to engineer a paradigm shift in the current educational model in Chile (and also in other Latin American countries) and to promote cognitive and social justice in schools.

The conceptual proposal of school practices of pluriverse sense-thoughts (of my own invention drawing from the work developed by Freire, 2000; De Sousa Santos, 2012; Escobar, 2014; Fals Borda, 2015; Mavisoy, 2018; Salazar, 2018, etc.) emerges with the writing of this chapter and proposes a paradigm shift in order to talk about educational *ecosystems* instead of simply educational systems, and to conceive pluriverse sense-thoughts in the broad sense of ecology (De Sousa Santos, 2012; Rodríguez, 2017), Mother Earth (Boff, 2017; Steinhäuser, 2020), and Pachamama (Zaffaroni, 2011).

According to Pérez (2009), the school as an institution seeks to guarantee social and cultural reproduction for the survival of society; therefore, cultural assimilation educational model is adopted and then imposed by the modern nation-state (Quijano, 2008). This conceptual proposal of school practices of pluriverse sense-thoughts counteracts the cognitive injustices that constitute the origin of all the injustices that exist in today's world by ignoring all the knowledge of the peoples historically colonized by Europe (De Sousa Santos, 2011). Cognitive injustice is produced when Western hegemonic thought takes over and forecloses spaces for knowledge that do not fit 'Western' logics and traditions excluding them by what De Sousa Santos (2009) calls abyssal thinking. When the pluriverse sense-thoughts of children are made invisible and excluded in schools, there is no democracy or cognitive justice because the monoculture of knowledge considered legitimate is imposed.

The Eurocentric cognitive perspective has been re-produced for decades in the world of colonial/modern capitalism (Antonacci, 2015) to regulate people by hegemonic patterns, which seek to naturalize the socially constructed reality and present this reality as something inevitable, unquestionable, and assumed as truth. This is why a change of paradigm in the current educational model in Chile is urgent, in order to generate more just, humane, and equitable educational conditions. By practicing school cultures attentive to pluriverse sense-thoughts, possibilities open up to construct educational ecosystems of multiplicitous worlds. This would be an avenue to overcome the fragmented vision of the 'others' and to make visible their own places of enunciation (Sosa, 2009).

Conclusion

The logic of Western hegemonic thought in Chilean education exacerbates individualism, generates the fragmentation of the person, and re-produces hierarchical social relations, competition among students, and deep disconnection with Mother Earth. The schools impose on students the duty to be, the duty to do, and the knowledge to do, with the aim of giving society a certain type of person; therefore, the school tends to homogenize, standardize, and discipline students through institutionalized school practices.

In the research that this chapter draws from, the implementation of institutionalized school practices in the three participating schools involved the actions of the educational community, their ideological positions, their tensions, their agreements, and their resistance. Therefore, the socially constructed reality in these schools is dynamic and unstable. When the people of the educational community who participated in this study resist the imposition of institutionalized school practices, they open the possibility of knowing the multiplicity of worlds and generate more horizontal social relations to develop our humanity.

According to the results of the research, the school practices institutionalized in the participating schools are implemented with different intensity by the adults interviewed: teachers, principals, and discipline inspectors. Of the total number of interviewees (No. 20), 60% were teachers and 15% were directives. Among the group of teachers interviewed, two of them lived in exile outside Chile (during the military dictatorship[21]), and these teachers expressed a critical view of the re-production of institutionalized school practices and the construction of new 'others' in schools. The life experience of these teachers contributed to their sensitivity and empathy about the migratory phenomenon and, therefore, greater possibility of reversing the situations of cultural assimilation experienced by children of migrant backgrounds in Chile.

In Chile, all public elementary schools are governed by the guidelines of the Chilean Ministry of National Education; however, the intensity or decrease of social control of students and power-knowledge relations will depend on the educational paradigm of each school and the critical vision of the educational actors and their resistance actions (students, teachers, discipline inspectors, and directors). The social control of students and the power-knowledge relations in schools can only be reversed in the future when a profound change in the educational paradigm takes place. This profound change in the educational paradigm will depend on political decisions, ideological elements, economic, and socio-cultural elements of those who make educational decisions at the national and local levels.

For the above reasons, the proposal of school practices of pluriverse sense-thoughts in this chapter is a contribution to promote the cognitive justice (De Sousa Santos, 2009), because it promotes the harmonic processes with Mother Earth and the reestablishment of the integral balance of the human-culture-nature relationship (Mavisoy, 2018). The school practices of pluriverse sense-thoughts produce an integral balance between man-culture-nature when the interrelationship and complementarity that exists between human beings and the other worlds that surround the human world are re-known (Escobar, 2014). The schools practices of pluriverses senses-thoughts facilitate people's reconnection to their territories of origin, their histories and their places of enunciation, to construct forms of social meaning where other knowledge and cosmovisions coexist (ancestral traditions, beliefs, aesthetics, etc.).

Precisely the conceptual proposal of school practices of pluriverse sense-thought is proposed as a relevant possibility to promote a paradigm shift in school education of the 21st century, not only in the case of Chile but in other Latin American countries.

Notes

1 The use of the word "children" in this chapter includes several genders and breaks the binominal norm of 'girls and boys.'
2 At the time of production of this chapter, the migration bill was still pending in the Chilean Congress.
3 The conceptualization of the new 'other' emerges from the theoretical horizon of the other (Rojas & Castillo, 2005) as a place of essential otherness that establishes hierarchies (dominant and dominated).
4 Sense-thoughts link persons to their territory, their community and the diverse forms of existence in the world. Therefore, it also involves the locus of enunciation of the persons, in addition to their accents, volumes of voice, rhythms (speed) of speech, and use of local lexicon.
5 Ancestral existential possibilities, epistemic, spiritual, social, aesthetic, political, and economic, among others.
6 Chile is characterized by being a long and narrow country, located on the western edge of South America.
7 According to the latest statistics, the city of Santiago (Chile's capital) concentrates 59.4% of the country's immigrants (Godoy, 2020).
8 Immigration is conceptualized from the transnational perspective of contemporary migration, taking into account ties to the country of origin, cross-border links and community-territory interconnections (Velasco, 1998; Portes, 1997).
9 According to reports provided by the Chilean Ministry of National Education (2018), the enrollment of children of migrant backgrounds is concentrated in public schools with 58% in basic education.
10 This type of practice is researched in public schools, because these are where the enrollment of children of migrant backgrounds in Chile is concentrated (Ministerio de Educación, Centro de Estudios, Mineduc, 2018).
11 According to Escobar (2014), there is a multiplicity of possible worlds, a pluriverse where practices of inter existence emerge.
12 The Nasa inhabit the Andean region of the southwest of Colombia.
13 The complete description of Humanitarian Plan for the orderly return is published at https://www.chileatiende.gob.cl/fichas/56635-plan-humanitario-de-regreso-ordenado.

14 Among the most debatable aspects of this plan are the requirements that must be declared under promise or oath of faith by whoever is interested: (a) not to have children born in Chile or minors under personal care or curatorship in Chile; (b) to renounce any application for residence in Chile (that he or she may have made), as well as any application for refuge or refugee status if he or she has it (as applicable); and (c) to accept the commitment and prohibition not to return to Chile, for the course of the next nine years from the materialization of the date of departure from the country.

15 This plan responds to what is stated in the political constitution of Chile in 1828 in the chapter referred to 'Of the Nation' in its article No. 1, that 'The Chilean Nation is the political meeting of all natural and legal Chileans. It is free and independent of any foreign power. Sovereignty resides in it essentially (…).' (Chile, 1828, p. 8).

16 According to the National Library of Chile, the School of Naturals opened in 1700 first in Chillán (until 1723), then in Santiago (1723–1767, 1775–1786), and then back again in Chillán (1786–1811).

17 The Pacific War between 1879 and 1883 pitted Chile against Peru and Bolivia.

18 For this research, political discourse refers to institutional forms of text and speech that have political implications. This discourse occurs in concrete circumstances and has legal implications (Van Dijk & Mendizábal, 1999).

19 For this research, educational discourse refers to the pedagogical discourse implemented in school settings whose function is to educate students.

20 This refers to the soul, the idiosyncrasies of a Chilean way of being (Larraín, 2014).

21 The Chilean military dictatorship took place between September 11, 1973 and March 11, 1990.

References

Althusser, L. (2015). *Sobre la reproducción* [On reproduction]. México: Akal.

Amuchástegui, M. (1995). Los rituales patrióticos en la escuela pública. In Puiggrós, A. (dir.), *Historia de la educación en Argentina* [History of education in Argentina]. Volume II. Buenos Aires: Galerna.

Aninat, I., & Vergara, R. (Eds). (2019). *Inmigración en Chile. Una mirada multidimensional* [Immigration in Chile. A multidimensional look]. Santiago de Chile: FCE, CEP.

Antonacci, M. (2015). Decolonialidade de Corpos e saberes: ensaio sobre a diáspora do eurocentrado [Decoloniality of Bodies and Knowledge: an essay on the diaspora of the eurocentric]. In M. Antonacci (Ed.), *Memórias ancoradas em corpos negros*. 2ª ed. São Paulo: Educ.

Apple, M. (1994). *Educación y Poder* [Education and Power]. Barcelona: Paidós/Mec.

Bellei C. (2013). El estudio de la segregación socioeconómica y académica de la educación chilena [The study of the socioeconomic and academic segregation of Chilean education]. *Estudios pedagógicos* (Valdivia), 39(1). pp. 325–345.

Bello, G. (2010). Alteridad, vulnerabilidad migratoria y responsabilidad asimétrica. *Revista Dilemata*, 3. pp. 119–127.

Bidaseca, K. (2017). ¿Dónde está Ana Mendieta? Estéticas afro-descoloniales feministas y poéticas eróticas caribeñas y anitillanas [Where is Ana Mendieta? Afro-decolonial feminist aesthetics and erotic poetics from the Caribbean and the West Indies]. In Campoalegre, R. & Bidaseca, K., *Más allá del decenio de los pueblos afrodescendientes*. Buenos Aires: Clacso.

Boff, L. (2017). *Una ética de la Madre Tierra. Cómo cuidar la casa común* [An ethic of Mother Earth. How to take care of the common home]. Madrid: Trotta.
Carrillo-Sánchez, C. (2020). *Niños/as de la inmigración en la educación chilena del siglo XXI. Prácticas escolares institucionalizadas en los procesos socio-culturales y políticos de las escuelas de la Región Metropolitana* [Children of immigration in the Chilean education of the 21st century. Institutionalized school practices in the socio-cultural and political processes of schools in the Metropolitan Region]. Unpublished PhD Thesis, Facultad de Ciencias Sociales FACSO de la Universidad de Chile, Santiago de Chile.
Cepeda, S. (2019). ¿Es posible la protección de los Derechos Humanos de niños, niñas y adolescentes migrantes en el marco de la regulación migratoria actual? [Is it possible to protect the human rights of migrant children and adolescents within the framework of current regulations on migration?]. *Revista Señales*, XIII (21). pp. 4–18.
De la Hoz, A., & Rentería, D. (2018). Capital Afro. Construcción de marca a partir de la reivindicación social. Caso Miss Balanta [Afro-Capital. Brand building from the social claim. The case of Miss Balanta]. Monograph. Available at: https://repository.javeriana.edu.co/handle/10554/40054.
De Sousa Santos, B. (2009). Más allá del pensamiento abismal: de las líneas globales a una ecología de saberes [Beyond abyssal thinking: from global lines to an ecology of knowledge]. In *Pluralismo epistemológico*. La Paz: CLACSO; CIDES-UMSA. La Paz, Bolivia: Muela del Diablo Editores.
_____. (2010). *Para descolonizar Occidente. Más allá del pensamiento abismal* [To decolonize the West. Beyond abyssal thinking]. Buenos Aires: Clacso.
_____. (2011). Epistemologías del Sur [Epistemologies from the South]. *Utopía y Praxis Latinoamericana*, 16(54). pp. 17–39.
_____. (2012). De las dualidades a las ecologías [From dualities to ecologies]. In *Cuaderno de Trabajo*. No. 18. Bolivia: Remte.
Dewey, J. (1967). *Democracia y Educación* [Democracy and Education]. Buenos Aires: Losada.
Díaz, A., & Ruz, R. (2009). Estado, escuela chilena y población andina en la ex Subdelegación de Putre. Acciones y reacciones durante el período post Guerra del Pacífico (1883-1929) [State, Chilean school and Andean population in the former Subdelegation of Putre. Actions and reactions during the post Pacific War period (1883-1929)]. *Polis, Revista de la Universidad Bolivariana*, 8(24). pp. 311–340.
Escobar, A. (2014). *Sentipensar con la tierra: nuevas lecturas sobre desarrollo, territorio y diferencia* [Feeling and thinking with the Earth: New Readings on Development, Territory and Difference]. Medellín: Ediciones Unaula.
Fals Borda, O. (2015). *Una sociología sentipensante para america latina* [A sentient and thinking sociology for Latin America]. Buenos Aires: Siglo XXI.
Foucault, M. (1998). *Vigilar y Castigar. Nacimiento de la prisión* [Discipline and Punishment- The Birth of the Prison]. Mexico: Siglo XXI.
Freire, P. (2000). *Pedagogía del oprimido* [Pedagogy of the Oppressed]. Madrid: Siglo XXI.
Fuentes, M., & Castellanos, P. (2020). El problema migratorio, un fenómeno global [The migration problem, a global phenomenon]. *Revista Metropolitana de Ciencias Aplicadas*, 3(1). pp. 169–176.
Gallego, A. (2010). *Formación de nación y educación* [Nation building and education]. Bogotá: Siglo del Hombre Editores S.A.

Gillborn, D. (2006). Teoría y educación crítica de la raza: Racismo y antirracismo en la teoría y la praxis educativa [Race Theory and Critical Education: Racism and Anti-racism in Educational Theory and Practice]. *Discurso: Estudios en la política cultural de la educación*, 27(1). pp. 11–32.
Giroux, H. (1990). Los profesores como intelectuales [Professors as intellectuals]. Barcelona: Paidós/Mec.
Godoy, G. (2020). Según estimaciones, la cantidad de personas extranjeras residentes habituales en Chile bordea los 1,5 millones al 31 de diciembre de 2019 [According to estimates, the number of foreign residents in Chile is around 1.5 million as of December 31, 2019]. *Prensa Ine.* Available at: https://www.ine.cl/prensa/2020/03/12/seg%C3%BAn-estimaciones-la-cantidad-de-personas-extranjeras-residentes-habituales-en-chile-bordea-los-1-5-millones-al-31-de-diciembre-de-2019.
González, S. (2002). Chilenizando a Tunupa. La escuela pública en el Tarapacá Andino 1880-1990 [Doing Tunupa Chilean. The public school in the Andean Tarapacá 1880-1990]. Santiago de, Chile: Colección Sociedad y Cultura.
Green, A. (2006). La educación desde la Madre Tierra: un compromiso con la humanidad [Education from Mother Earth: a commitment to humanity]. In *Memorias del Congreso Internacional de educación, investigación y formación docente.* Medellín: Facultad de Educación, Universidad de Antioquia-Colombia.
Green, A. (2011). *Propuesta de formación en la Licenciatura Pedagogía de la Madre Tierra* [Proposal for training in a Degree on the Pedagogy of Mother Earth]. Medellín: Universidad de Antioquia (Udea).
Grosfoguel, R. (2011). Racismo epistémico, islamofobia epistémica y ciencias sociales coloniales [Epistemic racism, epistemic islamophobia and colonial social sciences]. *Tabula Rasa,* (14). pp. 341–355. Available at: https://revistas.unicolmayor.edu.co/index.php/tabularasa/article/view/1418.
Herrera, L., & González, C. (2011). Problemáticas y perspectivas en torno a la migración [Migration challenges and perspectives]. *Frontera norte.* Mexico: Colegio de Chihuahua.
Jackson, P. (1992). *La vida en las aulas* [Life in the classroom]. Madrid: Ediciones Morata.
Larraín, J. (2014). *Identidad Chilena* [Chilean Identity]. Santiago de Chile: Lom.
Leyton, C. & Huertas, R. (2012). Reforma urbana e higiene social en Santiago de Chile: La tecno-utopía liberal de Benjamín Vicuña Mackenna (1872-1875) [Urban reform and social hygiene in Santiago de Chile: The liberal techno-utopia of Benjamín Vicuña Mackenna (1872-1875)]. *Dynamis,* 32(1). pp. 21–44.
López de Lara, A. (2017). La construcción de lo nacional en la escuela: espacio en disputa [the construction of the national in the school: space in dispute]. *Pacarina del Sur. Revista de Pensamiento Crítico Latinoamericano.* Available at: http://pacarinadelsur.com/editorial/62-dossiers/dossier-20/1420-la-construccion-de-lo-nacional-en-la-escuela-espacio-en-disputa.
Margarit, D., & Bijit, A. (2014). Barrios y población inmigrantes: el caso de la comuna de Santiago [Neighborhoods and immigrant population: the case of the municipality of Santiago]. *Revista INVI,* 29(81). pp. 19–77.
Martinez-Oña, M. & Muñoz, A. (2015). Iconografía, estereotipos y manipulación fotográfica de la belleza femenina [Iconography, stereotypes and photographic manipulation of female beauty]. *Estudios sobre el Mensaje Periodístico.* Madrid, Servicio de Publicaciones de la Universidad Complutense, 21(1). pp. 369–384.

Mavisoy, W. (2018). El conocimiento indígena para descolonizar el territorio. La experiencia Kamëntšá1 (Colombia) [The indigenous knowledge to decolonize the territory. The experience Kamëntšá1 (Colombia)]. *Revista Nómadas*, 48(4). pp. 239–248.

McLaren, P. (1995). *La escuela como un performance ritual. Hacia una economía política de los símbolos y gestos educativos* [The school as a ritual performance. Towards a political economy of educational symbols and gestures]. Mexico. Siglo XXI.

Mignolo, W. (2015). La comunidad, entre el lenguaje y el territorio [The community, between language and territory]. *Revista Colombiana de Sociología*, 38(2). pp. 167–182.

Ministerio de Educación, Centro de Estudios (Mineduc, 2018). Mapa del estudiantado extranjero en el sistema escolar chileno (2015-2017) [Map of foreign students in the Chilean school system (2015-2017)]. *Documento de trabajo N° 12*. Santiago de Chile.

Montoya, J. (2018). *Temas y problemas de geografía humana: una perspectiva contemporánea* [Themes and problems of human geography: a contemporary perspective]. Bogotá: Facultad de Ciencias Humanas, Universidad Nacional de Colombia.

Mucchielli, A. (2001). *Diccionario de Métodos Cualitativos en Ciencias Humanas y Sociales* [Dictionary of Qualitative Methods in Human and Social Sciences]. Madrid: Síntesis.

Muñoz, M. (2015). La educación en la construcción de la idea de ciudadano, 1910-1948 [Education in the construction of the idea of citizen, 1910-1948]. *Anuario de Historia Regional y de las Fronteras*, 20(2). pp. 183–213.

Navarrete, B. (2019). La inmigración en la agenda de seguridad en Chile. Las nuevas amenazas en los libros de la defensa nacional [Immigration on the Security Agenda in Chile. New Threats in the Books of National Defense]. *Estudios internacionales*, 51(193). pp. 37–63.

Palacios, N. (1918). *Raza Chilena. Libro escrito por un chileno y para chilenos* [Chilean Race. Book written by a Chilean and for Chileans]. Santiago de Chile: Editorial Chilena.

Pérez, A. (2009). *Las funciones sociales de la escuela: de la reproducción a la reconstrucción crítica del conocimiento y la experiencia* [The social functions of school: from reproduction to critical reconstruction of knowledge and experience]. Buenos Aires: LPP, Laboratorio de Políticas Públicas.

Pinheiro, L. (2015). Resistencia histórica y memorias colectivas en américa latina: construyendo pedagogías insumisas, insumiéndose desde otras educaciones [Historical Resistance and Collective Memories in Latin America: Building Unsubstantiated Pedagogies, Using Other Educations]. In P. Medina (Ed.), *Pedagogías insumisas: movimientos político-pedagógicos y memorias colectivas de educaciones otras en América Latina*. Mexico: Universidad de Ciencias y Artes de Chiapas, Centro de Estudios Superiores de México y Centroamérica, Educación para las Ciencias en Chiapas. pp. 300–325.

Portes, A. (1997). *Globalization from Below: The Rise of Transnational Communities*. USA: Princeton University. pp. 1–26.

Prussing, C., & Salazar, C. (2009): *Belleza y publicidad* [Beauty and advertising]. Thesis to obtain the degree on journalism. Universidad de ARCIS, Santiago de Chile.

Quijano, A. (2008). El movimiento indígena y las cuestiones pendientes en América Latina [The indigenous movement and outstanding issues in Latin America]. *El Cotidiano*, 151. pp. 107–120.

Quijano, A. (2014). Colonialidad del poder, eurocentrismo y América Latina [Coloniality of Power, Eurocentrism and Latin America]. In *Cuestiones y horizontes: de la dependencia histórico-estructural a lacolonialidad/descolonialidad del poder*. Buenos Aires: Clacso.

Rivera, S. (2018). *Un mundo ch'ixi es posible. Ensayos desde un presente en crisis* [A Ch'ixi World is Possible. Essays from a Present in Crisis]. Buenos Aires: Tinta Limón.

Rodríguez, E. (2017). La ecología de saberes en la sistematización de experiencias educativas como una apuesta pedagógica decolonial [The ecology of knowledge in the systematization of educational experiences as a decolonial pedagogical bet]. *Intersticios De La Política y la Cultura. Intervenciones Latinoamericanas*, 6(11). pp. 95–118.

Rojas, A., & Castillo, E. (2005). *Educar a los otros Estado, políticas educativas y diferencia cultural en Colombia* [Educating the Other States, Educational Policies and Cultural Difference in Colombia]. Cali: Editorial Universidad del Cauca.

Sagredo, R. (2013). La invención de un clásico: los recuerdos del pasado de Pérez Rosales [The invention of a classic: memories from Pérez Rosales]. *Anales de Literatura Chilena*, 14(19). pp. 41–60.

Salazar, M. (2018). Micropolíticas y pluriversos: interrogantes y construcción de posibles [Micropolitics and multi-verses: questions and construction of possible]. *Revista investigación & desarrollo*, 26(1). pp. 162–181.

Sánchez, C. (2000). El surgimiento de los Estados-Nación y las políticas pedagógicas como herramientas de integración social y de control en Iberoamérica en el siglo xix [The Emergence of Nation-States and Pedagogical Policies as Tools of Social Integration and Control in Ibero-America in the 19th Century]. In A. Roig. (Ed.), *El pensamiento social y político iberoamericano del siglo XIX*. Vol. 111. Madrid: Editorial Trotta. pp. 109–126.

Santos, M. (2000). *Por uma outra globalização. Do pensamento único a conciencia universal* [For another globalization. From one thought to universal consciousness]. Río de Janeiro: Editora Record.

Sarango, L. (2014). *El paradigma educativo de Abya Yala. Continuidad histórica, avances y desafíos* [The educational paradigm of Abya Yala. Historical continuity, advances and challenges]. Managua: Uraccan.

Sexton, J. (2012). Ante-Anti-Blackness: Afterthoughts. *Lateral*, 1. Available at: http://lateral.culturalstudiesassociation.org/issue1/content/sexton.html.

Silvia, L., & Allori, A. (2005). Los actos escolares como prácticas rituales: ¿conservar o redefinir? [School Acts as Ritual Practices: Preserve or Redefine?]. *Educación, Lenguaje y Sociedad*, III(3). pp. 197–206.

Sosa, E. (2009). La otredad: una visión del pensamiento latinoamericano contemporáneo [Otherness: a vision of contemporary Latin American thought]. *Letras* (Caracas), 1. pp. 51–80.

Steinhäuser, C. (2020). Los saberes de los ancestros: clave para los vínculos con la Madre Tierra en una comunidad andina en Argentina [The knowledge of the ancestors: key to the links with Mother Earth in an Andean community in Argentina]. *Documents d'Anàlisi Geogràfica* [S.l.], 66(2). pp. 307–324.

Stenhouse, L. (1991). *Investigación y desarrollo del curriculum* [Research and curriculum development]. Madrid: Morata.

Tijoux, M. (2014). El Otro inmigrante "negro" y el Nosotros chileno. Un lazo cotidiano pleno de significaciones [The Other "Black" Immigrant and the Chilean Us. A daily bond full of meanings]. *Boletín Onteaiken*, 17. Available at: http://onteaiken.com.ar/ver/boletin17/art-tijoux.pd.

Todorov, T. (2010). *Nosotros y los otros. Reflexión sobre la diversidad humana* [On Human Diversity]. Spain: Siglo XXI.

Van Dijk, T., & Mendizábal, I. (1999). *Análisis del discurso social y político* [Analysis of social and political discourse]. Ecuador: Abya-Yala.

Velasco, L. (1998). Identidad cultural y territorio: una reflexión en torno a las comunidades transnacionales entre México y Estados Unidos [Cultural Identity and Territory: A Reflection on Transnational Communities between Mexico and the United States]. *Región y Sociedad*, Sonora, Mexico, IX (15). pp. 105–130.

Vicuña, M. (1872). *La transformación de Santiago. Notas e indicaciones* [The transformation of Santiago. Notes and indications]. Santiago de Chile: Imprenta de la Librería del Mercurio.

Villareal, K. (2017). Trenzando la identidad: cabello y mujeres negras [Braiding Identity: Black Hair and Women]. Thesis to obtain the degree of magister. Facultad de Ciencias Humanas de Departamento de Antropología de la Universidad Nacional de Colombia, Bogotá.

Wynter, S. (2009). En torno al principio sociogénico. Fanon, la identidad y el rompecabezas de la experiencia consciente y cómo ser "negro" [Around the sociogenic principle. Fanon, the identity and puzzle of conscious experience and how to be "black"]. In F. Fanon, *Piel negra, máscaras blancas*. Madrid: Akal.

Zaffaroni, E. (2011). *La Pachamama y el humano* [Pachamama and the human]. Buenos Aires: Ediciones Colihue.

Zamora, J. (2005). Políticas de inmigración, ciudadanía y estado de excepción [Immigration, citizenship and state of emergency policies]. *Arbor*, 181(713). pp. 53–66.

Zarate, R. (2017). Somos Mexicanos, no Somos Negros: Educar para Visibilizar el Racismo "Anti-Negro" [We are Mexicans, not Blacks: Educating to Make "Anti-Black" Racism Visible]. *Revista Latinoamericana de Educación Inclusiva*, 11(1). pp. 57–72.

Chapter 3

Indigenous Mexican Migrant Youth School Testimonios in the Florida Heartland

Farmwork, Migration, Language, Discrimination, and Extracurricular Activities

Yenny Saldaña, Mariana Santiago, Ana Guevara, Liliana Mata, Eduardo Morales, Briana Salazar, Cristina Saldaña, Adolfo Saldaña, and Rebecca Campbell-Montalvo

Introduction

Recent work has documented the educational circumstances of Indigenous Mexican migrant farmworking students in the US (Perez, 2009; Salas & Portes, 2017; Perez, Vásquez, & Buriel, 2016; Vásquez, 2019; Urrieta, Mesinas, & Martínez, 2019), a multiply-minoritized and culturally rich population. Migrant farmworkers move in conjunction with the crop seasons in order to work in agriculture to make a living. Since 1965, the US has had a federally funded program to support educational success of migrant students, known as Title 1 Part C: Migrant Education Program (Florida Department of Education, 2020).

In considering how Indigenous Mexican migrant farmworking students experience schooling, one vein of scholarship has focused on how students' linguistic, racial, and ethnic identities are perceived by educators, who then provide educational services based on those perceptions (Barillas Chón et al., 2021; Baquedano-López & Borge Janetti, 2017; Baquedano-López, 2019; Machado-Casas, 2012; Campbell-Montalvo, 2020a; Campbell-Montalvo, 2020b; Campbell-Montalvo & Castañeda, 2019; Campbell-Montalvo et al., forthcoming). In the US, the law requires that schools identify student and parent language information to support educational efforts (Education Commission of the States, 2014). Subtractionist policies, such as those found at the research site (Campbell, 2016), generally attempt to shame away home language use among Latinos and other children (Valenzuela, 1999) and reward the learning of 'foreign' languages among non-Latino White students, a phenomenon known as 'elite bilingualism' (Fuller, 2012). At the same time, previous work has

DOI: 10.4324/9781003090519-4

found that many Indigenous Latino parents want their children to learn English for improved chances at upward social mobility (Bishop & Kelley, 2013; Velasco, 2010).

In a county in the Florida Heartland anonymized as 'Central County,' Indigenous Latino families who reported using Náhuatl and other Indigenous languages had their languages re-formed in school records as 'Spanish' (Campbell-Montalvo, 2020b). This occurred in part due to language ideologies that cast Indigenous languages as 'dialects' compared to the higher status Spanish as a 'language' (Meek & Messing, 2007). For every 19 students who had a parent who spoke an Indigenous Mexican language, only one was documented in school records as doing so (Campbell-Montalvo, 2020b). At the same time, these students' racial status of American Indian is re-formed by the Florida Department of Education due to the state's policy that for Latino students, only their ethnicity is recorded (Campbell-Montalvo, 2020a). The assumption that people who are Latino do not have any additional racial or ethnic identities, including Indigenous identities, nor speak languages other than Spanish, is known as Latinization[1] (Salas & Portes, 2017). Indeed, recent research suggests that such Latinization processes that erase linguistic and racial Indigeneity at school may be widespread (Barillas Chón et al., 2021; Baquedano-López, 2019). Together, this existing research suggests a disconnect between how these students understand themselves and how educators understand them, directly impacting how they are served by schools. Indigenous Mexican farmworkers wanting to take advantage of Central County's robust Migrant Education Program that employs eight Migrant Advocates (with six of the eight being bilingual Latinas—though none speak an Indigenous language) face obstacles in receiving services in Indigenous languages and must find neighbors or others to interpret in order to access services (Campbell-Montalvo & Castañeda, 2019; Campbell-Montalvo & Pfister, 2021; Campbell-Montalvo, forthcoming).

To understand how Indigenous Mexican youths experience schooling and are served by schools in Central County, one must also pay attention to the other circumstances and relevant social and economic forces in these youth's lives. Previous fieldwork in the Florida Heartland has found that unequal opportunities for linguistic, racial, and ethnic groups are a primary feature of life in Central, spurred by historical and current social forces privileging students and adults from dominant groups (Campbell, 2016). For instance, a prior Central educator survey (n=81) showed that there was disconnect between how educators from various racial groups perceived racism. The majority of Latino and African American educators believed racism was a problem in the schools and county, while the majority of non-Latino White educators disagreed, with several noting that, if anything, 'reverse racism' was the issue. Observations in Central schools showed that people who made negative statements about farmworkers were predominantly non-Latino monolingual English-speaking White educators, while several Latino school employees reported that such negative sentiments were also expressed by people in the community. However, this previous research did not employ methodologies that allowed youth to share experiences in their own words.

Thus, this chapter presents a perspective missing in the literature by offering an account of these children's educational experiences through their own testimonios. Testimonios are an appropriate method for this chapter's purpose, given their established use by non-dominant groups to confront oppression and highlight injustice (Pérez Huber, 2012). The excerpts of testimonios included here were kept in their original form. Unlike other more in-depth testimonies (i.e. Blackmore, 2012), the testimonios included here were letters that did not go through multiple rounds of revisions or mediation and instead were singular drafts in which the youth organically shared their life experiences. As these Indigenous Mexican migrant youth share, their lives as students are affected by their positions in society as farmworkers and/or children of farmworkers, their movement to new places, their own language and identities and others' perceptions and treatment to their languages and identities, racially or ethnically motivated discrimination, and participation in schooling programs.

The testimonio letters were written in the first half of 2020 by eight self-identified Indigenous Mexican migrant youth who are receiving or have received schooling in Central. The youth were aged 14–19, and the ages of the testimonio writers are a strength of this work, given that many testimonios and other work on the issues in this chapter are done with older individuals (except such work as Blackmore, 2012). The letter writers all come from families where an Indigenous Mexican language is spoken by some members of the family. Some youth were born in Mexico while others were US-born. These youth and their families are part of an Indigenous Latin American diaspora to the US (Clifford, 2007), and their experiences are impacted by global forces in the lands from which they and/or their parents come (e.g., Guerrero, San Luis Potosí, and Querétaro).

Setting

The Florida Heartland is an agricultural area in central Florida that is more culturally US Southern, rural, religious, and politically conservative than many other parts of the state. Central has experienced marked Latino migration since the 1950s, with Tejanos (Mexicans and Mexican Americans from Texas, US) coming to harvest watermelon at that time (Mize & Swords, 2010; Campbell-Montalvo & Castañeda, 2019). More recently, Mexicans, many Indigenous, have come directly from Mexico to seek better lives and education for their families (Campbell, 2016).

Table 3.1 Demographic characteristics for selected schools and the district for the 2014–2015 school year, according to the Florida Department of Education

Level	Latino**	White	Black	Asian	American Indian	Pacific Islander	Multiracial	Migrant	English language learner	Economically disadvantaged	Total students
Apple Elementary School	61%	28%	7%	*	*	0%	2%	12%	21%	83%	547
Emerald Elementary School	80%	17%	*	*	0%	0%	*	21%	48%	87%	373
Central Junior High	61%	31%	6%	*	*	0%	2%	11%	5%	80%	1209
Central School District	61%	30%	6%	1%	<1%	0%	2%	12%	12%	79%	–

* A group containing fewer than 10 students but greater than zero.
** Latinos are counted in the Latino category and in no racial group.

Sixty-one percent of Central County's students are Latino, as shown in Table 3.1, which also provides information on additional student characteristics. The county's school district has a predominantly non-Latino monolingual English-speaking White teaching workforce, as well as the active Migrant Education Program serving hundreds of students each year.

Central emblemizes aspects of *Friday Night Lights: A Town, a Team, and a Dream* (Bissinger, 1990) in the ways that the culture of rural communities is connected to or emerges from the local schools, including the weekly high school football game (Campbell, 2016). In Central, critical spheres of social life in the county revolve around the schools and their high-ranking social actors. For example, the Back-to-School Tailgate Party is a public event in Central's capital town held by the Central County School District. Several thousand residents attend The Tailgate Party at the beginning of each school year. It offers a venue for school board members and business owners to set up tables to get their names and businesses out into the public domain. The event features performances by the high school's cheerleading team and an appearance by Miss Central, a high school junior crowned with the title by a panel of judges.

In Central, school resources and place are largely and critically affected by students' positions in racial, ethnic, language, socioeconomic, and citizenship status groups (Campbell, 2016). For instance, around the time of the Back-to-School Tailgate Party, a local non-profit organization holds a smaller back-to-school event with the goal of providing school supplies that is attended by hundreds of students and families. Most attendees are families racialized as African American/Black or Latino, and many are economically disadvantaged. School board members similarly haul out their professional banners and set up tents to hand out pencils and other items. The county sheriff's department passes out bike helmets, and a foodbank gives away loaves of bread.

Testimonios, Testimonio Gathering, and Author Positionality

Emerging from Critical Race Theory, the field of LatCrit emphasizes an examination of the experiences of Latinos in areas often relevant to their lives, including immigration, language, and ethnicity (Pérez Huber, 2010; Solórzano & Delgado Bernal, 2001). Within LatCrit, testimonios, 'politically urgent life stories' (Prieto, 2016, p. 96), is a conceptual tool and method (Fuentes & Pérez, 2016) using participants' own words or writing to express their experiences in contexts of inequality (Booker, 2002; Beverly, 2000; Blackmore, 2012; González et al., 2003; Mangual Figueroa, 2013; Kleyn et al., 2018; Smith, 2010). Various scholars deploy differing conceptions of testimonios (Pérez Huber, 2009), calling them 'authentic narratives' (Yúdice, 1991, p. 17) or 'verbal journeys' (Brabeck, 2001, p. 3). The operationalization of testimonio we use was offered by Morales and colleagues (2001) as 'a way to create knowledge and theory through personal experiences' (Pérez Huber, 2009, p. 643), which is 'used by non-dominant groups to challenge oppression and brings attention to injustice' (Pérez Huber, 2012, p. 377). We employ testimonios in the form of letters to bring forth the stories of Indigenous Mexican migrant youth to document and speak back to injustices they have experienced relating to their social positions.

In addition to authoring a testimonio, first author Yenny Saldaña recruited testimonio writers from her network, emphasizing that she was looking for Indigenous Latino migrant youth. Potential contributors were given electronic flyers (in Spanish and English) asking them to share about: the language(s) they grew up speaking in their home; experiences in and out of the classroom that may have been influenced by their linguistic, racial, and ethnic identities; how their families came to live in Central; the kind of work their family does; and how that line of work has impacted their lives. Yenny collected the letters and read and organized their content into themes, then she and last author Rebecca Campbell-Montalvo presented them here layered by analysis. Co-authors Mariana Santiago, Ana Guevara, Liliana Mata, Eduardo Morales, Briana Salazar, Cristina Saldaña, and Adolfo Saldaña contributed one testimonio each to this chapter but did not take part in further mediation of the testimonios. Some authors preferred not to link their testimonios to their identities, so all testimonios are presented using pseudonyms. Although they were encouraged to write in English or Spanish, all writers submitted their letters in English.

Regarding the positionality of the lead authors, Yenny is an Indigenous Mexican who was born in Chilapa de Álvarez and grew up in Central. She is equally fluent in Spanish and English, having learned the latter in elementary school. Rebecca and Yenny first met while Rebecca was conducting home visits with Central County School District Migrant Advocates during ethnographic fieldwork beginning in 2014. Rebecca is a cultural anthropologist who is a non-Latina White woman who speaks English as her first language and who learned Spanish as an adult.

Testimonios: Work, Migration, Language, Discrimination, and School Activities

Characteristics of Work and Migration

In order to make a living, families usually had to relocate seasonally with crop cycles. In their letters, youth described the types of produce they harvested and the agricultural activities in which they and their parents participated.

Luisa, 17, wrote about how her parents work in an aquatic plant nursery after seeking to change their work environment when she was born:

> In 2003, I was born. So they had to find a different workplace from the one they had [where they were] picking chiles, *ejotes*, tomatoes, etc. My mother eventually started [working] for a company known for its aquatic plants in that same year. My father eventually joined in the year of 2004. The men's role in the work would be to plant plants around the coastline of some beaches in different states and sometimes to take out some of the plants in the lakes. The women's role is to plant seeds and take plants out of the lake.

Jorge, 19, wrote that his parents worked harvesting in the fields, but it was still difficult to always have enough money to purchase food. He noted that oftentimes the children would help their parents work, harvesting in the fields to make ends meet:

> My parents did field work, picking oranges, cucumbers, tomatoes, tobacco, etc. and at times it took us kids to help to bring more money in. I remember that it was difficult to just get food on the table and to make money.

The parents of Francisco, 14, also worked as harvesters, '[My parents] work in the fields, mainly in picking and sometimes planting. This makes us move every year between Florida and Michigan.'

The parents of Mariana, 16, similarly engaged in farm work:

> Since coming to the US, about 16 years ago, my parents have moved around a lot. We usually stay in Florida for most of the school year and move to Michigan in the summer. We do this because my parents work in the fields. They go where the work takes them. They have worked in planting, picking, and packing just about everything you would find in a grocery store.

Mía, 19, described in further detail her family's migratory past. Like Jorge, she wrote about working in the fields with her parents as a child. She equated her work alongside them in the fields with important life lessons that taught her the value of money.

> We have been migrating back and forth from Florida to Michigan for as long as I can remember. My family usually stays in Michigan for the entire summer and heads back to Florida at the end of fall. In Michigan, we pick and work in the packaging warehouses for blueberries. After the blueberry season ends, we pick apples. In Florida, my parents plant, weed, and pick a variety of fruits and vegetables (tomatoes, eggplants, squash, peas, okra, watermelon, etc.). Up until this year, I worked in the fields alongside my parents. I've prepared the soil, dug holes using my fingers for seeds, picked, packaged, and dug plastic from the raised beds. I am honestly grateful for all the experiences that I've had from working under the sun. From an early age, I learned the value of a single dollar bill and how important it was to be responsible with my money. My parents showed me that even though you have absolutely nothing, if you work hard enough, you can get by.

Natalia, 17, also described her family's migration route in detail. She noted that her family primarily moved between three states:

> Ever since I can remember I have been migrating with my family... However, Florida was different since we always came back to the same town in Central County and stayed there a little longer. You see, after my younger brother was born, my parents decided to settle down in Okeechobee, Florida. Later on, because of failed orange crops, we came to small Central County and we made our life here, although we never stopped migrating north for the summer. Now, let me explain what migrating means to me and my family. From November to May we live in Florida, picking whatever crops this state has to offer, from strawberries to tomatoes. During May and June, we reside in North Carolina for the blueberry season. Then comes July through October, which we spend in cold Michigan picking blueberries and apples.

Migration and Schooling

As shown, many of the families described in the letters traveled between two states, but others went to new areas yearly. Nearly all these youth noted how their educational experiences were affected by migration as members of migrant farmworking families.

The differing start and end times of academic years between states, such as Michigan and Florida, caused rising senior Natalia to lose out on a month of school every year:

> You might have noticed how this schedule affected me as a student, but in case you didn't catch on let me explain. School in Florida starts in August but because of the blueberry season, I am in Michigan during the first three months of school. You might say, 'Then attend school in Michigan.' But, you see, the problem with that is that school in this northern state does not begin until September. So, ever since kindergarten, I miss out on about a month or more of school. This gap made my learning a bit more difficult but not impossible.

Natalia noted the programs in which she participates to attempt to make up for time she misses in formal schooling:

> I was blessed with help from different programs, groups, and individual people who cared about my education and experience as a migrant student. The Van Buren NOMAD [Needs and Objectives for Migrant Advancement and Development] program is an example of the help I received. The NOMAD program was a summer school where kids like me attended and reviewed topics that we most likely missed out on the previous school year. However, not all migrant students get this help or know that the program exists.

Mía wrote about how older siblings in her family come back to Central earlier than the younger ones in order to avoid missing school:

> Once school starts in Florida, any one of us past 8th grade goes back. This is to ensure that we do not fall behind on Honors or AP classes. The rest of the family stays in Michigan until the apple season is over. This is usually the beginning of November.

Like Natalia, Mía also wrote about how she and her siblings participated in summer programs in other states:

> My younger siblings are enrolled in summer school and participate in a migrant program. The Van Buren Migrant Program [NOMAD] really

helps because my parents can work knowing that the little ones are safe at school. It also saves us money because we don't have to pay for a babysitter.

Mariana also noted participation in various migrant programs:

> In elementary school, my parents signed me and my brother up for an afterschool program that focused on migrants. We were in that program for one year before dropping it to work in the field with my parents. In sixth grade, I attended another migrant afterschool program before dropping that as well because the crop season was bad and we had to pitch in to help my family. The three youngest in the family (me and my younger brothers) also went to a migrant summer school program in Michigan.

Jorge also commented on how migration impacted his education, noting that he was not always placed at the same level and that schools used different curriculum:

> As early as I can remember, my family migrated from state to state for work. A result of that was the young ones in the family like myself changing schools constantly. The first time I went to school in Florida was in kindergarten…We migrated back and forth from northern states like Ohio and North Carolina for work, sometimes not always in the same city or county so almost every year was a different school…As for my educational experience, it was a mix. Sometimes I would be put in advanced classes while other times I would be put in the intensive classes. It was harder to learn because whenever we changed schools each one had their own curriculum, so we would either have to catch up or wait depending on how far we got in the previous school. Sometimes it was completely different. From my experience, we did try to seek help from migrant programs and such to receive help for school supplies or transportation.

The impacts of migration on social elements of schooling were apparent. For instance, Francisco wrote, 'In school I mostly avoided people in order to not get attached to anyone because I didn't want to feel sad when I moved. I feel like this pushed me towards my love for books.' Jorge similarly commented on how being enrolled in new schools each year impacted his relationships with peers, writing, 'To me that was one of the challenges. It was harder to make friends since you were always the new kid, and when you did make friends then you didn't know if you would see them again.'

Like most of her peers, Natalia wrote about moving a lot, but emphasized that her notion of home had more to do with who she was with:

> I have memories of different camps and houses that became a home for me and my family for the two months or so that we spent there. To me, home was not a what or a where but a who. I guess I truly live by the Spanish saying *'hogar es donde está la familia'* ['home is where your family is'].

Related to the theme of migration, three youth discussed border crossing. For instance, Camila, 15, wrote about how her parents came to the US:

> My parents are from Mexico and arrived to the United States in 2002 after two attempts. On their first attempt they were caught and deported back to Mexico. Despite not making it the first time they decided to try again. They successfully made it by the help of a border patroller. Eventually, they made it to Arizona where an old man offered them a ride and a place to stay. They agreed to stay for two weeks while they found a ride to Florida. Once they arrived to Florida they found a place to work picking oranges.

Mía also shared her immigration story:

> My parents, two older brothers, and I immigrated from Guerrero, Mexico. I crossed the border when I was 3 years old, so I have been living in the US for about 16 years. I don't recall much from that experience, but my parents tell me stories of the border crossing. We hired a coyote to guide us through. I was wearing my backpack and not allowed to put it down, otherwise I would lose it. We mainly traveled at night, dodging from one bush to another. After a close call with border patrol, our group got separated. We of course found each other and were more careful to stick together after that. The journey was particularly difficult on my mother. She was heavily pregnant at the time and was in charge of me and my two older brothers. The oldest, age 8 at the time, slept near a scorpion and was bitten on his leg.

Language and Schooling

In writing about language, several students discussed being bilingual in their letters. Mía wrote, 'Everyone in my family speaks both English and Spanish, but my mother is the only one who can fluently speak Náhuatl.' As noted in Camila's letter, 'I speak both English and Spanish. Both of my parents speak Spanish and a little bit of Náhuatl.' Jorge wrote, 'My parents spoke only Spanish and another native language, but my siblings and I did grow up learning English due to schooling, which I believe was my parents' goal.'

Like many of her peers, Mariana wrote about her family's use of an Indigenous language. She wrote:

> My parents had six kids. My older siblings [learned Spanish in the home and] had to learn English while in elementary school, but they now know both languages. While all of us kids and my dad are bilingual in English and Spanish, my mom on the other hand also speaks Náhuatl in addition to Spanish. At home we use a mix of English and Spanish, sometimes twisting them into the same sentence. Occasionally we will say 'thank you' in Náhuatl, but that's as far as we know that one.

In describing their language repertoires, other youth noted that they spoke Spanish far less well than their older siblings. For instance, Francisco wrote, 'My family has been in the United States for 15 years. I mostly speak English because I'm not exactly fluent in Spanish, most of my older siblings can speak Spanish better than me. My parents mainly speak Spanish.' Francisco and his younger brother had learned English from their four older siblings before they had entered school (Campbell, 2016).

Mía recalled in her letter what it was like to learn English in Central schools. She wrote:

> When I started at Apple Elementary School, I only knew Spanish. Even though I tried my best, I was failing language arts, spelling, and reading. I remember feeling ashamed for not knowing the language that came so easily to the other kids. The teachers didn't know how to communicate with me, so they mainly left me alone while they helped the other kids. I don't remember how long this continued for, but it all changed when I was introduced to a [bilingual Latina paraprofessional interpreter at the school]...She would regularly pull me out of class to teach me the basics of English. Her one-on-one teaching sessions continued until 3rd grade, when I caught up with my peers.

Melanie, 19, detailed a different linguistic and migratory experience than the other youth, writing:

> My father used to do migrant work before I was born. From what I was told, he would travel up and leave my mother here while he worked. I did not know what he did or where he went because once I was born, he didn't leave anymore. So, I did not grow up with the struggles that most immigrant children faced; however, with me being half Hispanic and half White, I faced different problems growing up.

Melanie indicated that she did not speak Spanish, but that others assumed that she did because of her name and appearance. She wrote about how others' assumptions of her language use impacted her in both school and work.

> A majority of my school paperwork was sent home in Spanish just because of my last name. I remember classmates talking to me in Spanish because they assumed I knew the language, all because of the color of my skin. This problem became more frequent when I went to high school and in Spanish class. People would believe that I already knew what I was doing when I didn't. I had to work hard in that class while others didn't. I can recall an issue during my AP English class my junior year where some of the guys were asking me if I knew what something meant just because they knew my last name and knew it was Spanish. They stated, 'I thought you knew what it meant because you speak it all the time' and no one in the room had ever heard me speak in Spanish. And now, with me being a working adult out in the community, I get it worse. People will have full conversations with me in Spanish and I only catch certain parts because of the Spanish classes I took in high school…I have had to learn to adapt in the work environment because of my language boundary. I've had to make gestures for things like an I.D. and had to pull up things [on my phone] as an example and pray that someone else in line could help me with the situation. I have tried countless times to help build my vocabulary, but I just can't find the time for it between school and work. For now, I just pick up on things here and there that I hear my friends say so that I can understand the people in my community better and communicate with them.

Discrimination at School and in the Community

In about half of the letters, the youth wrote that they had not experienced discrimination and felt connected to their community. For the other half, youth wrote about schooling and public contexts in which they experienced discrimination, or negative treatment because of their appearance. For example, while Luisa felt that, overall, she was happy with the schooling opportunities available to her and she took advantage of them, she noted that they were not free from discrimination and neglect. She wrote:

> My experiences in public schools are super amazing. Most teachers that I had are super understanding and hardworking. I try my best by participating in [as] many extracurricular activities as I can. This includes programs such as the STEM [Science, Technology, Engineering, and Math] program, Team Donnie, Key Club, Leo club, AVID [Advancement Via Individual Determination], and [more].[2] However, this does not mean I receive the same treatment as other students in one of the programs.

At the time, I was the only brown student in the group while the rest were White. Last year, I joined a program thinking I would have one of the best experiences with my instructor. However, I was wrong. Every time I would try to communicate with the instructor, she would avoid reading my messages and end up answering like two days or even a week later stating, 'Forgive me, I am just seeing your text.' I would check in with my group to see if they had gotten a response from the instructor and they stated they would receive emails and text messages on the same day they texted her. Most people that know me know that I am such a thoughtful and caring person. I never gave a reason for the instructor to ignore any of my messages or phone calls.

Mariana wrote about how she and her family frequently encounter people in public shopping areas who turn away from them, who could at any time make negative statements about them because of their ethnicity, or who might direct rude looks their way. She wrote:

We usually end up surrounded by family each time we move so I believe that most people just stick with their peoples. They just kind of live their life pretending the other doesn't exist and move on. We encounter them in daily life and if they see us sometimes they just turn the other way. Others will mumble under their breath about how Mexicans are stealing their jobs or say 'You should go back to where you came from.' Sometimes they don't say anything, but they give you a look, and you know what that look means. And anytime you see or hear those you just have to ignore it and move on with your life. You have better things to do than entertain ignorant people.

Mía also wrote about the negative comments heard from strangers in public places. In this case, these harassing comments and actions were directed specifically toward farmworkers.

The one time I've ever had a racist encounter with someone from my community was at Walmart. I will never forget this. It was a Saturday, because that was the only day that *campos* would use old school buses to transport their workers to shop and do laundry. So that day, Walmart was packed with Hispanic fieldworkers wearing dirty clothes and muddy shoes. I was walking past a classmate of mine when I noticed an older White woman who was staring at the fieldworkers in utter disgust. She turned to my classmate and loudly said, 'Look at them. Can't they at least take a shower, like normal human beings?' My classmate said nothing but elbowed her as if she was trying to get her to be quiet. I ignored them and continued to the next aisle. A short while later, I saw them again. The woman was making it quite obvious that she didn't want to be near a fieldworker. And every time she passed one, she would scrunch up her face as if she smelled something foul. At one point, she started complaining that there were no more bags of Hot Cheetos on the shelf. I heard her exclaim, 'They take our jobs, they take our schools,' she made eye contact with me when she said this part, 'and now they want to take our food!? Honestly! They should just go back to where they came from.' My classmate said, 'Mom! Stop it!' The woman glared at me and her daughter but finally got quiet. I started walking away, but out of the corner of my eye I saw the woman approach one of the workers. He had his back turned and did not notice her reach into his cart, take out two bags of Hot Cheetos, and place them in her cart. Her daughter saw this transaction but didn't say anything. I decided to wait for the woman to turn her back towards her cart. When she did, I quickly grabbed both bags of Hot Cheetos and returned them to the original cart. My classmate saw me do this and smiled.

Extracurricular School Activities

Youth wrote about the programs that helped them cope as students dealing with pressures experienced by any student, as well as those particularly affecting Indigenous, migrant, farmworking, English-learning Latinos. Regarding extracurricular activities, Camila wrote:

> I never had a bad experience at public school. I do the best of my ability in all my classes. I even joined a club and had a great experience. I was eager to know that everyone in that club wanted to help out the community. It felt good to share something in common with everyone.

Mía wrote about the Airforce Junior Reserve Officer's Training Corps (AFJROTC) in which she participated at her school. Mía described the equitable atmosphere crafted in his program:

> In high school, I was part of the AFJROTC program. I really loved it because everyone was given equal opportunities to advance in the Corps. Everyone started on an equal platform and when it was time to train, we trained as a group. Anytime a cadet was having difficulties, a higher ranking or a more experienced cadet would take the time to help them. The Corps had different races and ethnicities and was accepting to them all.

Mía also wrote of the Central High School's annual multicultural day event. Various student cultures were incorporated and expressed widely, including Mexican, Hmong, African American, and more. Some wore traditional

Hmong or Mexican folkloric clothing and performed dances from their cultures (Campbell, 2016). Mía wrote:

> My high school also had a yearly tradition called Multi-cultural Day. Different school clubs and sport teams would choose a country and bring in food originating from that country. During lunchtime, we could buy food from a lot of different cultures. Some students would participate in a talent show. They could dress up, sing and dance to music played in that country. It was a day our differences were celebrated.

Conclusion

These testimonios illustrate how Indigenous Mexican migrant youth experience schooling, bringing forward injustices, oppression, and resistance. As related to work, Jorge noted that at times it was difficult for his family to have enough food on the table, and that the children would work with their parents in order to make more money. Like Jorge and Mariana, Mía wrote about working in the fields with her parents as a child and how it taught her the value of money. The context of being in families making a living through laborious work (Holmes, 2013; Campbell-Montalvo & Castañeda, 2019) requiring children to work outside of the home would present challenges for any student.

As the youth noted, these challenges were compounded by the effects of having to relocate frequently. Natalia pointed out that she missed out on a month of school every year, which equates to more than a year (13 months) of missed schooling from kindergarten to 12th grade by the time she graduates. With the Central academic year starting in August, migrant students who are not physically present in schools at that time often do not have a spot saved for them (including in AP [Advanced Placement], Honors, and Advanced courses) when they return to the Central school district, usually in November (Campbell, 2016). Mía's family has adapted to polices that exclude late-arriving migrant students from honors or advanced classes by sending older siblings home earlier than the rest of the family, to be looked after by guardians or to live alone in the family home. Such adaptations are indicative of the high value placed upon schooling by such families, but surely exert an emotional and economic burden on families. Even with these adaptations, youth, like Jorge, noted that they are not always placed at the same level and different states use varying curriculum. Jorge and Francisco wrote about the emotional heartbreak they experience from having to leave friends when they move, and how it affected their tendency to make connections with others.

Most youth wrote about their linguistic resources, as shown in Camila's letter where she discussed how the multilingual speakers of her household interact by incorporating elements from multiple languages into a system, a practice also known as translanguaging (Canagarajah, 2011). Some youth, such as Melanie and Francisco, mentioned a lack of proficiency in Spanish and how that affected them. While Francisco uses English as a primary language, he still grew up with the same parents who raised him in the same Indigenous traditions and values as his siblings who had Spanish fluency (Campbell, 2016).

Several youth wrote about experiencing discrimination, whether it was in school (Luisa) or out in the community (Mariana and Mía). Luisa's note on being the only brown student in a school program is especially troublesome, given the district demographic make-up and differential participation in extracurriculars (Campbell, 2016). In her letter, she problematizes the teacher's behavior, noting she had not done anything to deserve the neglect. Additionally, Mía's resistance to the White woman's prejudiced comments and entitlement of groceries in a farmworker's shopping cart through her return of the Cheetos to the man's possession shows how youth often resist when they can. Similar to Mía's story, non-Latino White educators advised Campbell-Montalvo to shop at Walmart on weekdays to avoid shopping alongside farmworkers, and observations and survey showed prejudicial attitudes were present among educators (disproportionately so for non-Latino Whites) (Campbell, 2016).

While they pointed out specific injustices, the letter writers also showed how they dealt with many of them. Natalia's conception of home as where one's family is helped her cope with frequent moves. For most of the letter writers, school programs were helpful and they took advantage of these resources. Mía's engagement in the AFJROTC program helped her feel included at school. The efforts of the Central High School AFJROTC leader, a non-Latino White man with the military rank of Lieutenant Coronel, have been previously documented. He was often one of the only non-Latino White people at local community events, such as *quinceañeras* (coming-of-age celebrations/rites of passage in which girls become women) and graduations, having been invited by students (Campbell, 2016).

In sum, this chapter amplifies the voices of these youth to humanize people whose stories are often not told (Fuentes & Pérez, 2016). The examples of racist insults hurled at children in grocery store and experiences of discriminatory educational neglect are powerful glimpses into the social worlds that US society is crafting for these young people. In the tradition of the testimonio as a conceptual tool and method, we hope that positive outcomes will occur from our highlighting of the unjust schooling experiences of these youth in their own words.

Moving forward, this work has demonstrated that school and community improvements (and national changes) need to be made, and the adoption of school-community partnerships (López & Irizarry, 2019) that draw upon asset-based perspectives as well as interactions with majority communities to support change could further support better experiences for these students. Increased investment in attempts to ameliorate negative implications of migration on the social and educational wellbeing of children through such programs as those mentioned by students will likely be positive. We urge educators, peers, policy makers, and people in the world to consider, listen, and incorporate what has been communicated in these testimonios into their macro and micro decisions, ranging from decisions about school policies to decisions about how to treat farmworkers in the grocery store.

Notes

1 The claiming of Indigeneity by the youth in this chapter may be seen as a performance of a reconnection to an identity that was stolen, especially in light of the linguistic and racial re-formation and Latinization cited in text. Xón Riquiac (2020) notes that such 'processes of racialization' through which Indigenous peoples come to be constructed as non-Indigenous occur through capitalist, religious, and educational forces institutionalized by state and global forces. For further context, see López López's (2018) critique of how Indigeneity is constructed based on static early 20th century anthropological representations and her application of a more nuanced discussion on how markers of Indigeneity often reflect what it means to be Indigenous only in colonial terms. Gómez's (2018) and Menchaca's (2002) work on the various social forces making Mexican as a race provide additional insight. See also work on the use of mestizaje to erase Indigeneity (Castellanos, 2017; Chacón, 2017; Saldaña-Portillo, 2017; Urrieta & Calderón, 2019).
2 Each of these clubs and organizations are either local or chapters of national non-profit and similar organizations that have stated goals that seek to improve youths' educational attainment and social skills.

References

Baquedano-López, P. (2019). Indigenous Maya families from Yucatan in San Francisco: Hemispheric mobility and pedagogies of diaspora. In S. Gleeson, & X. Bada (Eds.), *Accountability across borders: Migrant rights in North America*. University of Texas Press. pp. 515–563.

Baquedano-López, P., & Borge Janetti, G. (2017). The Maya diaspora Yucatán-San Francisco: New Latino educational practices and possibilities. In S. Salas, & P. Portes (Eds.), *U.S. Latinization: Education and the New Latino South*. SUNY Press. pp. 161–186.

Beverly, J. (2000). *Testimonio: On the politics of truth*. University of Minnesota Press.

Bishop, L., & Kelley, P. (2013). Indigenous Mexican languages and the politics of language shift in the United States. In C. Benson, & K. Kosonen (Eds.), *Language issues in comparative education*. Sense. pp. 97–113.

Bissinger, H. G. (1990). *Friday night lights: A town, a team, and a dream*. Da Capo Press.

Blackmore, J. (Ed.). (2012). *DreamFields: A Peek into the world of migrant youth: An anthology by Mount Vernon migrant youth and their allies*. Janice Blackmore.

Booker, M. (2002). Stories of violence: Use of testimony in a support group for Latin American battered women. In L. H. Collins, M. R. Dunlop, & J. C. Chrisler (Eds.), *Charting a new course for feminist psychology*. Praeger. pp. 307–321.

Brabeck (2001). Testimonio: Bridging feminist ethics with activist research to create new spaces of collectivity. Bridging the Gap: Feminisms and Participatory Action Research Conference, Boston College.

Canagarajah, S. (2011). Translanguaging in the classroom: Emerging issues for research and pedagogy. *Applied linguistics review, 2.* pp. 1–28.

Campbell, R. (2016). *Reification, resistance, and transformation? The impact of migration and demographics on linguistic, racial, and ethnic identity and equity in educational systems: An applied approach* (Doctoral dissertation). Available at Scholar Commons (http://scholarcommons.usf.edu/etd/6474).

Campbell-Montalvo, R. (2020a). Being QuantCritical of U.S. K-12 demographic data: Using and reporting race/ethnicity in Florida Heartland schools. *Race Ethnicity and Education, 21.* pp. 180–199.

Campbell-Montalvo, R. (2020b). Linguistic re-formation in Florida Heartland schools: School erasures of Indigenous languages. *American Educational Research Journal, 58.* pp. 32–67.

Campbell-Montalvo, R. (Forthcoming). Saliendo adelante: Indigenous im/migrant family agency in navigating linguistic barriers to school resource access. In M. Strickland, & L. Roy (Eds.), *Composing storylines of possibilities: Immigrant and refugee families navigating school.* Charlotte, NC: Information Age Publishing.

Campbell-Montalvo, R., & Castañeda, H. (2019). School employees as health care brokers for multiply-marginalized migrant families. *Medical Anthropology, 39.* pp. 1–14.

Campbell-Montalvo, R., & Pfister, A. (2021). Access to K-12 school resources for Latino im/migrants in the Florida Heartland: The interstice of family cultural backgrounds and linguistic structural realities. In D. Warriner (Ed.), *Refugee education across the lifespan: Mapping experiences of language learning and language use.* New York, NY: Springer.

Campbell-Montalvo, R., Sidorova, O., Valdovinos, M., Lucas, R., & Cong, X. (Forthcoming). Healthcare access brokerage by school employees for Immigrant Mexican and Indigenous Guatemalan farmworking families in a Connecticut elementary school. *AERA Open.*

Castellanos, M. B. (2017). Rewriting the Mexican immigrant narrative: Situating indigeneity in Maya women's stories. *Latino Studies, 15.* pp. 219–241.

Chacón, G. E. (2017). Metamestizaje and the narration of political movements from the south. *Latino Studies, 15.* pp. 182–200.

Chón, D. W. B., Montes, P. D., & Landeros, J. (2021). Presencing While Absent: Indigenous Latinxs and Education. In E. G. Murillo, Jr, D. Delgado Bernal, S. Morales, L. Urrieta, Jr, E. Ruiz Bybee, J. Sánchez Muñoz, V. B. Saenz, D. Villanueva, M. Machado-Casas, & K. Espinoza (Eds.), *Handbook of Latinos and Education: Theory, Research, and Practice.* Routledge. pp. 135–145.

Clifford, J. (2007). Varieties of indigenous experience: Diasporas, homelands, sovereignties. In M. de la Cadena, & O. Starn (Eds.), *Indigenous Experience Today.* Routledge. pp. 197–224.

Education Commission of the States. (2014). 50-state comparison. *What methods are used to identify English language learners?* Available at: http://ecs.force.com/mbdata/mbquestNB2?rep=ELL1403.

Florida Department of Education. (2020). Title I, Part C: Migrant Education Program (MEP). Retrieved from http://www.fldoe.org/policy/federal-edu-programs/title-i-part-c-migrant-edu-program-mep/.

Fuentes, E. H. & Pérez, M. A. (2016). Testimonio as a radical story-telling and creative soulful resistance. *Association of Mexican American Educators*, *10*(2). pp. 5–14.
Fuller, J. M. (2012). *Spanish speakers in the USA*. Multilingual Matters.
Gómez, L. E. (2018). *Manifest destinies: The making of the Mexican American race*. NYU Press.
González, M. S., Plata, O., García, E., Torres, M., & Urrieta, L. (2003). Testimonios de inmigrantes: Students educating future teachers. *Journal of Latinos and Education*, *2*(4). pp. 233–243.
Holmes, S. (2013). *Fresh fruit, broken bodies: Migrant farmworkers in the United States*. Berkeley, CA: University of California Press.
Kleyn, T., Alulema, D., Khalifa, F., & Morales Romero, A. (2018). Learning from undocumented students: Testimonios for strategies to support and resist. *The New Educator*, *14*(1). pp. 24–41.
López, J., & Irizarry, J. G. (2019). *Somos pero no somos iguales*/we are but we are not the same: Unpacking Latinx indigeneity and the implications for urban schools. *Urban Education*. https://doi.org/10.1177/0042085919835292.
López López, L. L. (2018). *The making of indigeneity, curriculum history, and the limits of diversity*. Routledge.
Machado-Casas, M. (2012). Pedagogías del camaleón/Pedagogies of the chameleon: Identity and strategies of survival for transnational Latin immigrants in the US south. *Urban Review*, *44*. pp. 534–550.
Mangual Figueroa, A. (2013). ¡Hay que hablar!: Testimonio in the everyday lives of migrant mothers. *Language & Communication*, *33*(4). pp. 559–572.
Meek, B., & Messing, J. (2007). Framing Indigenous languages as secondary to matrix languages. *Anthropology and Education Quarterly*, *38*. pp. 99–118.
Menchaca, M. (2002). *Recovering history, constructing race: The Indian, black, and white roots of Mexican Americans*. University of Texas Press.
Mize, R. L., & Swords, A. C. S. (2010). *Consuming Mexican labor: From the Bracero program to NAFTA*. University of Toronto Press.
Morales, A. L., Zavella, P., Alarcon, N., Behar, R., del Alba Acevedo, L., Alvarez, C., Benmayor, R., Lomas, C., de Filippis, D. C., Cuadraz, G. H., & Fiol-Matta, L. (Eds.). (2001). *Telling to live: Latina feminist testimonios*. Duke University Press.
Perez, W. (2009). *We are Americans: Undocumented students pursuing the American dream*. Stylus Publishing, LLC.
Perez, W., Vásquez R., & Buriel, R. (2016). Zapotec, Mixtec, and Purepecha youth: Multilingualism and the marginalization of Indigenous immigrants in the United States. In H. S. Alim, J. R. Rickford, & A. F. Ball (Eds.), *Raciolinguistics: How language shapes our ideas about race*. Oxford University Press. pp. 255–272.
Pérez Huber, L. (2012). Testimonio as LatCrit methodology in education. In S. Delamont (Ed.), *Handbook of qualitative research in education*. Edward Elgar Publishing. pp. 377–390.
Pérez Huber, L. (2010). Using Latina/o critical race theory (LatCrit) and racist nativism to explore intersectionality in the educational experiences of undocumented Chicana college students. *Educational Foundations*, *24*. pp. 77–96.
Pérez Huber, L. P. (2009). Disrupting apartheid of knowledge: Testimonio as methodology in Latina/o critical race research in education. *International Journal of Qualitative Studies in Education*, *22*(6). pp. 639–654.

Prieto, L. (2016). *Testimonios* informing a human rights and social justice education framework. *Association of Mexican American Educators Journal*, 10(2). pp. 96–103.

Salas, S., & Portes, P. R. (Eds.). (2017). *US Latinization: Education and the new Latino south*. SUNY Press.

Saldaña-Portillo, M. J. (2017). Critical Latinx Indigeneities: A paradigm drift. *Latino Studies*, 15. pp. 138–155.

Smith, K. (2010). Female voice and feminist text: Testimonio as a form of resistance in Latin America. *Florida Atlantic Comparative Studies Journal*, 12(1). pp. 21–37.

Solórzano, D. G., & Delgado Bernal, D. (2001). Examining transformational resistance through a critical race and LatCrit theory framework: Chicana and Chicano students in an urban context. *Urban Education*, 36(3). pp. 308–342.

Urrieta, L., & Calderón, D. (2019). Critical Latinx Indigeneities: Unpacking Indigeneity from within and outside of Latinized entanglements. *Association of Mexican American Educators Journal*, 13(2). pp. 145–174.

Urrieta, L., Mesinas, M., & Martínez, R. A. (2019). Critical Latinx Indigeneities and education: An introduction. *Association of Mexican American Educators Journal*, 13(2). pp. 1–14.

Valenzuela, A. (1999). *Subtractive schooling: U.S.-Mexican youth and the politics of caring*. State University of New York Press.

Vásquez, R. (2019). Zapotec identity as a matter of schooling. *Association of Mexican American Educators Journal*, 13(2). pp. 66–90.

Velasco, P. (2010). Indigenous students in bilingual Spanish-English classrooms in New York: A teacher's mediation strategies. *International Journal of the Sociology of Language*, 206. pp. 255–271.

Xón Riquiac, M. J. (2020). Chi uwach loq'alaj q'ij saq: The sacred existing in knowing/learning from space/time. In L. L. López López & G. Coello (Eds.), *Indigenous Futures and Learnings Taking Place*. Routledge.

Yúdice, G. (1991). Testimonio and postmodernism. *Latin American Perspectives*, 18(3). pp. 15–31.

Chapter 4

Migration, Betterment, and Modernity

Encounters and Un-Encounters Between Mobility and Access to Education as Life Projects in Three Generations of Migrants from Loja, Ecuador[1]

María Mercedes Eguiguren

Introduction

In the second half of the 20th century, two social processes began, which profoundly influenced Ecuadorian society. The first is the considerable expansion of access to public education in all educational levels (Luna and Astorga 2011). The second is the configuration of an international migration movement that, at the end of the century, placed Ecuador at the top of emigration statistics in Latin America (Jockisch 2014).

Beginning in the 1950s, Ecuador implemented a governmental political project that pursued 'modernization' on various axes, including the expansion of access to public education. This project brought with it an ideology that assimilated modern national identity with a mestiza identity (Vallejo 2004; Whitten 1981). There have been debates around the implications of education policies and access to education in terms of its contribution, whether to the expansion of the middle class (Espinosa 2010) or to the reproduction of forms of class and ethnic domination (Vera 2009; Martínez Novo and de la Torre 2010). Nevertheless, these debates, which allude to the relationship between education and social mobility, have assumed that the subjects of education are 'national' subjects, fixed in space and whose cultural and identity references conform to the those of the nation-state.

At the same time, during the second half of the 20th century, important processes of internal migration began as well as international emigration. These movements of people inside the country, from rural areas to the city as well as between cities, pushed Ecuador into one of the fastest urbanization processes in Latin America (CEPAL 2012). In parallel, since the 1970s, Ecuadorians began relocating to various cities in the US, settling mostly in the East Coast region. This migratory tradition changed direction in the late '90s and early 2000s, when Ecuadorian emigration increased at an unprecedented rate, with Spain and Italy as the preferred destinations of migrants (FLACSO - UNFPA 2008).[2]

In this chapter, I establish a relationship between these historical processes through a perspective centered on the life projects of men and women from Loja, a city in the south of Ecuador. This region has gone through intense migratory and circulatory processes since the middle of the last century (Eguiguren 2019). I propose to understand migration and education as interconnected aspirations that motivate people's trajectories of spatial mobility. At the same time, I propose that examining how these aspirations change over generations contributes to an interpretation of the relationship between sociopolitical regimes and personal biographies (Guhlich 2017), because different generations have different motivations for and give different meanings to mobility and education, relevant to the context in which they live.

The life projects that are studied here are situated socio-spatially in the south of the Ecuadorian Andes, and specifically in the city of Loja, as a space with a particular peripheral urban experience as the origin of translocal and transnational migrations. I propose that through a focus on the aspirations to earn an education and to leave one's place of origin, which are constructed in this particular location, we can better understand how historical experiences are permeated with the geographic inequality that marks local spaces.

Methodology

This work is part of a larger research.[3] Between 2013 and 2014, I carried out several visits to towns in Cañar and Loja, two provinces in the southern highlands of Ecuador, as well as to the principal urban destinations of internal and international migration from those provinces, in Ecuador and the US. I carried out biographical interviews with 42 men and women belonging to three generations: those born between 1930 and 1950, those born between 1951 and 1970, and those born between 1971 and 1995. I understand a generation as a group of people who share the same historical setting for their life experience, and as well share a common historical time for experiences associated with the stages of their life—childhood, adolescence, adulthood, and old age (Chirot 2000).

The focus of this chapter will be on interconnected stories of spatial and social mobility of several of the interviewed individuals,[4] originally from Loja, whose stories allow us to delve into the complex relations between social mobility, spatial mobility, and education.

Southern Ecuador: Spatial Inequality, Mobility, and Migration

Historically, Ecuador has had three political and economic centers in the cities of Quito, Guayaquil, and Cuenca, with a high concentration of population and capital flows. They divide the country into three political, economic, and cultural regions. At the same time, and similar to other Latin American countries, the urban/rural division has been important not only in administrative and economic terms, but also as the spatial organization of social differences (Kingman 1992; de la Cadena 2006).

The dominant historical narrative for the southern highlands of Ecuador has been that of the 'isolation' of those provinces from the national space. This has been so mainly due to the difficulties of transportation, the little contact between the capital and other parts of the country, and the predominance of older local power structures until the beginning of the 20th century (Fauroux 1983). Nevertheless, there is a long history of different types of movement and translocal and transnational connections with the southern provinces of the country, which challenge the national order inasmuch as they don't pass through the central powers, or contest them directly (Palomeque 1994; Eguiguren 2019).

During much of the 20th century and still today, the province of Loja has had high numbers of internal migration (CONADE-UNFPA, 1987) and, although there is a lack of statistical data, there is evidence of migratory chains from Loja to the US, Canada, and European countries that date from the 1970s (Eguiguren 2019). The role of mobility as a prevailing characteristic of the province can also be observed in the constant migration and circulation within the provincial space (Fauroux 1983).

The city of Loja is the capital of the province. It has become a center of movement and circulation due to several factors, such as the age of the colonial settlement in the city and the accompanying presence of centers of local political power, the settlement of elites in the urban center (Fauroux 1983), and as a result, the concentration of public and private services, including those of education (Sánchez 2004). Here I propose to view the specificity of Loja's space from the idea of an Andean city as presented by Kingman (1992), based on a criticism of the binary and static oppositions of the categories rural/urban, indigenous/mestizo, and Andean/Western. The Andean city is characterized by relations of 'trans-territoriality' (García Canclini in Kingman 1992, 18), which encompasses practices and identities that are indigenous, mestizo, European, and African, and which constructs processes of class formation understood as positions that result from power relations in multiple dimensions: ethnic, social, economic, and cultural. In the midst of these social relations, for Kingman, the city

> provides ... the learning necessary to survive in the modern world, the assimilation of certain behaviors, cultural forms, techniques, secrets and habits that belong to the other society; and even, in some cases, offers professionalization as a means to break ethnic dependence (Kingman 1992, 22).

Spatial and Social Mobility and Subjectivity in the Andes

Scholars of transnational studies have argued that people don't migrate between spatial and social entities that are isolated from each other (such as nation-states) but rather through social, economic, and cultural structures configured in a transnational way (Levitt and Glick Schiller 2004). Nevertheless, the study of older migratory processes through this perspective is not common, especially in the case of the Andean region.

A transnational perspective on history does not imply simply looking through this lens at migratory movements across national borders, but also to deconstruct the territorial limits that have been understood as 'containers' inside the national space (Taylor 2003): the region, province, and the border between city and countryside. This perspective implies bringing to the debate the history of connections and movement that has existed between regions that have been conceptualized as isolated and other spaces within the nation and beyond national borders.

In this attempt to view the history of national spaces from a transnational perspective, it is fundamental to trace the history of what Berg has called the configuration of 'mobile selves' (Berg 2015). In her ethnography of Peruvian Andean migrants in New Jersey and Miami, Berg shows that migration cannot be understood solely as the movement of labor, but rather that it is necessary to understand the configuration of a subjectivity oriented toward mobility (spatial as well as social) as one of the historical keys to the shaping of a subaltern race and class in the Andes.

In Sociology, the idea of subjectivity is linked to the concept of action as a behavior to which meaning is attached (Weber 2014), which can be understood simultaneously as the direction of the behavior itself as well as the endowment to it of meaning (Swedberg and Agevall 2016). Later on, subjectivity has been conceptualized as the internal realm of individuals in which they construct a conception of themselves, the self, which is intrinsically linked to their relationship with others (Goffman 1959; Schutz 1967).

In migration studies, giving attention to the life experiences of migrants, and the accompanying use of the methodological resource of life stories to collect these experiences, dates back to the classics of the Chicago School, Thomas and Znaniecki (Rivera Sánchez 2012; Pagnotta 2011; Guhlich 2017). This tradition of reclaiming the subjectivity of migrants through their experience has continued over time, demonstrating the importance of wishes, desires, and imagination in migration (Lawson 2000; Carling and Collins 2018; Velasco and Gianturco 2012). In this study, I understand subjectivity in this sense, highlighting the role of wishes and desires (Lawson 2000) to better understand the production of translocal linkages and their relationship with subjectivities that pursue education as a form of betterment of one's living conditions as well as of oneself.

The literature focused on the relationship between subjectivity and socio-political regimes in postcolonial contexts has given much attention to the narrative of *mejorar*—'advancement' or 'bettering oneself'—as a powerful subjective and social force that guides the life trajectories of their subjects (Berg 2015; Leinaweaver 2008; Vallejo 2004; de la Cadena 2006). For Vallejo (2004), the postcolonial State of the mid-20th century in Ecuador defined development as a path to reach a modernity represented as 'foreign,' with North American or Western European societies as models (Vallejo 2004). This conception of the role of the State as the driver of the national society toward modernity-development is then plunged into the background by globalization and neoliberalism, and Ecuadorian subjectivity is reconfigured according to neoliberal individualism, which turns its back on the State and promotes the idea that the subject is responsible for him/herself (2004).

Nevertheless, the ideas of 'betterment' and 'advancement,' as well as the connected idea of achieving a better life in another place (within or outside of the country), have permeated Andean history and aren't only emblematic of the neoliberal historical moment (Berg 2015; Eguiguren 2019; Leinaweaver 2008; de la Cadena 2006). In the case of Peru, de la Cadena (2006) demonstrates that, since the beginning of the 20th century, intellectual and political debates have included the idea that Indigenous elements could and should be transformed in order to be integrated into the nation. Such debates are linked from the mid-20th century to the governmental development paradigm, which positions education as the model instrument to achieve modern subjects and thus promote national development (de la Cadena 2006).

Education in National Projects of Modernity

A large part of the literature about education in Ecuador addresses its relationship with nation-state projects, understanding the education system that has been implemented in the country over time as a product of the disputes between political projects of the national elites (Goetschel 2007). Less research has been conducted on understanding how different social sectors have taken on the educational project in their culture and identity. Such an analysis is presented by Ana María Goetschel, who follows a Bourdieuan approach. Her work attempts to understand education as a social field, proposing that access to education in Ecuador in the first half of the 20th century constituted 'a struggle by the middle class to insert itself into the public sphere, which transcends the educational field into the social field' (Goetschel 2007, 20–21).

It is also important to focus on the spatial inequalities that education reveals, as part of a wider state project that, in the national development paradigm, has structured the national space in regional and local hierarchies (Eguiguren 2019). Regarding education, this structure implies the reproduction of a hierarchical order in institutions and educational content that projects spatially on all levels: the 'best' and most prestigious elementary schools, high schools, and universities that existed in Ecuador in the second half of the 20th century are concentrated in the three central cities (Quito, Guayaquil, and Cuenca). The prestige and 'quality' (perceived or real) of education decreases as the geographical location of institutions becomes farther toward the periphery.

This inequality in the location and type of educational institutions within the national space is linked to a functionalist understanding of education (Goetschel 2007). Education in peripheral spaces of the nation is oriented toward producing subjects functionally linked to national development, in economic terms (workers) as well as political terms (citizens with an embodied national culture) (Luna and Astorga 2011; Whitten 1981). In this sense, it is important to signal the tension between the instrumental objectives assigned to education by state projects and the significance conferred by subjects who see education as a potential path to achieve wider goals, not necessarily linked to a role as a gear in the process of national development, but rather linked to questions such as prestige, social recognition, and a more desirable way of living.

This inequality further influences in two ways the socio-spatial configuration of the country and its international connections: first, the existence of prestigious educational institutions contributes to reinforcing spatial imaginaries of cities as centers of civilization and opportunities for social mobility. At the same time, the lack of institutions deepens the opposing images of the countryside and small towns as places that are 'backwards' and 'isolated.' Second, a hierarchical and unequal education system, based on and at the same time reproducing geographical inequalities, becomes part of the socio-spatial dynamics that drive mobility in Ecuador (Miles 2004; Cantos 2012; Pagnotta 2011; Eguiguren 2019; Pérez Gañán and Pesántez Calle 2017). To leave the town or place of origin with the aspiration to study is thus converted into a form of seeking social mobility, but also into a form of seeking the transformation of one's own identity towards modernity; at the same time, it is the same ritual of mobility and circulation that individuals from the periphery with these life aspirations have followed over decades (Miles 2004; Cantos 2012; Eguiguren 2019).

A Generation Watching Education from Afar: Education and the Middle Class in the 20th Century

In the mid-20th century in Ecuador, education was endowed with a series of meanings that were, to a certain point, contradictory. Education represented an aspiration in terms of identity and self-transformation into a 'modern' person. But at the same time, especially among working classes and rural populations, as well as among small towns and cities, education represented an exclusive realm, reserved for urban upper classes. Thus, particularly for the generation that grew up in the periphery in the 1930s and '40s, to have an education was a marker of distinction and hierarchy (Kingman 1992).

Participants from this first generation refer to a university education as a clear sign of distinction, and they describe it among other naturalized signs that mark social hierarchies, such as being a landowner, being white, or having a last name among the local elites. At the same time, they see education as a goal that was difficult to reach in their own life trajectory. The majority of these individuals attended formal schooling through primary school,[5] after which they began working as merchants, employees, or owners of small businesses (Eguiguren 2019).

Pedro, a vendor from Loja with a long trajectory of internal migration, had his first migratory experience at twelve years old, when he moved with his mother and siblings from Cariamanga, a small town in the interior of the province, to the provincial capital. In that town, Pedro's mother began to work washing and ironing clothes, while he and his siblings sold merchandise in the street to supplement the family income. When asked if he had attended high school, Pedro responded, 'I didn't have the good fortune to reach those levels of education' (Pedro, interview, September 20, 2014).

Even though the participants denote one meaning of education as a class privilege reserved for elites, they also show in many ways how they have tried to challenge the subaltern positions to which they have been relegated by their exclusion, at least partially, from formal education.

Pedro defines himself as self-taught, someone who has achieved education through personal drive. Pedro says that having 'taught himself' and his desire to 'build himself' as well as his friendships with people of Loja's middle and upper classes have pushed him to get involved in what could be called the 'public space' of the city (Goetschel 2007: 26). Pedro recounts how, when he was about thirty, he and a group of friends created a public opinion newspaper in which he wrote articles. Later, he also collaborated with other similar newspapers (Pedro, interview, September 20, 2014).

What stands out from this experience is how in his telling the friendships he formed in Loja with men of middle and upper classes as well as his involvement in activities in the public sphere typical of men in Latin American cities (Guerra 1998 in Goetschel 2007)—in spaces with both cultural (local newspapers), as well as economic, influence—are closely linked to the upward social mobility he achieved during his years there. Although due to his humble origins Pedro did not attend high school, as an adult he was able to open businesses, manage a movie theater, write in local papers and was a member of the local Chamber of Commerce (Pedro, interview, September 20, 2014).

In Pedro's telling, all of these spaces are connected to his friendships and thus represent spaces that are meaningful as forms of sociability. Education, therefore, is not an end in itself but rather a cultural repertoire that allows for engagement with urban life.

In this generation, mobility as well as life projects are linked to other economic and social aspirations; education appears only tangentially (Eguiguren 2019). In the memory of the interviewees, education is given social significance, which turns it into a sign of distinction, and thus into a relatively distant objective. But in all cases, this conception is transformed in this generation's children. For them, education becomes a goal that shapes and organizes their family projects and is in close relationship to migration.

Mobility and Intergenerational Aspirations for a Better Life

In 1981, Pedro moved to Quito with his family. He tells about this move among other memories of life in Loja in the '60s and '70s, when Loja, in his memory, was a small city. Of that period, he says: 'only very well-off people could, for example, send their children to study here, in the capital. To give just one example, Benjamín Carrión[6] (…)' (Pedro, interview, September 20, 2014). Nevertheless, at the beginning of the 1980s, three of Pedro's children had finished secondary education and wanted to study in Quito; each had chosen a different degree and wanted to study in the prestigious Central University in the capital. Pedro explained that at that time, he had the resources to cover the costs of his children's studies in another city, and he began to rent an apartment for them. But in the end, his wife was emotionally affected by being far from her children, so the whole family immigrated to Quito.

At this point of the story, Pedro intertwines the ideas of education as an aspiration and as a class privilege in a continuous desire for 'betterment' that materializes in an emigration project: to access a prestigious education means going to study in Quito, a possibility that in his youth was reserved for elites. Additionally, in his testimony, his children's decision is expressed as a preference: they don't only want to study but also to do so in the degree programs that are in tune with their interests, future projects, and ideas of prestige. For Pedro, this decision is about satisfying his children and imagining for them a career that could manifest his own upward social trajectory: 'on the other hand, one of the other girls said she wanted journalism, and since I dabbled in journalism in Loja back then… it was my dream, I hoped that one of my children would choose that path' (Pedro, interview, September 20, 2014).

Among the internal and international migrants of the first generation, the education of their children becomes a goal that orients the family life. The second generation begins to value education as connected to the possibility to build a personal life project and identity, linked to one's professional life

(Eguiguren 2019). This second generation had more possibilities to access a professional career than their parents did. But their life projects, connected to a career resulting from their studies, faced many difficulties in the middle of the economic crisis that affected Ecuador, and further, their aspirations towards cosmopolitan values and the hope to have different experiences than those offered by the small cities where they lived weighed heavily on this generation.

Various interviewees of this generation coincided in highlighting different motivations for emigrating from Loja, based on their own experiences as well as those of their fellow citizens whom they mentioned in the interviews. Their testimonies described a migration with economic motivations but connected to frustration at not having been able to complete university studies or for not having found a job in their profession. For them, migration is also linked to questions which transcend economic necessity and which are defined in more abstract terms. Marcelo, for example, posed that society in Loja at the beginning of the '80s was 'very closed,' and Néstor concurred: 'for young people there were no alternatives, it was a very closed environment, a very closed society...' (Néstor, Marcelo, interviews, November 10, 2013).

They express a conjunction of processes that marked their common experience in the context of the '80s. On one hand, they are directly connected to global imaginaries that give a positive connotation to travel (Vallejo 2004, Cantos 2012). On the other hand, they experience the deterioration of the conditions that favor social mobility through education. For this generation, their educational projects must face economic crisis as well as the desire for different ways of life, for study, or for less traditional professions, which clashes with the reduced possibility they find in their place of origin (Eguiguren 2019).

Studies Abroad as Transnational Linkages

One way in which these aspirations were encouraged in the urban context, especially for the population with access to high school, was the option to study in foreign countries, which they could access through cultural exchanges and scholarships (Jijón 2015; Carrasco 2015; Epps 2009). Although these alternatives were not accessible to the majority of the population, they continue to be important for various reasons. First, because they are framed within strategies developed by the cultural institutions of governments, particularly those of powerful countries such as the US and the Soviet Union, to reach a greater cultural expansion through education in the context of the Cold War (O'Mara 2012; Epps 2009).

Second, these forms of student mobility, especially scholarships, were not exclusively reserved for members of the elite; rather, middle-class students were also able to access them. I refer, for example, to youth originally from small cities in the interior of the province. They belong to an emerging sector connected to the 'cultural public sphere' (Rodríguez 2015) or a 'plurality of public spheres' (Goetschel 2007, 26), made up of people who work in liberal professions, artists, and politicians, among others.

Travel for studies begins to become part of the imaginary of possibilities for this generation, which helps to make the experience of mobility more proximate and more desirable. For example, César, who immigrated as a child to Quito with his mother, and in 1971 to the US, recounts that in his adolescence he knew young people who studied in other countries:

> Students came who had already lived in the US, or who lived in Europe and… I met them in Quito, and then we talked, you know? that in the US this, that in Europe this, then I had this, like a dream, to say, 'I also want to immigrate there' (César, interview, November 18, 2013).

Furthermore, in several cases during fieldwork, students who left were the contacts for family members and friends to undertake their own migration, particularly in the context of relationships between social classes.

The migratory, social, and professional trajectories of the students of this time are heterogeneous. Although traditionally studying abroad has been a sign of prestige in Ecuador, it has not always indicated an increase in social, cultural, or academic capital for the interviewees. This is the case of José, another interviewee, who studied in Romania in the '70s. On his return to Loja, he wasn't able to find a job, and he migrated again, this time within the country. He worked for some years, but his employment trajectory depended more on 'contacts' with friends and people close to him for political activities than on his studies. Finally, he decided to immigrate to the US in the '80s in order to find work and support his family (José, interview, November 10, 2013).

Some students who traveled in this period did have a career in their place of origin that was connected to their studies, and some even followed a distinguished professional trajectory (Eguiguren 2019, 126). However, the variability of these experiences shows that in this generation, although the pursuit of professional fulfillment and traveling abroad were linked in the imaginary, the latter began to be seen as a wider opportunity, even if it meant leaving behind their studies and career. This was particularly in a context of increasing disjunction between the expectations of university studies and the real possibilities of supporting oneself with a university degree.

To Be a Migrant: Devaluation of Education and Narratives of Personal Achievement

Although the second generation of this study shows a turn towards education as an axis of life projects (Eguiguren 2019), the context of economic crisis linked to the rise of neoliberalism, along with the reinforcement of the social transnational space shaped between the south of Ecuador and the US, brought to many the dilemma between continuing their professional life or emigrating to join the US labor market as a low-skilled worker. Validating a university degree in the destination society was almost impossible (Coloma 2012). In César's story, before immigrating to the US, he studied Architecture in Quito and worked as a designer in businesses and wealthy families' houses. When asked if he arrived in the US seeking a specific job, he said:

> Nothing [special] (...) even now, after forty years of living here, I tell new people who come: if you came to work here, don't ask what the job is, ask how much they pay (...) Because (...) if I came with the idea that I'm going to be a doctor, that I'm this or I'm that, I want to work here, I'm going to starve to death. (...) Because this is a country, well, the same as any country; you need a license, a qualification, just because you're a doctor over there doesn't mean you're going to be a doctor here. (...) (César, interview, November 18, 2013).

Like César, the other interviewees expressed a very clear understanding of the place they could occupy, as immigrants, in the labor market of their country of arrival. Especially those who had achieved a certain social, economic, or cultural capital in their origin society, whether because they had graduated from university, or because they had attained a job that was well paid or well regarded in their original context, to join the economic and social life in their new context as a migrant implied a process of downward social mobility. This downward mobility is tangible in experiences such as taking on physically demanding jobs and long work days, sharing living space with family members or friends, maintaining strict patterns of savings and personal privation, among others.

This process leads to a reconfiguration of personal and familial projects, previously connected to studies and a professional job. The recorded testimonies reorient themselves through a narrative in which diverse achievements are highlighted, such as getting a job, a place to live, saving for a goal, helping someone from your family emigrate, achieving certain standards of comfort for your children, among others. These narratives about one's own trajectory are no longer confined to study and professionalization, rather the meanings of 'betterment' or 'advancement' are considerably diversified (Leinaweaver 2008).

Building a Personal Project in Neoliberal Times

Ecuadorians born in the decades of 1970–1990 live in a context of intensification of economic crisis, of increased poverty, and towards the end of this period, of a generalized loss of confidence in the life opportunities that the country could offer in the future (Goycoechea 2013). In contrast to the preceding generation, for this generation, education loses its centrality within life projects. This change happens in close relation with neoliberalism in two ways: due to the stagnation in the supply of education, which happens in the last two decades of the 20th century, and due to the expansion of a neoliberal mentality (Dean 2010; Nyenyezi Bisoka and Giraud 2020). This change also implies that neoliberalism does not only expand through mechanisms of force, but that these mechanisms interact with the transformation of subjectivities towards valuing flexibility and one's own capacity to assume risk and uncertainty.

In the life trajectories of the third generation, education does not stop being a desirable alternative and part of life aspirations, but it is subject to the conditions presented in the context of origin: crisis, migratory trajectories already established in the family or close environment, and in terms of the educational context and value of professional life, a decrease in the expectations of the future possibility to practice a profession and through that profession, to plan on a life of stability and continuity.

I examine these changes through the case of Andrea. Andrea was born in Loja, but her family moved to Quito when she was little. When she was five years old, she returned to Loja with her mother after the separation of her parents. Her mother worked as a secretary in a school in Loja, and immigrated to Madrid at the end of the '90s, where she worked as a live-in domestic worker until she could save enough to bring her children to Spain. Andrea arrived in Madrid with her brother in 2001, when she was 15 years old.

For this young woman, her experience of education was overrun with the transformation that emigration entailed and the stage of her life in which this change took place. The change of field in her high school studies can be seen as the starting point of a process of self-transformation, based on an assessment of her capacity for adaptation and autonomy, and on the simultaneity of her migratory experience (Levitt and Glick Schiller 2004). Andrea recalls, about her first experiences in a Madrid high school:

> The first year was super hard for me and I had to repeat it, and when I repeated it I saw it was so hard, I didn't understand them... I mean, I didn't understand physics like I did here [in Loja] because I think, from what I have studied, they do it a little differently (...). And I didn't understand it. (...) They always suspended me. So (...) I said 'no, I need to start from zero' and I started from zero (Andrea, interview, October 16, 2014).

'Start from zero,' to Andrea, meant to change the field of her studies. In Loja, she had chosen Chemistry and Physics, which she meant to continue in Madrid, but her initial difficulties led her to choose a technical high school diploma in Administration and Graphic Design. Andrea remembers these moments as a time of great disorientation in school, which she attributes not only to the differences in teaching methods but also to a larger 'non-understanding,' which included people's ways of speaking and relationships with classmates, but also to her own way of being: 'before I was like... I was more quiet, and I didn't know what to say or how to ask.' Thus, she chose to pursue the field in her school that was 'easier,' and she remembers, 'my friends told me Administration, and I went to Administration and really, it was easier' (Andrea, interview, October 16, 2014).

This change in the direction of her studies is part of a much wider process in which her principal concern was to 'understand' the social context in which she had to participate: being an adolescent in Madrid. It was a moment in her life in which, on one hand, the differences with life in Loja were evident to her, but on the other hand, she felt the process of racialization that categorized her as Latina and at the same time generated ways to resist this exclusion through a process of self-transformation that included styles of dress, of speaking, the effort to make friends of different origins. Andrea narrates these shifts as changes that she undertook alone, as well as a continuous before and after between 'being shy,' 'not getting it,' and getting 'clued-in' (Eguiguren 2019). These experiences can't be understood through ideas of adaptation or assimilation, but rather from the space of intimate experience, as a process of subjective transformation steeped in the tension between feeling the racism of the receiving society and feeling free of it. Thus, there are moments in which Andrea says she felt discrimination, and others in which she alienates her own experience:

> But me, I've always been told 'you're not like the Ecuadorians' but I don't think it has to do with my appearance (...) but rather that they... sometimes they categorize you, a little bit, just for how you look (...) I'm telling you, all the interviews I've gone to, they've always contacted me for some work (...). But I have seen friends that do have a very Latino look, and they've contacted me but not [my friends]... it's weird (Andrea, interview, October 16, 2014).

Over time in Andrea's immigrant experience, she develops a construction of self that shows a great willingness to change in order to avoid social exclusion. Andrea's schooling decision is part of that process. In this way, after she finished high school, Andrea looked to quickly enter the workforce. In her words, before turning 18, she started 'getting [her] resume out,' to help out at home as well as to earn her own money. Almost immediately she found a job as a checker in a supermarket, where her high school diploma in Administration allowed her to move up to manager. Four years later she changed jobs, to that of secretary in a doctor's office. When the global recession began, she lost that job and was unemployed for a time until she found work as a promoter and model for a jewelry store.

In this work history, Andrea emphasizes the personal qualities that in her perception have been important to achieve some stability. The capacity to handle several things at once, to get along well with her boss, to learn new tasks quickly, work independently, be available, and even her physical appearance is a profitable quality (as she is now a model for jewelry). Andrea sees all of these elements as personal advantages in the midst of the economic crisis and in a competitive work environment:

> Right now it's one month on, one month off, you see it go up and come down… and you see that in your company, where you work, and like, they're firing people, they're firing people, but you are getting to stay (…) [My boss] told me (…) 'look, if we've fired people who've been here 30 years, 15 years, 10 years (…) and we haven't fired you (…) it's because you have a good look, it's because you do things well for us, we're ok.' (Andrea, interview, October 16, 2014).

Thus, her outlook on the future is oriented toward flexible and insecure jobs, but which are undertaken as a gamble in which her personal qualities and abilities will weigh in. This outlook is a way of confronting the future which is shared by other members of the third generation (Eguiguren 2019). Reflecting on the crisis in Spain, Andrea says:

> You can have two degrees, you can have one degree, you can have three Master's, it's all the same (…) but if you don't have a job where… they've seen you're worth it, where they feel (…) [like in my case, how my bosses] feel comfortable with me, because I always fix their problems (Andrea, interview, October 16, 2014).

We see that studies are dismissed and minimized in a context where what matters is 'entrepreneurship of the self.' In this context, a last element that emerges in this third generation, and is reflected in Andrea's case, is the emphasis in one's 'personal project' or the personal decisions that one makes when facing an uncertain landscape (Eguiguren 2019). In the case of Andrea, she does not think about the future in terms of the route she will take but rather of the place in which she will live.

At the time of our interview, Andrea's sister had been living for several years back in Loja, her brother had left Madrid and was living in Berlin, some of her high school friends had returned to Latin America, while her mother continued to live in Madrid. To Andrea, who was in Loja on vacation, returning to Ecuador, staying in Madrid, or a new emigration to somewhere else are all possibilities, which she also weighed in relation to different life projects, of her own or of others of her generation: her brother and his job in Berlin for which he travels to many countries; her sister and her family life in Loja with her three children; friends in Loja, most of whom are married and have children; friends in Madrid, whom she saw as more focused on work; work colleagues who, like Andrea herself, had a good income but without future security. Except the idea of having a family, which she had decided to put off, any of these scenarios were options that Andrea was willing to 'try' without excluding any of them. The future seemed full of paths and possibilities, but also uncertainty.

Conclusions

In this chapter, I examined the construction of mobility projects of migrants from Loja from three different generations. These projects are situated within wider trends of social change that permeate the social structures in which these generational groups are positioned. The subjectivities captured through the interviews reflect that these mobility projects are constructed in relation to powers of different scales: education as connected to state projects, local social hierarchies, and a growing transnational space constructed not only by migration but also by the country's linkages with global markets.

In this work, a focus on education as an aspiration connected to social and cultural meanings stands out. Although the chapter addresses some ways in which education maintains and reproduces exclusionary social structures, it also examines how the people affected by that exclusion face it and pursue other social positions. Thus, this chapter adds to the debates about the relationship between education, inequality, and social mobility, by showing the importance of not assuming a homogeneous subject of education in the national space. On the contrary, the experience of aspiring to an education, accessing an education, and incorporating it in one's life projects is permeated with socio-spatial inequalities. Only taking this point into account can we understand how, in Ecuador in the second half of the 20th century, the position of subjects toward education is filled with translocal and transnational imaginaries and projects.

The mobility projects of the first generation pursue better positions within social structures, but at the same time, they create new spaces: as mid-sized property owners, merchants, or pioneering migrants, this generation contests its place in economic and social relations. In this conflict, education represents a form of social distinction, but at the same time, the venture into forms of urban sociability permits a response to that exclusionary representation. The second generation, which experienced greater access to education but also limitations on the possibility of carrying out life projects as urban professionals, particularly shows the contradictions between the transition to urbanization and a context of territorial hierarchies. The mobility of this generation reveals subjectivities anchored simultaneously in multiple spaces. For the third generation, mobility is constructed principally with regard to two transnational processes: neoliberalism and migration.

The reconfiguration of subjectivity that is produced in the confluence of these two processes intensifies tensions already present in the previous generation. This generation's mobility projects are constructed around education but with much greater emphasis on ideas of opportunity, risk, and individuality. In this sense, education is not valued as much for the degree obtained but rather for the teaching of certain abilities that permit one to face the present context of flexibility and risk.

This analysis debates and complicates the perspective on migration as a social process driven only by economic necessity and deprivation. In order to do so, it is fundamental to pay more attention to subjectivity and migration as a life project driven by aspirations that are socially, spatially, and historically constructed. As demonstrated by the case of Loja, an Andean city that for generations has been at the crossroads of immigration from the wider province and emigration toward other cities within Ecuador and worldwide, migration and education gain meaning for subjects in an unequal geography in which social and spatial mobility are interconnected.

Notes

1 I thank Joseline Rosero, student at the Central University of Ecuador, for her valuable assistance during the preparation of this chapter.
2 In 2013, the Ecuadorian population was in tenth place among national groups 'of Hispanic origin' living in the US (López 2015). In 2008, the Ecuadorian community in Spain was the largest community of Latin American origin in that country (FLACSO - UNFPA 2008).
3 This research was carried out for my doctoral thesis between 2010 and 2015 thanks to funding from the Académie de Recherche et d'Enseignement Supérieur, ARES (Belgium) and the Secretaría Nacional de Ciencia y Tecnología, SENESCYT (Ecuador).
4 I use pseudonyms for all of the people interviewed who are cited in this chapter. All interview subjects were informed about the academic objectives of the interview and were promised anonymity in the use of their testimonies.
5 In Ecuador, traditionally formal education is divided into primary education (6 grades from 5 to 12 years old), secondary basic education (three grades from 12 to 15 years old) and high school (3 grades from 15 to 18 years old). After completing high school, one can enter technical institutions or university.
6 Benjamín Carrión, originally from Loja, was a central person in Ecuadorian intellectual and political life beginning in the 1930s (Rodríguez 2015).

References

Berg, U. D. (2015). Mobile Selves: Race, Migration, and Belonging in Peru and the U.S. In *Social Transformations in American Anthropology*. New York: New York University Press.

Cantos, M. S. (2012). Ecuadorian Migration: An Ethnographic Approach to Analyzing Socio-Cultural Influences on Migration. *Paper 170*. Syracuse University Honors Program Capstone Projects. Syracuse University.

Carling, J. & Collins, F. (2018) Aspiration, Desire and Drivers of Migration. *Journal of Ethnic and Migration Studies* 44 (6). pp. 909–926. https://doi.org/10.1080/13 69183X.2017.1384134

Carrasco, A. (2015). *Análisis Histórico - Comparativo de Los Créditos Educativos Otorgados Por El IECE* [Historical - Comparative Analysis of Educational Credits Awarded by the IECE]. Guayaquil: Universidad de Guayaquil.

CEPAL. (2012). *Población, Territorio y Desarrollo Sostenible* [Population, Territory and Sustainable Development]. Santiago de Chile: CEPAL.

Chirot, D. (2000). The Social and Historical Landscape of Marc Bloch. In T. Skocpol (Ed.), *Vision and Method in Historical Sociology*. New York: Cambridge University Press. pp. 22–46.

Coloma, S. (2012). ¿Qué Tan Distintos Son Los Migrantes Calificados? Itinerarios Migratorios: Capital Cultural y Social Entre Migrantes Calificados Ecuatorianos En Estados Unidos [How Different Are Skilled Migrants? Migratory Itineraries: Cultural and Social Capital Among Skilled Ecuadorian Migrants in the United States.]. Thesis to obtain a master degree. Quito: Facultad Latinoamericana de Ciencias Sociales, FLACSO - Sede Ecuador.

CONADE – UNFPA. (1987). *Población y Cambios Sociales. Diagnóstico Sociodemográfico del Ecuador, 1950–1982* [Population and Social Changes. Sociodemographic Diagnostic of Ecuador, 1950–1982]. Quito: Corporación Editora Nacional.

Dean, M. (2010). *Governmentality: Power and Rule in Modern Society*. London: Sage.

de la Cadena, M. (2006). ¿Son Los Mestizos Híbridos? Las Políticas Conceptuales de Las Identidades Andinas [Are Mestizos Hybrid? The Conceptual Policies of Andean Identities]. *Universitas Humanística*, no. 61. pp. 51–84.

Eguiguren, M. M. (2019). *Movilidades y Poder En El Sur Del Ecuador, 1950 - 1990* [Mobilities and Power in Southern Ecuador, 1950 - 1990]. Atrio. Quito: Editorial FLACSO Ecuador.

Epps, W. T. (2009). *Maintaining the Empire: Diplomacy and Education in U.S.-Ecuadorian Relations, 1933 - 1963*. Dissertation. Austin: The University of Texas at Austin.

Espinosa, B. (2010). Configuración de Las Clases Medias En Ecuador: Soportes y Rupturas [Configuration of the Middle Classes in Ecuador: Supports and Ruptures]. In Burbano de Lara, F. (Ed.), *Transiciones y Rutpuras. El Ecuador En La Segunda Mitad Del Siglo XX*. Quito: FLACSO Ecuador - Ministerio de Cultura. pp. 377–411.

Fauroux, E. (1983). Poder Regional e Instituciones Regionales En La Provincia de Loja Desde Principios Del Siglo XX: Ejes de Una Investigación [Regional Power and Regional Institutions in the Province of Loja Since the Beginning of the 20th Century: Axes of Research]. *Cultura. Revista Del Banco Central Del Ecuador* V (15). pp. 235–253.

FLACSO - UNFPA. (2008). *Ecuador: La Migración Internacional En Cifras*. [Ecuador: International Migration by the Numbers]. Quito: FLACSO - UNFPA.

Goetschel, A. M. (2007). *Educación de Las Mujeres, Maestras y Esferas Públicas. Quito En La Primera Mitad Del Siglo XX* [Education of Women, Teachers and Public Spheres. Quito in the First Half of the 20th Century]. Quito: FLACSO Ecuador - Abya-Yala.

Goffman, E. (1959). *The Presentation of Self in Everyday Life*. New York: Doubleday.
Goycoechea, A. (2013). Se Fue, ¿a Volver? Imaginarios, Familia y Redes Sociales En La Migración Ecuatoriana a España (1997-2000) [Gone ¿For a While? Imaginaries, Family and Social Networks in Ecuadorian Migration to Spain (1997-2000)]. *Íconos - Revista de Ciencias Sociales*, no. 14. p. 32.
Guhlich, A. (2017). *Migration and Social Pathways: Biographies of Highly Educated People Moving East-West-East in Europe*. Verlag Barbara Budrich.
Jijón, M. (2015). *El Papel de La Cooperación Rusa En El Ecuador* [The Role of Russian Cooperation in Ecuador]. Quito: IAEN.
Jockisch, B. (2014). Ecuador: From Mass Emigration to Return Migration? *Migration Information Source*, November. https://www.migrationpolicy.org/article/ecuador-mass-emigration-return-migration.
Kingman, E. (1992). Ciudades de Los Andes: Homogenialización y Diversidad [Cities from the Andes: Homogenization and Diversity]. In E. Kingman, *Ciudades de Los Andes. Visión Histórica y Contemporánea*. Travaux de l'Institut Français d'Études Andines 72. Quito: IFEA; CIUDAD.
Lawson, V. (2000). Arguments within Geographies of Movement: The Theoretical Potential of Migrants' Stories. *Progress in Human Geography* 24 (2). pp. 173–189. https://doi.org/10.1191/030913200672491184.
Leinaweaver, J. (2008). Improving Oneself: Young People Getting Ahead in the Peruvian Andes. *Latin American Perspectives* 35 (4). pp. 60–78.
Levitt, P. & Glick Schiller, N. (2004). Conceptualizing Simultaneity: A Transnational Social Field Perspective on Society. *The International Migration Review* 38 (3). pp. 1002–1039.
López, G. (2015). *Hispanics of Ecuadorian Origin in the United States, 2013. Statistical Profile*. Washington D.C.: Pew Research Center. Available at: https://www.pewresearch.org/hispanic/wp-content/uploads/sites/5/2015/09/2015-09-15_ecuador-fact-sheet1.pdf.
Luna, M. & Astorga, A. 2011. Educación 1950 - 2010 [Education 1950-2010]. In *Estado Del País. Informe Cero. Ecuador 1950 - 2010*. Quito: Estado del País. pp. 291–306.
Martínez Novo, C. & De la Torre, C. (2010). Racial Discrimination and Citizenship in Ecuador's Educational System. *Latin American and Caribbean Ethnic Studies* 5 (1). pp. 1–26.
Miles, A. (2004). *From Cuenca to Queens: An Anthropological Story of Transnational Migration*. Austin: University of Texas Press.
Nyenyezi Bisoka, A. & Giraud, C. (2020). Michel Foucault à l'épreuve de la Globalisation [Michel Foucault at the Test of Globalisation]. In *Néolibéralisme et Subjectivités. Michel Foucault à l'épreuve de la Globalisation*. Presses Universitaires de Louvain. pp. 23–33.
O'Mara, M. (2012). The Uses of the Foreign Student. *Social Science History* 36 (4). pp. 583–615.
Pagnotta, C. (2011). Équatoriens à Montréal: étude de l'experience subjective de la migration à travers les récits de vie [Ecuadorians in Montreal: study of the subjective experience of migration through life stories]. *Diversité urbaine* 10 (2). pp. 111–128.
Palomeque, S. (1994). La Sierra Sur (1825 - 1990) [The Southern Sierra/Highlands]. In J. Maiguashca (Ed.), *Historia y Región En El Ecuador*. Quito: Corporación Editora Nacional. pp. 69–142.

Pérez Gañán, M.d.R. & Pesántez Calle, B.N. (2017). Impacto Migratorio en las Aspiraciones y Expectativas Educativas y de Movilidad Social de Jóvenes Sigseños [Impact of Migration in the Aspirations and Expectations of Education and Social Mobility of Sigseño Youth]. *Migraciones Internacionales* 33 (9). pp. 57–84. http://dx.doi.org/10.17428/rmi.v9i33.242

Rivera Sánchez, L. (2012). *Vínculos y Prácticas de Interconexión En Un Circuito Migratorio Entre México y Nueva York* [Links and Practices of Interconnection in a Migratory Circuit between Mexico and New York] Colección Becas de Investigación. Buenos Aires: CLACSO. Available at: http://bibliotecavirtual.clacso.org.ar/clacso/becas/20120507115705/RiveraSanchez.pdf.

Rodríguez, M. C. (2015). *Cultura y Política En Ecuador: Estudio Sobre La Creación de La Casa de La Cultura* [Culture and Politics in Ecuador: Study on the Creation of the House of Culture]. Thesis. Quito: FLACSO Ecuador.

Sánchez, B. (2004). El Impacto de La Emigración En Loja [The Impact of Emigration in Loja]. In F. Hidalgo, *Migraciones. Un Juego Con Cartas Marcadas*. Abya-Yala - ILDIS-FES - Plan Migración, Comunicación y Desarrollo. pp. 347–366.

Schutz, A. (1967). *The Phenomenology of the Social World*. Northwestern University Press.

Swedberg, R. & Agevall, O. (2016). *The Max Weber Dictionary. Key Words and Central Concepts*. Stanford: Stanford University Press.

Taylor, P. J. (2003). The State as Container: Territoriality in the Modern World-System. In N. Brenner, B. Jessop, M. Jones & G. MacLeod. (Eds.), *State/Space*. Malden, MA, USA: Blackwell Publishing. pp. 101–114.

Vallejo, A. (2004). El Viaje al Norte. Migración Transnacional y Desarrollo En Ecuador [The Journey to the North. Transnational Migration and Development in Ecuador]. In A. Escrivá & N. Ribas, *Migración y Desarrollo. Estudios Sobre Remesas y Otras Prácticas Transnacionales En España*. Córdoba: Consejo Superior de Investigaciones Científicas.

Velasco, L. & Gianturco, G. (2012). Migración Internacional y Biografías Multiespaciales. Una Reflexión Metodológica [International Migration and Multi-Spatial Biographies: A Methodological Reflection]. In M. Ariza & L. Velasco, *Métodos cualitativos y su aplicación empírica: por los caminos de la investigación sobre migración internacional*. México: UNAM - Instituto de Investigaciones Sociales - El Colegio de la Frontera Norte. pp. 115–150.

Vera, M. P. (2009). Rituales de Admisión. La Reproducción de La Diferencia En El Sistema Escolar Ecuatoriano [Admission Rituals. The Reproduction of Difference in the Ecuadorian School System]. In A. M. Goetschel, *Perspectivas de La Educación En América Latina*. FLACSO Ecuador - Ministerio de Cultura. pp. 311–328.

Weber, M. (2014). *Economía y sociedad [Economy and Society]*. México: Fondo de Cultura Económica.

Whitten, N. E. Jr. (1981). Introduction. In *Cultural Transformations and Ethnicity in Modern Ecuador*. Urbana: University of Illinois Press. pp. 1–44.

Chapter 5

Indigenous Women of Chiapas Migrating

Transformation and Education

Irasema Villanueva and María Elena Tovar

Introduction

Since the 16th century, European expansion has divided territories and people, determined local routes, and defined borders at will in America; this phenomenon intensified in the 19th century. In modern times, in the 20th and 21st centuries, part of the world's migration has been affected by organized crime and human trafficking. The United States decided to solve the problem by building a wall on the border with Mexico. As a part of globalization, countries must see the phenomenon of migration not only from an economic and security perspective, but also from an educational and legal perspective toward the respect of human rights, as a principle of equity and equality.

In the last 40 years, the neoliberal model imposed changes in the Mexican economy and culture, including changes in the social structures of the Indigenous population (Fabregas Puig, 2006). The transmigration to the United States makes Mexico the second-largest country in the world, in migratory terms, after India. Thirteen million Mexicans live outside of Mexico (Ling et al., 2020). Remittances sent to Mexico ranked fourth in the world and as of January 2020 were the second-largest source of national income after oil.

The state of Chiapas, located on Mexico's southeastern border, is characterized by the cultural diversity of its population, which comprises eleven ethnic groups and periodically receives temporary Guatemalan migrants who have been arriving to work on the coffee farms since the end of the 19th century (Tovar González, 2006). In the 20th century, despite the expansion of the migration phenomenon to the United States by people from other continents, the Indigenous population of Chiapas remained on the margins of migration to the United States. However, in the last three decades, with the implementation of the North American Free Trade Agreement, the number of Indigenous migrants from Chiapas to the United States increased due to the conditions of poverty fueled by the neoliberal economy, which has left the fields and their populations unprotected through the promotion of economic projects (Villafuerte Solís, 2001).

DOI: 10.4324/9781003090519-6

Within the growing migrant population in search of employment opportunities in the United States, there has been a notable increase in the flow of migrants returning to Chiapas (Martínez Caballero, 2020). This situation reflects the fact that the rural population is migrating without the experience, documentation, and education that would allow them to remain in the United States.

The present chapter presents a series of studies on migration, which includes both research and our own experiences focused on the migration of Indigenous women of the Tsotsil, Tseltal, and Zoque ethnicities. Tsotsil women have migrated for economic, political, and religious reasons since 1970, while Zoque women have migrated due to natural disasters in 1980. Women from the ethnic groups analyzed in this chapter first migrated internally within Chiapas, and a decade later, they migrated to other Mexican states. During the following decade, between 1995 and 2010, they began to migrate to the United States. The intergenerational accumulation of migratory experiences has caused pain and suffering to these women, as they have been forced to leave their territory. However, this migration has also contributed to new learning and education that has served to transform their reality.

This chapter is divided into four sections. The first section is an introduction to the topic of migration and its impact on Mexico. The second section focuses on the state of Chiapas and seeks to understand the marginalization imposed by the Colony on Indigenous women through the end of the 20th century. The third section addresses the cultural transformations faced by Tsotsil and Tseltal women during their migrations between 1970 and 2010. First, they migrated within Chiapas, forced by internal agrarian conflicts and by the fact that Mexico's prevailing economic model was incompatible with their own self-consumption-based model; later, they migrated beyond national borders but with greater work and educational experience due to changes in globalization. The fourth section includes a reflection on the Zoque women who migrated to the interior of Chiapas due to natural disasters in 1982, where their new semi-urban settlements opened up educational spaces and opportunities that allowed them to enter the labor market, first locally, then regionally; in the following decade, they transmigrated to the United States, driven by better income-earning potential. Finally, the last section offers reflections on the impact of migration on Indigenous women and their educational development.

The information in this chapter is based on unpublished fieldwork carried out by Irasema Villanueva between 1984 and 1985. During that time, Villanueva participated in the government's Social Assistance and Training Program for Vegetable Gardens of the Undersecretary of Indigenous Affairs (*Asistencia Social y Capacitación para Hortalizas de la Subsecretaría de Asuntos Indígenas*); this fieldwork provided relevant data on Tsotsil and

Tseltal women. The chapter also contains research undertaken by María Elena Tovar on the rights and history of women in Chiapas. The chapter also includes interviews with women of the Tsotsil, Tseltal, and Zoque ethnicities conducted by both of the authors. These interviews were carried out between 1985 and 2017, and they have allowed us to appreciate the progress made by some women who, having obtained greater access to education in this century within their localities, and having experienced migration to other regions, have gained a wider access to the fulfillment of their potential as women.

To interpret the reality of these women, other articles and analyses focused on education and female migration were also consulted. This research allowed us to look more closely at the history of three generations, allowing us to observe their migratory processes and changes in their level of education. With this literature review, we were able to reflect more deeply on the process of cultural transformation that these Indigenous women have undergone within processes of globalization.

Chiapas Migration and Its Impact on Mexico

Chiapas is one of Mexico's 32 states. It is located on the country's southeastern border and is the crossing point for Central American migrants, mainly by way of the Suchiate River. Chiapas is home to diverse Indigenous peoples; in 2010, a third of the total population of Chiapas spoke an Indigenous language (INEGI, 2010). Among the ethnic groups still inhabiting the region are the Zoques and 11 Mayan groups: Tsotsiles, Tseltales, Tojolabales, Mames, Kakchiqueles, Lacandones, Mochós, Jaltecos, Chujes, and Kanjobales. These ethnic groups were displaced from their lands during the colonial period and were forced to migrate for more than 300 years; this phenomenon contributed to isolation and economic stagnation for these populations (de Vos, 1994).

Currently, the state is characterized by a substantial educational, economic, and social lag; Chiapas was ranked first nationally in poverty in 2019. Reports from Coneval published in the newspaper *El Economista* (García and Ayala Espinosa, 2019) reveal that public policies for social development do not have a significant impact on the well-being of its population. Nevertheless, the Energy Information System 2020 indicates that Chiapas is the third-largest producer of oil in the country; it holds 70% of the country's water resources, which has allowed for the construction of three hydroelectric dams to supply electricity to a part of the national territory and even Guatemala between 1970 and 2000. The economic exploitation of its resources, however, is not reflected in the well-being of the population. Evidence of this statement is the economic stagnation based on extractive agriculture that the state underwent up until the 1990s. Currently, the economy is centered on tertiary activity represented mainly in services (72%), followed by secondary activity in construction and infrastructure (21%) and primary activity (7.3%), which reflects a low gross domestic product of only 1.7%. The economic entities employ a high percentage of women (44%), compared to men (56%), within a population of 456,000 agricultural workers (INEGI, 2016).

With regard to schooling, the National Institute of Statistics and Geography (INEGI, 2016) highlights that Indigenous communities show a higher incidence of poverty in the school-age population and low levels of education; this situation is exacerbated in the female population. According to the National Institute for Educational Evaluation (Instituto Nacional para la *Evaluación* de la *Educación*, 2018), in 2018, 26% of the Indigenous population was illiterate, such that UNICEF recommended that Mexico turn its attention to women in this group, considering that they have a lower level of school attendance than men, a difference that increases after the age of 12. Of the total number of girls over 12 years old, 95% dropped out of school due to pregnancy. Low school attendance rates and teenage pregnancy make them the most vulnerable group.

The situation of Indigenous women today is the result of the convergence between modernity and the historical consequences of colonization, particularly in the southeast of the country. Once the conquest was completed in 1524, the Spanish colony de-structured pre-Hispanic economies and took over Indigenous territories. With the Christianization of 'the natives,' the Church imposed a female model of fertility and submission that impeded their ability to make decisions for themselves. In Chiapas, the Hispanic male-chauvinist paradigm reproduced a system of domination based on servility, submission, obedience, and female dependency. Women were left with the Christian obligation to bear children, who would then become future payers of tribute, obedient to the authority of the father, the landlord, the government, the king, and God. As a result, Indigenous women became servants of the Spanish empire, of the landlords, and of their intermediaries (Olivera Bustamante, 2004). Thus, Indigenous women were subjected to domination throughout the viceroyalty; this phenomenon continued during the 19th and 20th centuries, leading to their ever-increasing marginalization. This subjugation remained in place throughout the generations, as evidenced throughout this chapter. Nevertheless, some women broke the rule by going beyond their cultural boundaries.

The marginalization of Indigenous women is evident in data collected by economists and labor experts focused on income, who agree that Chiapas reveals an asymmetrical behavior in terms of gender. This is reflected in the restriction of freedoms, educational delays, and the exercise of women's rights. For example, in the labor-income gap, women earn an average of $1,612 USD, as compared to $5,803 USD for men, that is, 72% less (Coporo Quintana & Villafuerte Solis, 2017).

Tsotsil and Tseltal Migrant Women

The historical-cultural settlement of the Tsotsil and Tseltal ethnic groups of the Mayan family includes several municipalities, historically located in the Los Altos region of Chiapas. The analysis in this chapter includes the fieldwork carried out by Irasema Villanueva with migrant women in two municipalities within the Northern Region: Simojovel and Huitiupán. These municipalities were expropriated and sold to mestizos in the last third of the 19th century, which gave them a 'coffee-growing sector' character based on 'servant-master' relationships, which lasted until the 1970s (Tovar González, 2006).

In 2015, Los Altos had the largest Indigenous population in the state of Chiapas, with 32% of the population identified as Indigenous (INEGI, 2016). In Los Altos, the use of land is mainly for self-consumption. In this social structure, women are recognized as members of the community but do not receive equal treatment to men, especially in the municipality of Chamula. In Chamula, there are high rates of family and community violence, where discrimination, polygamy, and selling of girls is a common practice. Life in Chamula takes place within a masculine context, legitimized by customary law (Ulloa, Montiel & Baeza, 2012).

Since the end of the 19th century, the Tsotsiles of the Los Altos region have migrated to the Soconusco region in southeastern Chiapas for coffee harvesting (Tovar González, 2006). During the 20th century, oil and coffee brought foreign revenues to the country, which required a large local and foreign workforce, bringing Guatemalans to the region during the harvesting season. Earning an income was the primary motivator for Indigenous families to migrate south to Soconusco. Women and children, both Tsotsiles and Tseltales, traditionally occupied in domestic work and in the harvesting of corn, would migrate to cut, pulp, and dry the coffee. However, by the 1970s, with the drastic fall in coffee prices and the weakening of the rural economy, labor recruitment decreased. This instigated new migrations of Indigenous people from the regions, as well as Central Americans, to the United States.

Internal Indigenous migration to different parts of the state began in 1930, and in the 1970s, internal migration was notorious due to demographic growth and modernization of the country, which included the development of hydroelectric projects. After a prolonged period of marginalization, Chiapas became the center of the country's economic development, given its oil and large rivers, which allowed for the construction of dams. These constructions affected various municipalities such as Simojovel and Huitipán and, as a consequence, Tseltal populations. The Tseltal populations became a social laboratory of gradual transformations for Indigenous women, who were impelled by the political culture of social participation. Attempts were made to displace this population to the jungle; however, there were political mobilizations accompanied by violence that prevented massive movements of this population (Villanueva Guzmán, 1984). These towns were the antecedent of the Zapatista Army of Liberation, EZLN, which began its struggle from 1970 until 2000, when the Itzantún hydroelectric project was cancelled.

Also, in the Los Altos region of Chiapas, there were violent intra-community movements that led to massive migrations due to religious differences between Catholics and Protestants. The latter group was evicted from the region for breaking with the 'usages and customs' of the community. As refugees, the Indigenous families moved to warmer regions with better soil for crops, as well as to parts of the jungle, which was beginning to be an option for mestizo migrants from other regions of the country (Uribe Cortez & Martínez Velasco, 2012).

First- and Second-Generation Internal Migration of Tsotsil and Tseltal Women

The pandora's box opened by the State of Chiapas in 1970 revived long-unresolved conflicts by giving priority to the country's economic development over addressing the needs of vulnerable groups in the Chiapas, among them the Indigenous population of the Northern Region of Chiapas, near the jungle. A hydroelectric dam was built, which the Indigenous communities rejected with the support of political organizations such as CIOAC (*Central Independiente de Obreros Agrícolas y Campesinos*) and CTM (*Confederación de Trabajadores de México*), among others. Farmers and other members of the community also joined in, hindering the project for three decades. The majority of the Indigenous population returned to their territory. The conflict came to an end by the end of the 20th century, preventing the construction of the dam (Villanueva Guzmán, 2009).

The Indigenous women of the Northern Region frame a living portrait of the 19th century (almost to the end of the 20th century) both economically and culturally. Schools were not located close to the coffee farms, as they were considered irrelevant within the coffee economy, characterized by 19th-century-style labor structures (Tovar González, 2006). By the 1980s, the Indigenous women of Simojovel and Huitiupán were living under control and domination exercised over mothers and daughters, in a reproduction of the machismo characteristic of the colonial era.

During the fieldwork, an Indigenous woman catechist of the Catholic Church moved around the region of Simojovel and Huitiupán, gathering women to tell about their lives and experiences; she translated their narratives into Spanish. These women said that when they migrated to the jungle, they were forced to return to their places of origin because of the lack of appropriate living conditions; this was due to the lack of agreements with the government since they were against the government's plan to construct the Itzantun hydroelectric dam (Villanueva Guzmán, 1984).

In our reflections on two generations—mother and daughter—of Tsotsil migrants from the Los Altos region (corresponding to the period from 1970 to 1994) we noted gradual changes in their customs as they became involved in social mobilizations in defense of their lands, or as they were expelled for professing Protestant beliefs contrary to the uses and customs of their community. These migrants were violently forced to leave toward the central valleys and the Chiapas jungle; in many cases, their homes were burned down. In the valleys, these women were treated as refugees because in their communities, the local authorities, under the excuse that they were violating the custom of religious festivals of the Patron Saint, repudiated them. It is necessary to point out that the communities collectively resolve to respect 'uses and customs' and, undoubtedly, religious intolerance had political motives for the growing young population, who began to demand land to work.

The conflicts themselves created certain conditions and alternatives of refuge to several Indigenous localities of Los Altos; in this way, the Indigenous population found a suitable forum for denouncing the accumulation of injustices that overwhelmed them within the regional and national organizations. One of these events was an Indigenous congress called 'Fray Bartolomé de las Casas,' held in 1974 in San Cristóbal de las Casas, which brought together four linguistic groups who were undervalued in the context of the national project—among them Tsotsiles and Tseltales—to discuss the dispossession of their lands.

In the dynamics of Indigenous mobilization, women were integrated, although without a voice, into the collective meetings. At the same time, in 1980, women's liberation emerged among Indigenous women. The women—with the limitations of monolingualism and lack of schooling—began to understand the importance of women's liberation; they were influenced by the proselytism of religious missionaries, as seen in the town of Simojovel in 1985. Together with academics and political leaders, they advocated for social justice and the liberation of Latin American populations. Women with a basic knowledge of the Spanish language played a leading role in translating the political message to other women. In the initial phase, men agreed to 'allow them' to participate in the peasant movement, informing and training them on how to demand their rights from the government (Villanueva Guzmán, 2009).

In the 20th century, rights of equality and justice were written into legal codes but were not implemented for everyone. From that point, social movements emerged, seeking to generate socio-political transformations in Chiapas with a focus on ethnic awareness. The unresolved agrarian conflicts of previous decades led to the uprising of Indigenous groups in various localities despite the persecution and imprisonment of men. Politically motivated women became involved in politics before the emergence of the EZLN in 1994, and gradually, as they left their territories, they began unleashing a past dominated by the uses and customs of male control.

Third Generation and the Tsotsiles' and Tseltales' Decision to Go Abroad

While still under the communal mandate of 'uses and customs,' rural communities gradually began to open up space for collective discussions, in which the voices of women were taken into account. In these spaces, the women acquired new notions to recreate their worlds, and ways to question government officials and to confront their adversaries (Toledo Tello, 2013). The long history of pain, but also of learning with empirical education inside the family home, helped to modify colonial cultural patterns inculcated in women for centuries. These learnings contributed to personal growth and a conscious awakening through education that are reflected in the social and workspace in which young Indigenous women now venture.

Zapatista Army of National Liberation (1994)

Despite all of the difficulties and obstacles, women organized themselves and, in a short period of time, the conditions were created for the communities of Chiapas to join the Zapatista movement in 1994. The nomination of Commander Ramona as a member of the EZLN was emblematic for the Indigenous people, considering that an Indigenous woman had never reached a position of such magnitude (Pacheco Ladrón de Guevara, 2019). The broad participation of indigenous women in political organization and their struggle against gender and social abuses transformed their domestic and social life. They passed this experience on to their descendants with new ways of thinking about their reality; thus, the vision of Indigenous children was disrupted by the clamour of the agrarian movement raised up by their parents.

Immersed in years of agrarian dispute, women and children saw how their spouses and fathers fought for their land. These emerging generations, trained in the protest mobilizations, denunciations, and confrontations of their parents, transmitted a sense of respect for the land to the following generations, but as time went by, that sentiment began to fade; food produce was devalued and the income they earned was insufficient to invest in the land. There was then a certain impulse to migrate to the United States in search of a higher level of income.

The encounter between the EZLN and the government led to changes in Chiapas. In a short period of time, highways replaced country roads, and various localities were provided with electricity and plumbing services, as well as educational infrastructure at all levels. With the Zapatistas, the people not only demanded basic services that had been denied for decades, but also respect for their territories by claiming their autonomy.

At the end of the 20th century and the beginning of the current one, the Mexican government provided university services to the main cities of Chiapas; two universities were built especially for Indigenous students, one in Ocosingo and the other in San Cristóbal las Casas. The building of electric infrastructure also made it possible to access media in the communities with communications towers, which enabled access to television, internet, cellular phones, electronic games, and so on, which contributed to meaningful changes for these younger generations of women (Cruz Pérez, Esteban Silvestre & García Lara, 2018).

Family experiences accumulated over the preceding four decades made it possible for some parents to allow their daughters to attend school. Although only a minority of these women were able to access higher education, this enabled them to have aspirations for the future. As of 2012 and 2015, Indigenous women participated in the elections, in accordance with gender parity, but this participation was accompanied by political violence. Thus, two women presidents of the municipalities of Oxchuc and Chenalhó, elected by popular vote, were forced to step down from their posts, under the gaze of 'usages and customs' and were replaced by men to preserve the peace, in spite of a legal ruling in the women's favor (Tovar González & Villanueva Guzmán, 2019).

How Tsotsil and Tseltal Women Began to Migrate to the United States

Beginning in 1990, heads of families started to migrate northward, followed by young people between the ages of 15 and 18, and later by single women, whose migration increased steadily after 2000 (Instituto Nacional de las Mujeres, n.d.). It is important to emphasize that young women from these ethnic groups have a high sense of solidarity and it is difficult for them to travel on their own. Within a short period of time, Tsotil and Tseltal groups made up a significant percentage of the population of Chiapas that chose to migrate across international borders. According to testimonies from Indigenous Chiapanecan migrant women, the migratory experience of Central Americans and Oaxacans helped them to make the transition to the United States to overcome economic and cultural obstacles with their languages, while also being supported by their families and friends. Angulo Barredo (2016) also confirms these testimonies in the Sierra Region. Other migrants lived the painful experience of crossing the desert and, once they found themselves at the opposite geographical limits, they were abandoned to their fate by the polleros.

Given the difficulties inherent to migration due to legal restrictions in the United States, cases of the arrival of complete families of spouses and children into that country are minimal (Angulo Barredo, 2016). First, the young married men migrated alone, and then their wives followed. Once the men had secured some stability in the United States, the Tsotsil and Tseltal women followed them to Los Angeles, San Francisco, New York, Chicago, and Miami (Fabregas Puig, 2006). It was common that the couple acquired debts in their communities back in Chiapas to cover the expenses of their relocation. The women were mainly employed in domestic and service work in the United States.

The dollars earned by the first generations of middle-aged married farmers flowed to their places of origin. These remittances quickly reached their wives; when both the husband and wife had migrated, the remittances were administered by the migrants' parents, who looked after the grandchildren back home. The remittances supplied food, clothing, education, and housing; they also helped to pay off the debt incurred in the trip north. It is estimated that two years of work in the United States were required to pay off the debts, which meant that migrants could not return to Mexico during that period of time (Coporo Quintana & Villafuerte Solis, 2017).

It should be noted that Chiapas's migration to the United States was gaining momentum and becoming a more-organized practice when restrictive migration policies on the northern border were implemented during the economic crisis of 2008–2009. Since that time, studies have been carried out regarding the migrants' return to Mexico, their maintenance of social networks, the overall socio-cultural framework of the family. By 2014, 43% of the population over 15 years of age in the Indigenous groups analyzed in this chapter (Tsotsiles, Tseltales, and Zoques) was illiterate and 23% of children between 6 and 14 years of age did not attend school. This situation negatively affected their employment and income opportunities abroad. However, by the first decade of the 21st century, a small percentage of the female population had completed university studies and, along with the migratory experiences of their families, sought opportunities beyond their local territory.

The women from these ethnic groups have managed to stand out. For instance, outstanding women weavers have obtained experience outside the country, and others have positioned themselves prominently within regional culinary scene, and other Indigenous women stand out in architecture, among other professions.

Zoque Women, Migration, and Education

We now turn to the women in the northwestern region, the deeply historical and cultural territory of the Zoques. The Zoques migrated from Franciso León and Chapultengango, due to the eruption of the Chichonal volcano in 1982, which destroyed entire villages and took the lives of thousands of people. The catastrophe generated a Zoque diaspora that resulted in settlements far from their original lands and had brutal consequences for men and women. Nevertheless, they managed to develop resilience thanks to the emergence of new forms of social organization and the re-creation of collective cultural mechanisms in their new settlements, as we will describe later.

Some families took refuge in the inner part of the state, near the affected areas, such as the municipal hub of Tecpatán. Other families left for southeastern regions such as the Riviera Maya, drawing from the prior experience of family members who years earlier sought work in the Riviera when the country was investing in tourism development. Fewer families went to Guadalajara, Mexico's central-western capital (Domínguez Rueda, 2014). By the mid-1990s, with more experience and income, women and men began to transmigrate to the United States.

The socio-cultural account of the Zoque women that we describe in this study intertwines stories from interviews collected between 1995 and 2017. They include informal and personal narratives of Zoque women from communities in El Naranjo (a community of Francisco León), and Nuevo Carmen Tonapac (a community of Chapultenango); both of these communities vanished with the eruption of the Chichonal volcano. Nuevo Naranjo is now part of the municipality of Tectapán, which is relatively close to Francisco León (Domínguez Rueda, 2014). The women of Nuevo Carmen Tonapac relocated to the municipality of Chiapa de Corzo, an urban region that contributed to the future-building of women who still maintained their traditions. With the communication infrastructure afforded to them in their places of resettlement, the women are better positioned to increase their participation in the schools (Villanueva Guzmán, 2017).

Migratory Experiences Within Chiapas of First- and Second-Generation Zoque Women

The family impoverishment resulting from the natural disaster forced migrant mothers and daughters to reinvent their existence. Without resources, the monolingual and illiterate young women went to the cities to work. They were relatively successful and managed to overcome the discriminatory obstacles of the workplace. Given the unstable income earned by their parents, women from Nuevo Naranjo worked in solidarity as domestic workers in Tecpatán and learned Spanish in the process. Women from Nuevo Carmen Tonapac, and other locations, drew the attention of women from Tecpatán to Tuxtla Gutiérrez to improve their income.

Second-Generation Zoque Migration to the United States

Some Zoque women of the second generation of Chichonal transmigrated to the United States, unlike the Tsotsiles and Tseltales who did not do so until the third generation. In the past, these Zoque women were aware that in the United States, they could earn a higher income. Thus, their preference was to accompany their husbands, but with the desire to return home to build their houses in their assigned territories. Supported by family networks, some women from El Naranjo migrated to South Carolina in the United States. This information was obtained in informal talks with Zoque women who were domestic workers in Tuxtla and is corroborated in the statistics of the IMER (*Instituto Mexicano del Exterior*) from 2010, which confirm the geographic location and the family networks that they established among relatives in the United States. We lost touch with them, some because they returned to their community years later. None of them had any schooling, and some of them were unable to read and write in conventional literacy terms. Their savings from their internal- and external-migration incomes allowed them to finance their own relocation to their communities of origin, as well as that of other women. The women who managed to cross the border into the United States were employed as domestic workers; one of them reported that her brother migrated with his entire family. Even though they suffered discrimination in the new location, they remained in the country. This, however, was not the case with the youngest child, who could not adapt to the United States' system and fell into drug addiction; he was deported when he was 14 years old, and he was taken in by his aunt and uncle's family upon his return to Chiapas. The father returned a few years later because one of his parents died, and he stayed to take care of the cattle. The wife stayed in the United States, hoping to see her other daughters through their studies, since the United States' system provided them with a free education.

Indicators from 2010 of the National Council for the Evaluation of Social Development Policy (*Coneval*) placed 98% of the population of the thirteen Zoque municipalities of Chiapas in conditions of extreme poverty. Based on these statistics, it is understood that at the end of the last century, hundreds of men and women sought employment options beyond the national borders. As they left their lands, they began to travel for the first time to the United States; the Zoques, specifically, went to Boston and other areas within Massachusetts. From 2006 to 2012, a total of 1,276 Zoques migrated there, according to data from the Institute of Mexicans Abroad.

The second generation of Zoques who lived near the capital of Chiapas, in places such as Carmen Tonapac, were soon able to acquire better access to educational resources than their mothers had, so that the mothers of the first generation were more inclined to push their daughters into schooling. Some earned higher degrees at the Indigenous University in San Cristóbal, thanks to financial support through scholarships, while others studied at public universities in Tuxtla. Nowadays, those who are mothers lead language-maintenance projects through the maintenance of social networks with families who have left for other parts of the country. Together, they preserve traditional festivals, such as the Mequé, and make their Zomés, or offerings to the divinity (Tovar González, 1987). Through interviews we conducted with some of the Zoque women of Chapultenango and Carmen Tonapac, women of the third generation reflected a greater awareness of the value of their ethnicity, carrying it with dignity and pride. We noted that this is not necessarily the case for the mothers of the first generation, who often hid their origins to avoid being ridiculed by the mestizos.

The Second and Third Generation of Zoques in Their New Settlements

Those migrant girls from Chichonal, now aunts and mothers, seek to improve their children's quality of life through education, despite the existing unemployment and low professional wages in Mexico. In 2010, the INEGI indicated that the communities affected by the municipal dump had more than five thousand inhabitants, most of whom were children.

The education that women of Nuevo Carmen Tonapac had received informed the mobilizations towards closing and relocating a municipal garbage dump in Chiapa de Corzo. The way the dump operated produced hazardous solid waste that carried health consequences to nearby populations. The demand for the closure and relocation of the municipal dump was led by a small group of Zoque women, who had graduated from public universities in environmental engineering, anthropology, and social work. Others had a high school education and had participated in workshops on human rights. The women made relocation of the dump possible by organizing themselves with leaders from six other surrounding locations, given that the dump was affecting the health of their communities as well.

These young women organized four localities made up of diverse cultural groups: Zoques, Tsotsiles, and two relocated mestizo groups. In April 2016, they confronted the municipal president of Chiapa de Corzo to condemn the damage being inflicted upon their environment. Given the Mayor's indifferent response, they opted to promote strategic litigation as a mechanism for the integral defense of their human rights with legal accompaniment (Villanueva Guzmán, 2017).

The residents of the affected localities filed several complaints with the State Human Rights Commission (CEDH), the Federal Environmental Prosecutor's Office (Profepa), the Chiapas State Environmental Prosecutor's Office (PAECH), and the General Secretariat of the State Government, all of which ignored the petitions. Generally, the authorities do not listen to the citizens and even less to the Indigenous women. This fact was evident in the case of the dump, in which the authorities continuously avoided a solution. Instead, Indigenous women were obliged to provide proof that their health had been affected, even though environmental regulations only required a formal complaint from the community to open a case.

This indifference to Indigenous women's demands happens despite the fact that there has been a law for *Access to a Life Free of Violence* for women and a *Prosecutor's Office for the Defense of Women's Rights* in operation in Chiapas since 2009. Due to threats against Indigenous women by municipal authorities, male leaders of the affected populations decided to follow the procedures for closing the dump; this situation served as an excuse to limit the participation of Indigenous women in the case. The young women of Carmen Tonapac did not cease and carried out parallel actions such as complaints on social networks (Facebook, WhatsApp, etc.). In addition, and in order to supplement the work of the legal defense, they independently developed a historical memory of the case with the aim of setting a precedent for future generations.

The environmental and legal knowledge that these Indigenous women acquired through the secondary education was key to mounting a case for why the municipal dump did not comply with official standards and was uninformed by environmental impact studies. By the end of October 2016, affected populations and authorities agreed on a definitive closure of the dump. Additionally, garbage removal would be guaranteed for all of the communities. These actions were pursued in response to the recommendations of the National Human Rights Commission (CNDH). The legal accompaniment was documented in a master's thesis (Villanueva Guzmán, 2017).

This case of the dump highlights the importance of women's right to social participation, and the significance of education for protection against gender-based violence, especially in vulnerable Indigenous populations. In this sense, the *Convention on the Elimination of All Forms of Discrimination against Women* (CEDAW) establishes the importance of engaging this population in social and political participation, as it leads to creating solutions to community problems. It is undeniable, as evidenced in the case discussed, that the educational preparation and social sensitivity of young professionals favors community action of Indigenous women as a whole, which in turn generates a better standard of living for all, with a healthy environment, and the fostering of a cordial coexistence.

Unfortunately, in Chiapas, the marginalization of women in their communities and the mestizo world still prevails; a problem that is aggravated by the conditions of poverty and low educational levels. International agreements such as Belém do Pará and the CEDAW have called for addressing this marginalization of women's issues.

According to data collected between 2005 and 2006 by Cruz Pérez, Esteban Silvestre & García Lara, 2018, young Indigenous women already had more access to education and other public services such as running water, and some even had access to the internet and tele-education. All of this was possible thanks to social programs such as *Oportunidades*, which is a student scholarship program. The third generation of Zoque women we engaged with in this study also attested to the fact that access to education and services had become available. As part of the school curriculum at the high school level, the women had access to human rights and environmental protections through ecological actions that are now promoted at the Colegio de Bachilleres de Chiapas in the community of Nuevo Guayabal (Alonso-Bolaños, 2015). Nevertheless, there is still work to be done.

Regarding 'uses and customs' codes, today Zoque women with a school education are working to maintain their traditions and mother tongue within networks and organizations in their territories or in the communities in which they resettled. Some women are empowered to participate in community assemblies where their opinions are respected. Some examples of Indigenous women's empowerment can be found in the municipality of Chapultenango, where women struggled against a mega-oil-extraction project, which would have put their river at risk after failing to follow the ILO's Indigenous Consultation Agreement 169.

Conclusions

The problems that Indigenous women face when migrating are multi-causal. We can conclude that some of the Tsotsiles, Tseltales, and Zoques women had remarkable transformations against adversity, which they faced with their intelligence and the transformative educational tools that they were able to acquire. The journey to achieving gender equity is still long, especially when Chiapas has the lowest rates of educational attainment, where Indigenous women are the most affected. This educational challenge is due, among other things, to early pregnancy rates, especially in the Los Altos region. Early pregnancy often forces women to leave school, leaving them without the educational tools to eradicate the impoverished conditions experienced by their parents.

Mexico has been the signatory of multiple international agreements and accords—the CEDAW, the 1995 Beijing Agreement, and the 2007 Law on Violence against Women—aiming to promote equality for women and confronting the discrimination and violence experienced by women and girls. However, these agreements are not respected in Mexico. The progress made through political disputes, as well as the life experiences of these women, have positively impacted these populations, but are still insufficient. Nevertheless, they are bridges and signs of light to encourage comprehensive education programs that strengthen the dignity of Indigenous women, without putting the 'uses and customs' at risk.

The guidelines and mandates derived from international frameworks and active community participation have influenced processes of gender equity in Mexico. The messages have been conveyed through talks, workshops, and social networks, which indicates that education is not confined solely to schools or classrooms. Technology enabling distance learning is facilitating educational processes. These important steps towards educational access require a more significant commitment from all parties—especially the authorities—and a more concerted effort in the communities where women, men, and children are involved. Effective learning reforms that combine 'uses and customs' and respect for human rights are urgently needed. These learning reforms must promote access to education for women as critical guardians of culture.

The experience of the first-generation Tsotsiles, Tseltales, and Zoques parents—in terms of family support, access to education, and gender awareness—have enabled the empowerment of the new generations in defense of their rights. In the case of the Tsotsiles, empowerment of women is evidenced from the first generation with the emergence of the emblematic figure of EZLN commander Ramona, who influenced the strengthening of the next generation. This empowerment was also evident in Zoque women from Carmen Tonapac and Chapultenango, as well as in other Indigenous women who had relocated to the Chiapas jungle. The former took social and political action in favor of their community in, for instance, the 'ecological march' movement against the authorization of irregular municipal garbage dumps. Through this movement, they have sought to stop water contamination and the rampant exploitation of forest resources. As part of high-school education in the jungle region, environmental and ecological issues were noted and were reflected in the movements engineered by these Indigenous women.

The approach to cities and other borders through migration, as well as the experience that Indigenous women had upon entering the labor market, helped them to empower themselves. The prevailing wave of digital technologization is rapidly transforming the culture through the massive influence of social media. The internet as a means of communication informs Indigenous cultures, while serving as an educational tool. The relevance of social networks to cultural movement in the region is evidenced in its benefits to the Zoque women from Carmen Tonapac and their mobilization in garbage dump case. However, the use of the internet has also become risky when young people venture into it without safety information. In Chiapas, high rates of human trafficking have been reported, including crimes that have been committed aided by the use of social media. Further access to education for Indigenous people, especially women, regarding the use of these digital resources is of vital importance.

Finally, it is important to note that Indigenous women's migration from the Zoque, Tsotsil, and Tseltal communities to the United States is not sufficient to raise their quality of life. Those who have migrated to the United States find themselves in a dilemma because the remittances they send only alleviate the poverty of their families and pay off the debts that they acquired when financing their migratory journey. Within this recent process of globalization, Indigenous migration is inevitable, but it must be redirected towards education and producing experiences that are a source of personal and collective growth.

References

Alonso-Bolaños, M. (2015). Somos otros, pero recordamos de dónde venimos como zoques: Aproximaciones a las generaciones post-erupción y sus dinámicas regionales [We are others, but we remember where we come from as Zoques: Approaches to post-eruption generations and their regional dynamics]. *Entre Diversidades Revista de Ciencias Sociales y Humanidades*, 1(4). pp. 59–82.

Angulo Barredo, J. I. (2016). *Migraciones, organización familiar y cambio sociodemográfico en la Sierra Madre de Chiapas* [Migration, family organization and socio-demographic change in the Sierra Madre de Chiapas]. Tuxtla Gutiérrez, Chiapas, Mexico: UNACH.

Coporo Quintana, G. & Villafuerte Solis, D. (2017). Chamula: pueblo de migrantes en Los Altos de Chiapas [Chamula: a migrant town in Los Altos de Chiapas]. *Migración y Desarrollo*, 15(2). pp. 97–121.

Cruz Pérez, O., Esteban Silvestre, H. & García Lara, G. A. (2018). Opresión y resistencia. Vivencias de mujeres indígenas universitarias [Oppression and resistance. Experiences of indigenous university women]. *RICSH Revista Iberoamericana de las Ciencias Sociales y Humanísticas*, 7(14). pp. 25–40.

Domínguez Rueda, F. (2014). Zoques urbanos en Guadalajara, Jalisco México: migración, racismo y prácticas culturales en el hogar [Urban Zoques in Guadalajara, Jalisco Mexico: migration, racism and cultural practices in the home]. *Revista nuestrAmérica*, 2(4). pp. 111–132.

Fabregas Puig, A. (2006). *Las migraciones y la interculturalidad en la actualidad [Migration and interculturalism today]*. In C. Miranda, E. Rodríguez & J. Artola (Eds.), *Los Nuevos Rostros de la migración en el mundo*. Tuxtla Gutiérrez, Chiapas, Mexico: Gobierno de Chiapas, Instituto de Migración. pp. 17–32.

García, A. K. & Ayala Espinosa C. (2019, August 6). Chiapas, el estado más pobre del país en la última década [Chiapas, the poorest state in the country in the last decade]. *El Economista*. Available at: https://www.eleconomista.com.mx/estados/Chiapas-el-estado-mas-pobre-del-pais-en-la-ultima-decada-20190807-0010.html.

Instituto Nacional de las Mujeres. (n.d.) La migración México-Estados Unidos: un enfoque de género [Mexico-United States migration: a gender approach]. Available at: http://cedoc.inmujeres.gob.mx/documentos_download/100918.pdf.

Instituto Nacional para la Evaluación de la Educación. (2018). Panorama educativo de la población indígena estatal [Educational panorama of the state's indigenous population]. Retrieved from https://www.inee.edu.mx/wp-content/uploads/2019/08/P3B113.pdf.

INEGI. (2010). Cuéntame Población [Tell me Population]. Available at: http://www.cuentame.inegi.org.mx/monografias/informacion/chis/poblacion/default.aspx?tema=me&e=07.

INEGI. (2016). Cuéntame Economía [Tell me Economy]. Available at: http://www.cuentame.inegi.org.mx/monografias/informacion/chis/economia/default.aspx?tema=me&e=07.

Ling, J. J., Cárdenas Salgado, G., Espinosa Carrasco L. A., López Vega R., Reyes Miranda, A., Isidro Luna, V. M., ... Segura Ramírez, A. V. (2020). Anuario de migración y remesas 2020 [Yearbook of Migration and Remittances Mexico 2020]. Available at: https://www.bbvaresearch.com/wp-content/uploads/2020/10/Anuario_Migracion_y_Remesas_2020.pdf.

Martínez Caballero, G. (2020). Estadísticas Migratorias, Síntesis 2020 [Migration Statistics, 2020 Synthesis]. Available at: http://portales.segob.gob.mx/work/models/PoliticaMigratoria/CEM/Estadisticas/Sintesis_Graficas/Sintesis_2020.pdf.

Olivera Bustamante, M. (2004). *De sumisiones, cambios y rebeldías: mujeres indígenas de Chiapas, Volumen 1 [Of Surrender, Change and Rebellion: Indigenous Women of Chiapas, Volume 1]*. Tuxtla Gutiérrez, Chiapas, Mexico: UNICACH, CONACyT, UNACH.

Pacheco Ladrón de Guevara, L. C. (2019). Nosotras ya estábamos muertas: Comandanta Ramona y otras insurgentas del Ejército Zapatista de Liberación Nacional [We were already dead: Comandanta Ramona and other insurgents of the Zapatista Army of National Liberation]. *Transcontinental Human Trajectories*, 6. pp. 66–79.

Toledo Tello, S. (2013). De peones de fincas a campesinos, Transformaciones agrarias y domésticas en el norte de Chiapas (siglos XX y XXI) [From farm workers to peasants, agrarian and domestic transformations in northern Chiapas (20th-21st centuries)]. *EntreDiversidades Revista de Ciencias Sociales y Humanidades*, 1. pp. 13–41.

Tovar González, M. E. (1987). *Copoya, vivencia de una tradición zoque* [Copoya, experience of a zoque tradition]. Tuxtla Gutiérrez, Chiapas, Mexico: SEC, Gobierno de Chiapas.

Tovar González, M. E. (2006). *Finqueros extranjeros en el Soconusco, durante el porfiriato* [Foreign farmers in the Soconusco, during the Porfiriato]. Tuxtla Gutiérrez, Chiapas, Mexico: UNICACH, CONACyT.

Tovar González, M. E. & Villanueva Guzmán, I. A. (2019). *La participación de las mujeres en la Política de la entidad de Chiapas y su impacto en la sociedad* [Women's Participation in Politics in Chiapas and its Impact on Society]. Retrieved from Nueva Alianza database.

Ulloa, T., Montiel, O. & Baeza, G. (2012). *Visibilización de la violencia contra las mujeres en los usos y costumbres de las comunidades indígenas* [Visibility of violence against women in the usages and customs of indigenous communities]. Mexico City, Mexico: CNPEVM.

Uribe Cortez, J., & Martínez Velasco, G. (2012). Cambio religioso, expulsiones indígenas y conformación de organizaciones evangélicas en Los Altos de Chiapas [Religious Change, Indigenous Expulsions and the Formation of Evangelical Organizations in the Los Altos region of Chiapas]. *Política y Cultura, 38*. pp. 141–161.

Villafuerte Solís, D. (2001). *Integraciones comerciales en la frontera sur, Chiapas frente al tratado de Libre Comercio México-Centroamérica* [Trade integrations on the southern border, Chiapas in the face of the Mexico-Central America Free Trade Agreement]. Mexico City, México: UNAM.

Villanueva Guzmán, I. A. (1984). Monografía de Simojovel y Huitiupán [Simojovel and Huitiupán Monograph]. Unpublished manuscript, *Subsecretaría de Asuntos Indígenas*, SDR, San Cristóbal las Casas, Chiapas, Mexico.

Villanueva Guzmán, I. A. (2009). *Simojovel en la sombra de la globalización* [Simojovel in the shadow of globalization] (Unpublished Bachelor's thesis). UNAM, Mexico City, Mexico.

Villanueva Guzmán, I. A. (2017). *Defensa y exigibilidad del derecho humano a una calidad de vida digna para los grupos vulnerables* [Defense and enforceability of the human right to a dignified quality of life for vulnerable groups] (Unpublished Master's thesis). UNACH, Tuxtla Gutiérrez, Chiapas, Mexico.

de Vos, J. (1994). *Vivir en Frontera. La experiencia de los indios de Chiapas* [Living in the Border. The experience of the Indians of Chiapas]. San Cristóbal de las Casas, Chiapas, Mexico: CIESAS.

Chapter 6

Forced Migration, Violence, Education, and Testimony: For a Place in the World

Miguel Angel Martínez Martínez

Given the political order of invisibilization of human rights violations that prevails in Mexico, memory emerges as a strategy to resist historical exclusions. The *Brigadas Nacionales de Búsqueda de Personas Desaparecidas* (National Brigades for the Search of Disappeared Persons)[1]—carried out in Mexico since 2016—have taken this argument as their objective and have intended to create solidarity between migrants and civil society so that the voices of marginalized people can be heard, and the cruelest strategies of power can be resisted. These brigades have shown that it is impossible to suppress the pain felt for the missing ones.

In these scenarios of human rights violations, we face two very distinct situations: first, we encounter the wounds shared throughout Latin America that intertwine to bring together solutions to achieve *good living*[2] amid tragedy, violence, and abuse; second, we face the confluence of experiences that give rise to the transversality of disaster. Through the disappearances of people, there are also forced migrations filled with pain, suffering, and mockery.

As people flee situations, life weaves itself on very specific looms. Threads come and go with the words and testimonies of the relatives of disappeared persons and human rights defenders who accompany those who experience forced migration. Their actions intend to dismantle the insignias of power and the alibis of the hegemonic and neocolonial system in violence-organized territories (Bolaños Guerra, 2015; Mignolo & Walsh, 2018; Quijano, 1988).

In violent settings, political and social constructions of insecurity benefit the elite and create processes of violation and *precarization* of human lives. Children, adolescents, and women are the most affected. Additionally, organized violence is systematically and collectively deployed on certain sectors of the population. Physical protection is suspended, as is access to formal education, clean water, and healthcare. Continuity of livelihoods is annulled, and exposure, defenselessness, and anguish are intensified.

In order to expose the nodes of the most atrocious violence, families and collectives exercise a differentiated function of education. Through the search for disappeared persons in clandestine graves and the accompaniment of

DOI: 10.4324/9781003090519-7

people who suffer forced internal displacement[3], families and collectives seek education that promotes and defends human rights. In this sense I ask: what educational alternatives are deployed in situations of danger? What challenges does invisibility imply for the understanding of human rights when it is both a strategy to protect lives and a political tactic? What challenges does invisibility imply for the care of people in conditions of displacement and forced migration? What actions and attitudes mobilize the most vulnerable people when the security mechanisms of the State never materialize or are covered with suspicion and complicity?

This chapter presents the crossovers between forced internal displacement in conditions of direct persecution and educational practices that mobilize unprecedented efforts of displaced people to hold on to the world, in their mobile rooting with the land and the community. In these contexts, the educational function exceeds the instructional and institutional demand and acquires a more significant historical function (Olivo, 2009). When people are besieged, persecuted and when they urge for life, their words and narratives become an acute and profound critique of the historical conditions under which life emerges. They become ethical positions that seek to restore history, departing from places that make traditional forms of resistance inoperative and that subvert Western rationality.

Education, Violence, and Internal Displacement: An Introduction

Although the concept of forced internal displacement refers to a great number of situations linked to physical, emotional, and material threats, this chapter focuses on mobilizations that are driven by human violence, that is, by intimidation, threats, beatings, mistreatment, persecution, and even murder. According to data from the International Displacement Monitoring Centre (IDMC, 2015), Mexico has 345,000 people internally displaced because of conflict and violence. In contrast, the latest report by the National Human Rights Commission in Mexico (*Comisión Nacional de Derechos Humanos [CNDH]*, 2016) only reports 37,217. There is no official figure in Mexico due to the absence of a census and a reliable institutional diagnosis. Efforts have not ceased, however, and in 2019, the Mexican Commission for the Defense and Promotion of Human Rights (*Comisión Mexicana de Defensa y Promoción de los Derechos Humanos*, 2019 [CMDPDH]) estimated that 8,726,375 people were forced to move between 2011 and 2017 because of crime and the threat of organized crime. Likewise, Salazar Cruz & Álvarez Lobato (2017) counted 740,000 displaced people based on media reports from December 1, 2006, to December 31, 2013, in national newspapers and from the Mexican states with the highest displacement numbers (Michoacán, Guerrero, Tamaulipas, Chiapas, Oaxaca, Veracruz). Furthermore, 'the figures for displaced persons after the six-year term of

[President] Calderón, and until 2018, are tracked by case' (Salazar Cruz & Álvarez Lobato, 2017, p. 30) without any accurate estimates.

The lack of a consistent diagnosis of forced displacement in Mexico, of operational protocols, and the persecution of migrants are examples of the institutional shortcomings regarding human rights. Moreover, when the Mexican government deploys its practices in specific situations of forced internal displacement through the design of public policies aimed at prevention, protection, and assistance for victims of displacement, intending to guarantee these same rights, it exercises greater intimidation and surveillance of migrants.

In contrast to an absence in federal law, two states have specific laws on forced internal displacement: Chiapas and Guerrero. These states also produce the greatest number of displaced peoples (CNDH, 2016; Salazar Cruz & Álvarez Lobato, 2017). It should be noted that the category outlined in the General Law of Victims (forced internal displacement) is determined by the legal, political and institutional conditions established by the State and guided by a figure that dissolves and naturalizes the historical conditions of precariousness that these populations (in contexts of violence associated with organized crime[4]) face. The statistics count according to the way they are interpreted, hence a critical approach to the concept of internal displacement and the conditions of their structural and historical exposition is fundamental in order to address the precariousness of the social, political, and economic arrangements that guide the crystallization of this historical debt.

Violence produces and organizes internal displacement. Violence normalizes and intensifies displacement through intersectional components where 'race,' 'social class,' 'age,' 'territory of origin,' and 'gender' radicalize the infringements upon girls, boys, adolescents, and women's rights. These intersectional elements also intensify the multiple forms of stigmatization, and 'are accentuated in the new places where displaced populations are settled [...] Xenophobic attitudes and, at times, outright racism and confrontation with the local communities where they settle emerge' (Mercado Mondragón, 2018, p. 11). The long-awaited implementation (since 2001) of public policies by the Regional Conference on the Protection of Displaced Persons and Refugees has driven families and collectives to forego the expectation that the State would indeed enforce effective actions that would protect them. Instead, they have worked with organized civil society actors to implement the needed measures.

For many collectives in Mexico, it is clear that the main causes of forced internal displacement are violence and armed conflict, especially since 2006 (Durin, 2019; 2018a; 2018b; 2018c). The perception of widespread violence, the overlooking of human rights, the suspension of schooling due to the armed conflict, and the territorial expansion of organized crime (tied to religious beliefs, traditional political affiliation, and ethnic origin) among other factors, cause people to move stealthily, as if dripping, one by one, family member by family member, and to leave their belongings and their stories, in homes and territories that come to be remembered with nostalgia. This is especially the case in states such as Guerrero, Veracruz, Tamaulipas, Sinaloa, Oaxaca, Michoacán, and Chiapas, where displacement is carried out as a strategy and where crime is rising (Mercado Mondragón, 2018).

In the case of forced migration in Mexico, Salazar Cruz & Álvarez Lobato (2017) consider that forced displacement:

> Is a survival resource for the civilian population in the face of regional or local violent regimes [...] it is an action and a reaction to extreme situations in order to guarantee life [...] it is a political decision because in the territorial scenarios of conflicts and in the face of disputed hegemonic actors, one cannot remain neutral [...] it is a process of various mobilizations that begins with the rapid and untimely departure of a large numbers of family members, with few belongings and in secret, leaving property and assets abandoned [...] From then on, those who flee face a set of challenges linked to insecurity, uprooting, residential and labor instability, compromising traditional ways of life, and health conditions (Salazar Cruz & Álvarez Lobato, 2017, pp. 29–30).

Francis Deng, former representative of the United Nations Secretary General on Internally Displaced Persons, notes that forced internal displacement 'causes family breakdown, cuts social, and cultural ties, ends strong employment relationships, disrupts educational opportunities, denies access to vital needs such as food, shelter, and medicine, and exposes innocent people to violence in the form of attacks on campsites, disappearances, and rape' (CNDH, 2016, p. 8).

As previously stated, the approach of this chapter takes into consideration the work done by the National Brigades in Search of Disappeared Persons (2015–2020) as a meeting point for a variety of groups and collectives that look to promote and defend human rights. This place of encounter is anchored in the territories most besieged by organized crime, where crime and the acquiescence of authorities intensify the risks for harassment, persecution, and siege. This makes the space that is intended to defend and promote human rights, an area where defendants are actually more exposed and visible to criminals. Under such circumstances, several workshops were held to provide psychosocial care, engage in decision-making and the rights of forcibly displaced persons, and the families of disappeared persons. These activities serve as practical interference for resistance and historical restoration and to show that there is not only a concern for survival in the face of violent regimes, but also that symbolic and political actions can be carried out to dismantle the predisposition to accumulation.

Thus, the experience of education for internal displaced populations is not organized by the international agenda established by global recommendations, nor by the formalization of competencies and institutional standards, but by the experience of the historical reality of those inflicted by insecurity. The aim of this education is to create alternative ways of life that can restore communities and their relationships with the territory, ensuring their protection from the imminent radical exposure to violence. Hence, the community's experience of accompanying people in situations of forced internal displacement, through the promotion of human rights, produces a transversal agency that is not reduced to flight or evasion[5]. Although the problem is not totally eradicated, agency opens a field of intervention and protection that is a positive peace (García-González, 2017, 2019). Education for peace is carried out in situations of migration. It is not only guided by the development of theoretical and practical skills in strictly academic terms. It also mobilizes certain ethical attitudes in order to experience human rights and the construction of social and communal links. In the areas where criminal and State violence is effective, education for peace calls for versatility and an intersectional approach that accounts not only for lived histories, but for the possibility to produce new histories.

In the midst of violence, the processes of accompaniment that collectives provide to persons and groups within the condition of forced internal displacement are always flexible and specific, responding to unique situations and not to normative standardizations. These practices are oriented by the processes of production of meaning, of connection with the land and others in a common space. They do not limit their effort to mere survival, but also promote ethical positions that help to understand the current historical reality with the responsibility of generating new beginnings—always unpredictable and novel because this responsibility is linked to the condition of witnessing. The selection of the meeting spaces as such, aligned with the organization and collaboration within the accompaniment process are part of the ways in which reflection and analysis of the specific situation is formulated. The process of accompaniment that is carried out is not based on the mastery of teaching, nor as an educational exercise that promotes scientific efficiency where the fight against ignorance allows access to progress and cultural promises. The accompaniment practices are oriented toward the care for *life entirely*. The elements traditionally considered as educational are suspended by questions that articulate the spontaneous, open, and frank dialogue about the specific situations that the person faces. Life and its circumstances are decoded under peace and human rights terms in a flexible way, where the times and themes are schemes adaptable to specific circumstances.

The doctrinal aspirations in which competencies are articulated in order to achieve a full and productive life in the future (in accordance with the domain of global standards) are suspended and valued depending on each unique way of inhabiting the Earth, of relating openly with others, and of mobilizing processes of meaning-making that transform the communal bonds. Such practices open up effective possibilities for mitigating the impact of forced internal displacement and installing symbolic inter-generational dynamics on the experience of territory, body care, and communality. Education, through these workshops, opens up as a modality of transformation and resistance in spaces where people become disposable and where states of exception fluctuate, in a 'no-man's land between public law and political action, and between the legal order and life' (Agamben, 2005, p. 24). It is in this way that the experiences of accompaniment of persons within the situation of forced internal displacement subvert the discourses and practices of harassment to show not only the deadly character that comes along with such discourses, but also to assert a life that insists, from its concrete political, social, and economic disparity, on affirming itself. The reduction of risks is processed from a historical dimension that does not subscribe to a strengthening of capacities, but rather prioritizes an intervention before injustices and aggravations.

The high sense of belonging to a territory, to a culture, is not deactivated by forced displacement. Education acquires different tones with respect to global ideological and economic criteria in order to make the educational experience unique. In other words, schooling's cultural capital is not measured by quality tests, but by the sense of community and the experience and relationship to the land. The mobile roots of forced migrants greatly differ from universalized criteria of quality that prevails in educational institutions. In these specific contexts, education reaches out as an interpretative mechanism with which the contradictions inherent to a generalized way of life are woven with the ways in which thoughts, attitudes, fears, and hopes are shaped into the situation of persecution. The communal creation of social fulfillment generates a space of protection and shelter. The effort to 'communalize life entirely' (Martínez Luna, 2015, p. 102) is deployed in particular and concrete conditions and is offered 'to comparatively enunciate our natural way of making life and the necessary reasoning we should assume in order to face the vicissitudes of our current times' (Martínez Luna, 2015, p. 100). In this way, education mobilizes forced displaced people's agency to install communal relations between community members and the land. This educational function emphasizes corporeality, place, and experience as meeting points for deeper experiences of human and political interrelationship. This function of education interrupts the consolidated flows of meaning to make them more flexible and to open up new instances in which life could be desirable to be lived.

It would be naive to deny that in Mexico the most precarious communities are attacked with the impunity that characterizes the rogue systems that become complicit in these situations (Derrida, 2005; Chomsky, 2002).

Besides, Indigenous and *campesino* communities, and some other social and political sectors have to strive to resist the suffocating assault of market-based policies and principles of a *totaliterarian*[6] (Martínez Martínez, 2019) and centralist education. *Totaliterarian* education was first imposed by the Mexican State in a neo-liberal and extractive economic logic; its values are opposed to those learned from generation to generation. The constant aggression against the communal experience and the symbolic links to land evinces that theirs is a life model to be destroyed. If *totaliterarian* education installs a discursive empire and generates the coordinates for a standardization of the meanings of the world, the body, social relationships, and human experience, education is the element that should interrupt this standardization, mobilize other meanings, and open up the experience of singularity as an ethical event, rooted in symbolic dialogical instances where other words, other narratives, and other livable lives emerge.

In situations of forced internal displacement, the processes of exchanging experiences and coexistence have also matured, strengthening the mechanisms of resistance to an economic model oriented towards privatization, not only of the economy, but also of politics and thought, and whose most sinister face is organized crime. If the ultimate causes of forced internal displacement are organized from a rationality that is consolidated in the individualization and privatization of life, 'communalizing is thinking about others and for others, it is the search for a more harmonious world, it is understanding that we are the result of others and not of our individuality' (Martínez Luna, 2009, p. 137). From these coordinates, communality appears as a tactic against persecution, aggression, and dispossession, as a defense and safeguard of all human aspirations oriented towards good living. Communalization is a way in which education is deployed as resistance, and aggrieved life is mobilized to prevail and insist in the midst of projects oriented by contempt. In this sense, education is a way of communicating life as a whole, in order to articulate unique ways of inhabiting the Earth, of making living with others and articulating thoughts to confront the usual fears and hopes of every human experience.

The Place of Forced Internal Displacement

> 'We just want to be part of the community, as we can no longer live where we used to live, now we want to live and die in this little piece of land where we are.'
>
> Women in forced internal displacement

The precariousness and infringement on people's living conditions are the factors that organize the historical experience in situations of danger. Flight from death as the ultimate experience is inevitable. It is not only the rejection by those who live in the communities, but also the risk that the criminal group(s) that displaced them in the first place will take over the place where they are now refugees, while the collectives, having to move to the place where the families are sheltered, run the risk of being ambushed, disappeared, and killed. Within this framework, the process of accompaniment inherently entails a formation of commitment to collectives and supportive people that places them in the line of fire. Although human rights defenders avoid their exposure, they act undauntedly, facing the known modes of attack from different criminal groups.

In scenarios of conflict, both displaced persons and human rights defenders act as witnesses who generate elements of memory configuration and search for justice in Mexico. The use of testimonies, the emergence of biographies and contextual narratives are educational resources that allow the re-signification of experiences and the re-articulation of social fabric. The interest in the present chapter lies in the political dimension centered on orality and communal communication as ways of sharing complaints and disseminating collective memory in contexts of violence and democratic transitions[7]. The sharing of testimonies allows people to understand and consider the way in which solidarity, forms of communality, and struggles for memory and truth are articulated in situations of specific persecution. In contexts marked by high rates of insecurity and criminality, children, adolescents, and women are the most vulnerable groups[8] (CNDH, 2019). In this regard, the CNDH considers that 'these forms of violence are based on a structure and a discourse in which there are dominated and dominating people, immersed in unequal dynamics of exchange where the weakest are exploited [...] Subjugated person are violated by the power of the dominant one, they have limited or segmented access to reality, and they live an excluded, fragmented, or alienated life from other dominated people' (2019, p. 185).

The construction of meaning for those who suffer unwanted situations can slip into a victim conception that cancels out all possibility and 'opens up an inexhaustible line of credit in the present' (Todorov, 2000, p. 54). For this reason, the creation of programs, the supplying of public services, technical provisions, and specialized interventions situate the victim at the epicenter in the form of 'a new field of public action' (Hartog, 2012, p. 17) to design, in a vertical and discursive manner, the specific protocols to mobilize the political force of the victim's memory. Without undermining the humanitarian reasons for the victim's status, it becomes a way in which rights could be effectively enforced through the State's recognition of them as the center of public programs and policies.

Mexico has implemented victimization strategies based on the 'politics of suffering' characterized by a double entry: victimization and the individualization of the offenses. According to Fassin (1997), this double feature 'defines a new form of subjectivation of social inequalities' (p. 35). Therefore, the positions of both the government and the institutions producing this discourse show the paradigm of the democratic and capitalist State:

> There is no discussion of the paradigm, but rather an adaptation of it so that the effects on the most vulnerable are a little less harsh. We can talk about internal arrangements that imply minimal corrections, which means that currently it is considered practically impossible to fight against inequalities; we only fight against their more visible consequences. Second, within this paradigm, the margin of action of local agents is very restricted, which creates much frustration (Fassin, 1997, p. 36).

This process of victimization implies certain anthropological and political consequences that go beyond the claims of this chapter, but we should emphasize that people and groups who suffer forced internal displacement are not awaiting the subsidiary strategies of the State, but rather the accompaniment and commitment of various supportive actors. The static defenselessness (that governments and perpetrators wrongly claim) of those who find themselves in forced internal displacement[9] becomes the starting point of a practice that is based on vulnerability.

In the midst of effective hostilities, of the harassment of politics of suffering, the passage from victimhood to testimony is made through a communality that is enacted with very specific words and actions:

> Realization [of testimony] is given according to the ground [the victim] steps on, to the people and families who live on that soil, to the daily work the inhabitants of that earth perform, and to the enjoyment or welfare that the same work provides to the community. At each moment, its manifestations will be in articulation with society and nature all around (Martínez Luna, 2015: 101).

The aim is not to arrange ideas through a discursive order, but to take a glimpse at risk, to border the edges of life and death, to recklessly touch words, lives and bodies, to be touched by them with thought, to wait for the other, perhaps another with another voice, who also listens and thinks that someone is talking, and responds from the depths to one's claims.

Education Amidst Violence: Workshops, Collectives, and Testimony

In spaces of persecution, where life itself is at risk, where cultural, ethical, social, and economic differences are a badge of aggression and displacement, education is relativized and organized from other coordinates.

The impositions of ideological character of education and the reproduction of governing systems are eliminated in such situations. Although Latin American countries are considered formally democratic, the majority still maintain vectors of the socio-political and economic dynamics (including their institutions) linked to high degrees of normalized violence associated with the same processes of democratization. The encroachment of democracy is made evident in forced internal displacements and yet from their seeming location of powerlessness, displaced people narrate the simulation and break down the fiction of 'civilized' values, values that elevate as discourses of truth and encounter the pain and cry of the unfairness. Territorial belonging and political membership (Benhabib, 2005) is not attained by its achievements, but by the living flaws that refute them. The democratic experience has built its history on the concept of dignity, which is evident in the overcoming of one's obstacles, the access to new knowledge, and the deployment of possibilities and competencies of the human being to the achievement of goals, both individual and collective objectives, but this democratic experience has a cost; in this case, the cost is a sedentary democracy[10] that is mainly supported by migrants.

In Mexico, forced displacement is not a new phenomenon; it is part of a tragic repetition. In Michoacán and Guerrero, as well as in Chiapas and Oaxaca, displacement has intensified, mainly in the northern areas of Mexico and the more gentrified cities. According to a report by the Coalition for the Defense of the Migrant and the American Friends Service Committee, the crisis of forced displacement is haunting our territories like a ghost (CPDM & AFSC-LAC, 2016). In the midst of such circumstances, people seem to have no alternative. However, human rights promoters specifically provide education support to vulnerable groups as a means to understand both forced disappearance and forced migration. They also foster the maintenance of rooting to the territory and the validity of human rights despite their constant detraction. Although people in situations of forced internal displacement have gone through a history of dispossession, their relationship with land and territory retains a symbolic strength. Such strength becomes a fundamental part of the structure of people's lives that carves out a resistance against the looming paradigm of property. Understanding the symbolic and semantic movements of Indigenous peoples[11], *campesinos* and semi-urban dwellers is an academic challenge; however, the work of Corroy Moral (2020) proposes that changes 'in the relationship with the land and its value have been attributed, initially, to the unequal relations—of race and class—mediated by labor activity in the countryside, between the colonizers and the native inhabitants' (pp. 290–291). Drawing from that and the accompaniment work we undertook in the workshops, I identify three stages in the educational and shared experiences of groups and persons in situations of forced displacement:

1 Safety in the face of imminent risk. Displaced persons are offered mechanisms for identifying risks, security strategies, and rights guarantees, as well as instances of engagement in the new receiving scenarios, designed according to the particularity of each case, as well as to the risk conditions, from the moment they leave one territory to take refuge in another.
2 The design of a safe integration process into the receiving community. To this aim, different workshops are held where diverse historic specific instruments (such as newspapers and storybooks) are analyzed in a reconciliatory and assisting manner. Therefore, the discussions are open, informal, and seek to generate three other interwoven moments that guide the reflections:

   a *Historization*. The aim of this moment is to demystify the images, figures, and stereotypes in the receiving community. Displaced people experience certain harmful messages from the inhabitants of the territories where they arrive. Therefore, the workshops address these messages and emphasize the importance of narrative in the construction of justice and truth.
   b *Denaturalization*. This is the second moment to highlight the multitude of conditions and forms of articulating life in moments of risk, as well as the necessities that extreme precariousness posits on displaced populations, to whom the conditions of dignified life seem to be extinguished. The denaturalization of the displaced people tears down social and individual guilt. The willingness to consider the situation from the standpoint of externalities or collateral damage, encouraged by the media and stylized and well-thought-out positions, transforms the historical conditions of displacement into inevitable incidents. For this reason, this moment becomes fundamental in the construction of experiences organized from another position in the face of the specific conditions of that *collective* encounter.
   c *Visibilization*. This moment is motivated by play between the visibility of the motivations, situations, and actors that caused the internal displacement, as well as the shelter, the secrecy, and the discretion to guarantee better protection. The task of showing, revealing, and narrating the various forms of violence by perpetrators and processes of human rights abuses requires the participation of a community that is rooted in the possibility of other forms of life. In this way, the attention is focused on observing and

thinking about the political and social origins from the perspective of disparity and asymmetry, their meanings and sensations, in order to transform the field of intervention so that forced displaced people can discern, in a critical and sharp manner, the ways in which power is deployed, both by the State and by organized crime, in a constant dynamic of negotiation and demand.

3 Differentiated approach. Intersectionality means that displaced persons are likely to identify with certain characteristics that increase their vulnerability such as gender, race, and age.

In this context, the human rights workshops become a set of theoretical-practical strategies that are deployed in communal work spaces whose contents are guided by a critical reflection of specific historical realities. The content of the human rights workshops is based on the danger each displaced community faces, so the relevance of the traditional modes of education is left aside to focus the reflection on the urgency of the economic, political, and social situation where the singular experience of each group of forced displaced people is emphasized. The previously discussed workshop elements serve as transversal criteria that play an ethical and political function that restores the world from alternative forms of understanding and intervention. The purpose of education in forced displacement conditions, thus, is not led by technical reasons of pedagogy. Instead, education has a historical biographical concern that can, and indeed does, operate from an ethical and political position of the testimony (Abad Faciolince, 2017; Calveiro, 2006; Franco 2002; De Marinis & Macleod, 2018; Sarlo, 2006; Yúdice, 2002).

Based on the considerations previously mentioned, the supposed and imposed truths about liberal democracy, progress, and the consumerist society are dismantled. People who undergo forced internal displacement describe the historical and structural movement that develops from politics to the destruction of subjectivity as a not-wanting-to-know attitude about their historical experience (Ellacuría, 1991). This mobilization is experienced in such a way that people can resist positions of domination and which in the same vein is oriented towards a space where power relations become inactive through the interruption of the continuum with practices from powerlessness and vulnerability, from the failure of displacement and the communality of uprooting. In forced internal displacement, when human rights are often suspended, when precariousness becomes more radical, in moments of great danger, displaced people mobilize a radical questioning to respond to the impossible. They do so from educational spaces that resist the onslaught of aggressions. A different mode of education, characterized by accompaniment, shows an affective and freeing sensibility in the midst of the complexity produced by the violence and persecution. It also emphasizes the strength and importance of the lives of migrants.

The asymmetry of these practices carried out within the collectives has registered in two ways in educational terms: the first one is in regard to the concepts of victim and testimony, and internal conflict and violence. The second one is related to forms of discernment of the concrete manifestations of violence by the state and organized crime. In this context, dialogues and strategies to keep themselves safe increase. The exposure to danger is greater when the accompaniment offered to relatives of displaced persons in a community (victims of aggressions by armed groups) is intensified by the presence of the police in the area, which increases the risks of more human rights violations. T[12] shares her experience:

> When armed forces arrive to take over the square, you don't know who to watch out for, whether it's them or the police. Last time when the National Guard and the State Police came to help us, after halting the aggressions perpetrated by the criminals, they just left the place despite the risk that the aggressors would return, as often happens. The community members blocked the exit to prevent authorities from leaving the town, and in response the police began to forcibly remove them, beating them, chasing them, and threatening them with firearms. They then asked for people's identification, and when the State Police were leaving the site, some came back for us and took away our computers, phones, backpacks and documents. A van we had hired had its tires slashed, its mirrors broken, and its lights cracked. I was pulled over by a state trooper and was thoroughly checked. He lifted my blouse to look for weapons, pulled down my bra and the leggings I was wearing in front of the family I was staying with. I was as ashamed as I was outraged (Human Rights Defender, personal communication, February 22, 2020).

In the midst of the altercation and territorial dislocation, of the dissolution of social ties and impunity, another space for relationship building and creating understanding is opened. This new space of relationship and understanding building resists dissolution and insists on strengthening itself. Drawing from a communal education, people that have been displaced relate the loss of their territory with the territory found. They do so at the very extreme of feeling impotence and at the center of common resistance. The victimized become witnesses where 'the circulation of testimony goes beyond the victim, creates bonds of solidarity and commitment with those who witness the events, and the political effects of the testimony expand [...] testimony allows for the reconstruction of memory, reparation, and the search for non-repetition' (De Marinis and Macleod, 2018, p. 14–15).

From a Western point of view, power detaches experience and leaves out existence in order to adapt it to an idea of self-founded autonomy. Martínez Luna (2015) reminds us that

> Resorting to autonomy has been a strategy to live with the rest of the world, to stop aggressions placed on the most vulnerable communities, to strengthen our concrete unity. However, we must recognize that we demand it within a foreign language. We want autonomy to be decreed, without demanding that we make it concrete in our daily lives (Martínez Luna, 2015, p. 111).

Thus, testimony as an educational practice ties to the community so that its members can take roots in the territory and inhabit it with words, so that migrants can integrate and be witnesses of the internal displacement. Words are then heard and lived, drawing from a sense of care for life from which knowledge is mobilized. In order to communalize life entirely, it is necessary to think and feel the world, from other possible worlds, for good coexistence.

No Conclusion

People that have been displaced are the subtle materiality of a political archaeology of truth, not only through the negativity of history, but also through a political order where violence is embodied in the images and representations that mechanically reproduce them. Moreover, forced displacement is an unstable, metastatic destruction that generates alliances and voids, creates impossible ruptures and emergencies, and engenders unpredictable relationships that go beyond instrumental rationality and the economies of preservation and proportionality. Itinerant bodies overflow and affect the nervous tissue in an emotion captured in a sign, a universe, and a nascent language every time they leave. Displacement is not absence, but subtraction turned into forced wandering. The forced wandering of those who have been displaced is a challenge and a question that is always open, not suspended, but accessible to the dynamics of life and history.

In these scenarios, marginalization, organized crime, manipulation, and state violence are combined, and the defenseless condition is exposed in a much harsher way. When everyone flees, the witnesses interpret and adapt tactics through social constructs of meaning, bonds of protection, and solidarity networks. They read the fabric of the world and the marauders to protect themselves from the imperative of forced migration. In the midst of this wound, a space is opened into the word that aspires to suture the aggressiveness of the violent migration of people.

Between the search for disappeared persons and forced internal displacement is the question of the place of education in situations of violence. The critical exercise of itinerant, persecuted and migrant education is part of the activities of collectives that challenge the institutional and instructional logic of traditional education. Within intimidation, siege, and persecution, education not only detonates the critical, communal, and supportive nature of the participants, but also questions the formal character of education that is deployed in privileged conditions from the consolidation of official instances and the political agendas of study programs. In this sense, it is necessary and urgent to emphasize that educational efforts in dangerous contexts recover the liberating function of education and make visible the consequences of an enlightened, instrumentalized, and globalized education.

Education, as discussed above, may articulate the historical testimony that is communally shaped. Those who participate in this form of education are witnesses to a historical reality and their testimony exposes others to a truth 'which demands a certain listening and social validation in order to be part of the socially constructed truth' (Calveiro, 2006, p. 79). In contexts of impunity and aggression, the configuration of truth faces major challenges and risks; risks that seek to be cancelled, hidden, and denied. If violence erodes trust and fragments the communal fabric, it is difficult to establish the exact limits or clear references between victims and witnesses. These limits are made even more indistinguishable by institutions and mechanisms of truth and justice. The institutional production of victims creates historical prejudices that still manifest themselves in their present totality. Therefore, the witness becomes a mechanism for the visibility of aggressions and contributes to the restoration not only of his or her biography, but also of history in situations of risk where it seems that all possibilities are closed because the only objective is to persist without further action. Hence, testimony surpasses the idea of a survival that becomes exhausted in the preservation of a body without attributes, without history, a body subtracted from all symbolic instances by the regimes of violence. The aim of testimony, thus, is not only to guarantee life, but also to communicate life entirely so that this constant flow of formal democratic processes is interrupted. These situations are shared with other experiences disseminated in Latin America that, as in Mexico, echo desires that take up the struggles for human rights.

Who said that everything is lost?

Notes

1 The National Brigade for the Search of Disappeared Persons is a strategy designed by groups of relatives of victims of forced disappearance. They are supported by different human rights groups and movements organized through the National Links Network. Since 2016, they meet in territories where the disappearance of persons has been proven and thus crystallizes the link with other human rights violations, such as forced migration. The searches are carried out in areas of high vulnerability due to state violence and organized crime groups. The last search brigade took place in Papantla, Veracruz, in February of 2020.

2 Good living or *buen vivir* refers to the Tseltal words *lekil kuxlejal*, a concept that seeks not only the individual wellbeing, but community health, peace, respect for different conceptions of work, organization, beliefs, spirituality, and environmental care practices.

3 People, families or populations in forced internal displacement are those who are forced to mobilize, temporarily or permanently, from their daily living spaces, because of the dynamics of violence and persecution that increase exposure to aggressions and coercion by legal or extra-legal groups (Salazar Cruz, 2014).

4 According to the National Survey on Victimization and Perception of Public Security (Encuesta Nacional de Victimización y Percepción sobre Seguridad Pública [ENVIPE]), in 2019, 11,000 displaced persons were added to the statistics of Mexico, especially associated with the violence generated by organized crime in Chiapas, Guerrero, Michoacán, Oaxaca, and Sinaloa.

5 'Agency refers to the socioculturally mediated capacity to act' (Ahearn, 2001, p. 112).

6 In Spanish, *totaletraria*. This neologism is formed by *totalitaria* (totalitarian) and *letra* (a reference to writing, literature, texts, but also to discourse, code, script).

7 'Since the mid-1980s, Mexico initiated a process of profound political change and social transformation. The increasingly competitive elections reflected a nation evolving to a more open and democratic political system' (Yeverino Juárez, 2005, p. 100).

8 An example of this is that the murders of minors have tripled and more than 30,000 youth have joined the ranks of organized crime (CNDH, 2019).

9 By static defenselessness in cases of forced internal displacement, I allude to the imaginary consideration of a propitious victim who is waiting to accept, without resistance, the vertical exercise of power.

10 I consider sedentary democracy the way in which forms of sovereignty and forms of the system of liberties become fixed and standardized.

11 The symbolic and semantic movements refer to the way in which meaning relates to narrative and identitary expressions within a community.

12 In order to maintain the participant's anonymity, I use T as a pseudonym.

References

Abad Faciolince, H. (2017). *El olvido que seremos* [The oblivion that we will be]. Spain: Alfaguara.

Agamben. G. (2005). *Homo Sacer II. Estado de excepción*, [Homo sacer II. state of exception] Buenos Aires: Adriana Hidalgo Editora.

Ahearn, L. (2020). *Annual Review of Anthropology, 30*. pp. 109–137.

Atuesta Becerra, L. (2018). Militarización de la lucha contra el narcotráfico: los operativos como estrategia para el combate del crimen organizado [Militarization of the Fight against Drug Trafficking: Operations as a Strategy to Combat Organized Crime]. *Las violencias: en busca de la política detrás de la guerra contra las drogas*. Mexico: Coyuntura.

Benhabib, S. (2005). *Los derechos de los otros. Extranjeros, residentes y ciudadanos*. [The Rights of Others]. Barcelona: Gedisa.

Bolaños Guerra, B. [Coord.]. (2015). *Biopolítica y migración. El eslabón perdido de la globalización* [Biopolitics and migration. The missing link of globalization]. Mexico: UAM Iztapalapa.

Calveiro, P. (2006). Testimonio y memoria en el relato histórico [Testimony and memory in the historical account]. *Acta Poética, 27* (2). pp. 65–86.

Chomsky, N. (2002). *Estados Canallas* [Rogue States. The Rule of Force in World Affairs]. Barcelona: Paidós.
Coalición Pro Defensa del Migrante A.C. & American Friends Service Committes-LAC. (2016). *Vidas en la incertidumbre: la migración forzada mexicana hacia la frontera norte de México ¿y nuestra solidaridad?* [Lives in Uncertainty: Mexican Forced Migration to Mexico's Northern Border. And Our solidarity?]. Available at: https://www.afsc.org/sites/default/files/documents/Vidas%20en%20la%20 Incertidumbre.pdf.
Comisión Mexicana de Defensa y Promoción de los Derechos Humanos. (2019). *Entre la invisibilidad y el abandono: un acercamiento cualitativo al desplazamiento interno forzado en México* [Between invisibility and abandonment: a qualitative approach to forced internal displacement in Mexico]. Available at: http://www.cmdpdh.org/publicaciones-pdf/cmdpdh-entre-la- invisibilidad-y-el-abandono-un-acercamiento-cualitativo-al-desplazamiento-interno- forzado-en-mexico.pdf.
Comisión Nacional de Derechos Humanos. (2016). *Informe especial sobre el desplazamiento forzado interno (DFI) en México* [Special report on forced internal displacement (IDP) in Mexico]. Mexico.
_____. (2019). *Niñas, niños y adolescentes: víctimas del crimen organizado en México* [Children and teenagers: victims of organized crime in Mexico]. Mexico.
Corroy Moral, A. (2020). Los ch'oles y la tierra: redefinición intergeneracional en tiempos de crisis y migración campesina [The Ch'oles and the Land: Intergenerational Redefinition in Times of Crisis and Peasant Migration]. *Estudios de Cultura Maya*, 55. pp. 281–318.
De Marinis, N. & Macleod, M. (2018). *Resisting Violence. Emotional Communities in Latin America*. Nueva York: Palgrave, Macmillan.
Derrida, J. (2005). *Canallas: dos ensayos sobre la razón* [Rogues: Two Essays on Reason]. Madrid: Trotta.
Durin, S. (2018a). Huir presos del terror. Masacres y desplazamiento forzado en los pueblos del noroeste de México [Fleeing Prisoners of Terror. Massacres and Forced Displacement in the Towns of Northwestern Mexico]. In E. Sandoval Hernández (coord.), *Violentar la vida en el norte de México. Estado, tráficos y migraciones en la frontera con Texas*. Mexico: CIESAS.
_____. (2018b). Las víctimas de la crisis de seguridad pública en busca del resguardo. Los desplazados por la violencia desde el Noreste de México [The victims of the public security crisis in search of protection. Those displaced by violence from the Northeast of Mexico]. In C. Flores (Coord.). *La crisis de seguridad y violencia en México; causas, efectos y dimensiones del problema*. Mexico: Colección México, CIESAS. pp. 220–254.
_____. (2018c). Sálvese quien pueda. Migración forzada, frontera internacional e interrupción de la circularidad en el noroeste [Save Yourself. Forced Migration, International Border and Disruption of Traffic in the Northwest]. In S. Arzaluz & E. Sandoval (Coords.) *Cruces y retornos en la región del noreste mexicano en el alba del siglo XXI*. Mexico: CIESAS, El Colegio de la Frontera Norte. pp. 135–172.
_____. (2019). Resistir la deshumanización. La sociedad civil ante las desapariciones, la coacción de la libertad y los desplazamientos forzados en México [Resisting Dehumanization. Civil Society in the Face of Disappearances, Coercion of Liberty and Forced Displacement in Mexico]. *Encartes Antropológicos 2* (3). pp. 3–12.

Ellacuría, I. (1991). *Filosofía de la realidad histórica* [Philosophy of historical reality]. Madrid: Trotta.
Encuesta Nacional de Victimización y Percepción sobre Seguridad Pública. (2019). https://www.inegi.org.mx/contenidos/programas/envipe/2019/doc/envipe2019_pres entacion_nacional.pdf.
Fassin, D. (1997). *La patetización del mundo. Ensayo de Antropología política del sufrimiento* [The Patetization of the World. Essay on Political Anthropology of Suffering]. Ponencia presentada en el VIII Congreso de Antropología en Colombia. Universidad Nacional de Colombia.
Franco, J. (2002). Si me permiten hablar: la lucha por el poder interpretativo [If I may speak: the struggle for interpretive power]. In J. Beverley & H. Achugar (coords.), *La voz del otro: testimonio, subalternidad y verdad narrativa*. Guatemala: Universidad Rafael Landívar. pp. 121–128.
García-González, D. E. (2017). Reflexiones críticas sobre la violencia en México desde la injusticia: proyectar imaginativamente para construir la paz [Critical Reflections on Violence in Mexico from the Perspective of Injustice: Projecting Imaginatively to Build Peace]. *Eidos 26*. pp. 149–177.
_____. (2019). *La paz como ideal moral. Una reconfiguración de la filosofía para la acción común* [Peace as a moral ideal. A reshaping of the philosophy for common action]. Madrid: Dykinson.
International Displacement Monitoring Centre. (2015). Global Estimates (2015). Available at: https://www.internal-displacement.org/sites/default/files/inline-files/20150713-gloal-estimates-2015-en-v1.pdf.
_____. (2012). Forced displacement linked to transnational crime in Mexico. Available at: https://www.internal-displacement.org/publications/forced-displacement-linked-to-transnational-organised-crime-in-mexico.
Hartog, F. (2012). El tiempo de las víctimas [The time of the victims]. *Revista de Estudios Sociales* 44. pp. 12–19.
Macleod, M. & De Marinis, N. (coords.). (2019). *Comunidades emocionales: resistiendo a las violencias en América Latina* [Emotional communities: resisting violence in Latin America]. Mexico and Colombia: Universidad Autónoma Metropolitana Xochimilco, Instituto Colombiano de Antropología e Historia.
Marston, J. (2019). The urban displaced: fleeing criminal violence in Latin American Cities. In IDMC. *Global Report on Internal Displacement*. Brown. Available at: https://www.internal-displacement.org/global-report/grid2019/downloads/background_papers/MarstonJerome_PaperUrbDispl_FinalPaper.pdf
Martínez Luna, J. (2009). *Eso que llaman comunalidad* [What they call communality]. Oaxaca: Culturas Populares, CONACULTA/Secretaría de Cultura, Gobierno de Oaxaca, Fundación Alfredo Harp Helú.
_____. (2015). Conocimiento y comunalidad [Knowledge and communality]. *Bajo el volcán 15* (23). pp. 99–112.
Martínez Martínez, M. A. (2019). Espectros de la violencia: necroescrituras y biografías de nuestro tiempo [Spectres of violence: necrowritings and biographies of our time]. *Reflexiones Marginales. Saberes de Frontera*. México: Facultad de Filosofía y Letras/UNAM.
Mercado Mondragón, J. (2018). La violencia y el desplazamiento interno forzado en México [Violence and forced internal displacement in Mexico]. *Cuicuilco Revista de Ciencias Antropológicas* (73). pp. 11–17.

Mignolo, W. & Walsh, C. E. (2018). *On Decoloniality: Concepts, Analytics, Praxis*. Londres: Duke University Press.

Olivo, P. (2009). *La bala y la escuela (Holocausto indígena): modos en el que la educación oficial la complementa el trabajo represivo de las fuerzas policiaco-militares en los pueblos indios de México* [The Bullet and the School (Indigenous Holocaust): Ways in which Official Education Is Complemented by the Repressive Work of the Police-Military Forces in Mexico's Indigenous Towns]. Spain: Editorial Virus.

Quijano, A. (1988). *Modernidad, identidad y utopía en América Latina* [Modernity, identity and utopia in Latin America]. Lima: Sociedad y Política Ediciones.

Salazar Cruz, L. M. (2014). *Organizaciones paramilitares, grupos de autodefensas y desplazamientos internos forzados en México 2006-2013* [Paramilitary organizations, self-defence groups and forced internal displacement in Mexico 2006-2013]. Project. Mexico.

Salazar Cruz, L. M. & Álvarez Lobato, J. (2017). *Desplazamiento interno forzado. Regiones y violencia en México, 2006-2013* [Forced Internal Displacement. Regions and Violence in Mexico, 2006-2013]. Zinacantepec: El Colegio Mexiquense, A.C./ Comisión de Derechos Humanos del Estado de México.

Sarlo, B. (2006). *Tiempo pasado. Cultura de la memoria y giro subjetivo. Una discusión*. [Past time. Memory culture and a subjective turn. A discussion]. Mexico: Siglo XXI Editores.

Todorov, T. (2000). *Los abusos de la memoria* [the abuse of memory]. Barcelona: Paidós.

Yeverino Juárez, (2005). The democratic transitions in Mexico and Latin American in the late 21st. Century. *Economía y Sociedad*. Año X, 16. pp. 99–116.

Yúdice, G. (2002). Testimonio y concientización [Testimony and awareness raising]. In J. Beverley & H. Achugar (coords.), *La voz del otro: testimonio, subalternidad y verdad narrativa*. Guatemala: Universidad Rafael Landívar.

Conclusion. The Relevance of the Body and Emotions in the Care for Migrating People: Experiences of Abiayala

Ivón Cepeda-Mayorga and María Emilia Tijoux

This book was originally conceived as a means for the voices from Abiayala to express our challenges, experiences, and knowledge about the convergence and the complexity of educational processes under circumstances of temporary or indefinite migration. This work gave us an opportunity to listen to other ways in which the task of defining identity—linked to particular perceptions of cultural traditions and roots—has been undertaken, while facing specific educational contexts in a situation where migration is provoked by varying causes and/or circumstances.

The International Organization for Migration (IOM) estimates that in the year 2020, 281 million people were displaced throughout the world (Organización Internacional para las Migraciones, 2021). This figure increases, trapped in the uncertainty of an existence influenced by the health crisis that capitalist management of lives unveils when bodies seem disposable. The consequences are fierce, and they allow the brutality of enslavement that brings about punishment with extreme exploitation—the illicit trading or trafficking of immigrants—to stick its head out. Meanwhile, the fear of invasion, the danger or the contagion that supposedly might do harm to the good, white, parts of society, takes hold in the word 'migrant,' which is underpinned by racism (Tijoux, 2016). Meanwhile, humanitarian politics maintain their attempts to 'help'—only to humiliate—by, for example, proposing 'friendly' deportations (Cátedra Racismos y Migraciones Contemporáneas, 2020).

In Abiayala, migration has many faces that are lost in the crowd of people who, for example, seek out unending caravans in search of dignity (López López, 2019; Laurent-Perrault, 2020; Salazar, 2019; Gandini, 2020). Some of those faces burst forth in this book: the face of one who flees from armed conflict to overcome the impossibility of living in their homelands; the face of one who does not wish to belong to criminal groups or organizations; the face of a child who journeys through towns and across landscapes looking for the family that they were separated from, without reason; or of a child who is trying to find their place in a 'new' school, having arrived in a cloud of shame; the face of one who looks for their partner, dreaming about the promise of a different life; the face of a family that risks its life in jungles, rivers, and deserts, chasing after the dream of a better future; of one who leaves behind the comfort of their village and their world, to face the anxieties of the city; or of the child who says goodbye to their land to follow their family in search of work. Borders incessantly announce the separation between superiority and inferiority (Gálvez, 2020), causing bodies and emotions to be intertwined with the fears constructed by the dominant logics in order to control (Figari & Scribano, 2009) those who dare to migrate—with or without permission—carrying out a voyage full of dangers. The barriers and obstacles that migrating people face are countless and seem to be repeated, woven into, and tangled up in their stories.

This book is born out of a desire to recognize the complexity of migration practices and of the experiences that are lived in the different 'Americas,' whose historical processes, participatory practices, and political-cultural lives have a particular rhythm that must be recognized and valued in order to find other ways to define a common society. Within this framework, our interest in the relationship that is woven between migration and education helps us to approach an understanding of the people migrating in order to dismantle the stereotypes that arise from antiquated practices of discrimination, precarization, and punishment—which ultimately stem from racism—against migrating people (Tijoux & Riveros, 2019).

Abiayala is inflicted by deep economic and social inequalities, inherited from colonial histories based on undervaluing people's own knowledges and situated knowledges. Claudia Zapata (2005) draws on the work of Indigenous intellectuals such as Silvia Rivera Cusicanqui (2018) to recognize the strength of a colonial structure conceived of what has been called 'development,' primarily thought of as Western development, where the powerful have been seeking to 'improve the race' in the southern parts of this land (Pérez Rosales, 1923). In this search for the 'improvement of the race,' many people have been left on the path of a punishment that comes from their presumed 'inferior position.' The footprints of a history of extermination require us to think, in light of the chapters of this book, about what 'progress' has done to us, and to reflect on how and how much we have bowed our heads hoping for the blessing of those who have attempted to rule us.

It would seem that in order for 'progress' to exist, it would be essential to look at other latitudes, at a 'North,' which has been constructed as a boundary to our sought-after existence as peoples of 'the South.' In that way, we look to imitate what is thought in said North, what is produced and discovered, without accounting for the fact that its 'Northern' reality does not fit in with the realities of the different Americas that form the southern portions of the continent. Faced with this irrelevant position, these Americas, that is to say Abiayala, are having to deal with the uncertainty, violence, and inequality that have amplified in the COVID-19 pandemic

(CEPAL-UNESCO, 2020; Naciones Unidas, 2020). The pandemic is not the cause of the inequalities, but rather a repetition of the uncountable sufferings experienced by those people whom states cast aside and expel. If indeed the virus is not the cause of the inequalities and injustices that are lived within the diverse communities of Abiayala, it has opened the stitching that covered up the scenes of precarization, discrimination, violence, xeno-antagonism, and racism. All of these violent practices break up and decimate the dignity of migrating people who were being punished long before the pandemic (Tijoux 2020; Cátedra 2020). The virus also makes manifest the relevance of thinking about migrating people in terms of their bodies, if only to recognize in them the part of their identity that is exposed to mockery, abuse, disdain, and violence (Anzaldúa, 2001). At the same time, this situation pushes us to accept the relevance that migrating people's bodies have to the configuration of public policies (De Sena & Scribano, 2019) and ways of approaching migration. In this sense, a profound reflection in this context of constant social suffering demands recognition of the ways in which the torment remains present in daily relationships and of its bodily and emotional expressions. In this way, the curtain is pulled away from the innumerable political, historical, and daily scenes that have normalized the violence and transgressions toward the dignity of migrating people.

At the same time, during this pandemic, a discourse of care has been propagated, aiming to keep distance between people (ACHS, 2020), implementing confinement, and using healthcare measures such as masks and various anti-bacterial products. Nevertheless, those who propagate this discourse disregard, yet again, the living conditions of thousands of people who do not have the means to access the resources that would protect them, nor the ability to care for themselves by sheltering in place. This ignores the problems faced by migrating people who remain in forced displacement, without housing, or living in overcrowded conditions (Tres & Rodríguez, 2020). At the same time, migrating people lack access to sanitary products and clean water to wash themselves (Tres & Rodríguez, 2020). Additionally, they lack access to healthcare because they are turned away from hospitals and clinics or because they are afraid of being deported (Ibañez & Rozo, 2020). Lack of care and vulnerability are made visible in how the bodies of migrating people are acted upon. How can we understand care in the context of the day-to-day reality that migrating people face? In what way is care given or expressed, if it is at all? What is the relationship between the need of recognition and care for migrating people and an educational process that would go beyond a specialization within a specific academic area?

Speaking about a need for care also implies an ethical reflection that should not be exclusive to our current pandemic circumstances. Thus, it is important to point out that the need for care for migrating people existed prior to the pandemic and it will remain well after it ends. Therefore, it is vital to reinforce a notion of care that accompanies different ways of relating with one other within migration contexts; that is, a notion of care that goes beyond a public discourse that promotes social distancing when in reality it speaks of a damaging physical separation between people. The ethical reflection on care implies a search for creating better societies, more just and dignified not only for some, but for all members of a given community.

In this way, and in line with the spirit of this book, we consider the body within the political and social boundaries of Abiayala from the perspective of Angélica De Sena and Adrian Scribano (2019), to later delve into the practice of care from the experience of different voices from Abiayala, such as those of the Brazilian philosopher Leonardo Boff (2012), as well as Cristina Vega Solís, Raquel Martínez Buján and Myriam Paredes Chauca (2018), Ibero-American thinkers who have woven their reflections into studies on gender, care, and migration, mainly in the Latin-American context. Drawing on this analysis, in this concluding chapter, we propose a pedagogy that considers migratory people's bodies and emotions through a notion of care. This pedagogical proposal implies showing different ways of weaving care based on educational practices that facilitate recognizing migrating people as valuable actors and interlocutors. In order to achieve this, in the final section of this chapter, we hazard a first approach for a pedagogy of care initially proposed by the Spanish philosopher Irene Comins-Mingol (2017) and complemented by pedagogical practices proposed within different educational practices, based on the work of lesbian Chicana writer Gloria Anzaldúa (Anzaldúa, 2001; Anzaldúa & Keating, 2013, Cantú-Sanchez, De León-Zepeda, & Cantú, 2020; Espinosa-Dulanto, Calderon-Berumen & O'Donald, 2020; Nuño, 2020).

Engaging Migrating Peoples, Bodies, and Emotions

One cannot explain a reality without turning to see what is happening in their community, to address (or try to address) the problems arising there. In terms of migrating people, it is critical to attend to their existence as people and not merely as bodies that express a particular origin or condition as foreigners. The search of recognition has been a common concern in contemporary western political philosophy from the defense of cultural diversity (Taylor, 1993), the political, social, and ethical development inside a society (Honneth, 1997), and the search for justice and fairness in political participation (Fraser & Honneth, 2003).

Nevertheless, speaking about recognition in the specific case of migrating people based on their experiences in Abiayala requires opening spaces for thought emerging from the territories that make up Abiayala. This opening allows us to reveal the need for recognition of a migrating person as a valuable interlocutor beyond their 'migrant' situation within a given territory, with the goal of confronting attitudes of violence, domination, exploitation, and racism. Following the reflections of Foucault (2001), Tijoux and Riveros (2019) emphasize the fact that racism is not a new phenomenon, but rather a response that has been normalized in regards to those who are considered outsiders based on notions of 'race' and 'racism.' This response has given strength to a discourse in which said 'outsider,' as a 'migrant,' is viewed as a threat to the political and economic order of a given society (Tijoux & Riveros, 2019). Further, Tijoux and Riveros shed light on the fact that racism is part of the capitalist structures of domination that are expressed in the bodies of migrating people as a labor force at their disposition to be exploited in a capitalist mode of production. This situation of exploitation is normalized as a part of the relationships between human beings. Nevertheless, it is necessary to think of imaginative and creative ways to access alterity that might allow us to reclaim common good through a different reading of the body (Camarena, 2020). This implies considering the body beyond its physiological condition or as a means of production.

We are proposing an orientation towards gaining an awareness of the body as the means we have for existing and inhabiting the world; indeed, it is the means by which a person understands and interacts with the world, with space, and with others who share said space (Cepeda-Mayorga, 2019). 'Human beings possess different dimensions: biological, social, cultural, economic, political, psychological, and ideological. The body materializes these dimensions as a reflexive and existential complexity in a project that is integral to human matters'[1] (Enríquez, 2019; p. 13). From this perspective, the reflection set forth by Sharon López-Araya (2017), in relation to Gloria Anzaldúa's text *La Prieta* (2001), gains meaning: 'if only crossing the border changed the color of one's skin; it is not where you are born, it is the color into which you are born'[2] (López-Araya, 2017 p. 162). Thus, your skin color can make the difference with respect to how you are considered and treated withing a society. 'Because it seems that looking is enough. Looking at one's body. That body that one 'sees'. These qualifications based on the state of being an immigrant, of one's origin, of one's color, the labor that [the migrating people] carry out, come to explain a way of being and to highlight the racism that once again defines cultural or psychological characteristics'[3] (Tijoux & Riveros, 2019, p. 402). In *La Prieta*, Anzaldúa reflects on how her identity and her way of relating with others and with the world is marked by her physical characteristics as an Indigenous woman and as a Latina, which give rise to discrimination and racism both in her daily life and in the academic environment (Anzaldúa, 2001). These types of actions remain present today and can be identified and highlighted within educational, judicial, economic, and market structures (Cantú-Sánchez, De León-Zepeda & Cantú, 2020), and allow us new ways to recognize the value of human beings.

Agamben (1998) pointed out that the human body was a receptacle of violence and of power exercised by other human beings as a form of domination. Scribano and De Sena (2020) go beyond this assertion and, drawing on lived experience in Argentina as an example, propose that the consideration of a life as expendable is tied to a model of production and maintenance of consumerism. In it, those who suffer the most are those who find themselves in a vulnerable position due to expulsion and dispossession. This is the enactment of a logic of exploitation that reaches the point of being normalized and reproduced (De Sena & Scribano, 2019). For that reason, it is necessary to find alternative social structures and ways of enacting education that to consider the relevance of the body. This consideration compels us to imagine and propose different and creative ways to access other people (Camarena, 2020), in order to develop greater empathy and care for us all (Echenberg, 2015; Castillo-González, 2017). This enactments may lead to other means of achieving social cohesion and social transformation (Camarena 2020; Scribano & Korstanje, 2020). Finally, the body is more than a physical support, it is 'the intensive, concrete reality of human existence, of consciousness, of thought, and even of freedom'[4] (Ramírez, 2017, p. 53). Likewise, it is necessary to bear in mind that it is through our bodies that we relate with the external world, find ourselves, and inhabit the world. 'Our body is outward experience above all: spatiality without argument, coexistence as a purpose and a truth'[5] (Ramírez, 2017, p. 55). Our body implies an intersubjectivity understood as a constant encounter with the other, which creates a reciprocal relationship between the definitions of both beings, as much of the individual as of the other with whom they find themselves (Garcés, 2013). At the same time, to open oneself up to an encounter with the other is to enter into a space of recognition, where a dialog—within which there exists the possibility of being wrong (López Sáenz, 2019), and of learning from the other—is established.

For De Sena and Scribano (2019), the body occupies a central location in the design and structuring of policies and strategies that consolidate a way of being in the world through consumption and the apparent immediate satisfaction of needs and desires. This way of seeing the body also corresponds with a superficial, reductionist, and impoverishing ideology of the body when it becomes a referent of domination and control over people (Ramírez, 2017). The body is seen as a territory where policies and means of exploitation that commodify their needs and affections are brought about and normalized. In this way, they transform said bodies into objects that are part of the chain of production (Cervio, Lisdero, & D'hers, 2020) into what Scribano (2009) calls social sensitivity. Along those lines, De Sena and Scribano propose a sociology of the body and its emotions capable of showing how violence is exercised structurally and daily (De Sena & Scribano, 2019), but which also serves as a bridge for recovering and proposing other ways of relating to each other. Following these authors, the sociology of emotions seeks to emphasize the importance of emotions and affections as an essential part of the decision-making process of individuals (De Sena & Scribano, 2019). Thus, emotions are considered 'rationally' based on mechanisms that are 'activated' within the experiences of an individual as a social actor and the influence of ideological models accepted within their society (De Sena & Scribano, 2019).

Since this assessment of the body and of emotions is broken by an instrumental and capitalistic logic, following Scribano, we propose a notion of recognition and care for others based on three key elements: (1) conscientious awareness of the fact that the body implies being in the world and in coexistence with others; (2) the intersubjectivity derived from this condition of spatiality; and (3) the relevance of emotions and affections as a part of the construction of a sensitivity and social action that recognizes bodies as 'territories of creativity, pleasure, and autonomy'[6] (Scribano, 2016, p. 161). Taking these three elements into account, we can undertake an ethical reflection on people's character and how it is shaped and expressed in the actions that their bodies take and suffer. In this way, the case of migrating people compels us to ask ourselves about their subjectivities and their location within this understanding of the body and its emotions. This questioning would imply recognizing ourselves in a different way, in order to give rise to different ways of living and coexisting.

This question would lead us to consider migrating people within the historical context of what has caused them to become a 'migrant,' and therefore within a category that has distanced them from humanity, but that requires the recognition in a historical-political moment that has forced them to leave their homelands. Being a migrating person forces one to appear as a body in movement, which implies considering the causes that bring them to move and that begin from an understanding of themselves and their reality. This approach to the body of migrating people takes into account how being in a strange territory also implies a different way-of-being in the world, as it also highlights the importance of language as an expression of that character. This requires considering the relevance of subtle elements like food, dance, artistic expressions (Irobi, 2006), and personal care, as expressions of how one behaves as a part of that body in movement. Then, understanding migrating people from their bodies allows us to see recognition or discrimination as two possible ways to create different relationships between people, in quotidian and academic environments. These bodily elements are not commonly considered within the educational strategies and projects involving migrating people, which underlines the criticism made by Scribano emphasizing that political and social structures define that which is considered to be an acceptable necessity and behavior, while other expressions remain overlooked (Scribano 2009; Scribano 2016; Cervio, Lisdero, & D'hers, 2020). Current educational practices seem concerned with including cultural diversity in educational discourses. In reality such concern seems to only be centered on the need to meet certain quotas, to which migrating people as a part of the educational process are expected to adapt (Di Caudo, 2016). Nevertheless, discounting the importance of the body, and its relationships with space and with others, implies a lack of awareness of bodily existence, and the role that feelings and emotions play in the shaping of relationships and affections between people.

Our bodies are our link to the reality in which we exist. Through our bodies we suffer, we become happy, we recognize other people and ourselves, we live. In the case of migrating people, there is a common perception that castes them as distant. They are seen as migrant bodies that can be used in the system of production. This perception has enabled abuses and harassment that denies their recognition as people. Hence, turning to the voices speaking of the different experiences in Abiayala is critical. This would account for diversity of perspectives, and exposing how migrating people live from the perspective of fore fronting the body in its spatiality, emotions, and affections. In this sense, a change of perspective is laid out suspending the figure of migrating people as 'miserable' (Scribano, 2016). This perspective is attentive to creative and imaginative means that allow us to analyze the problems of abuses and harassment mentioned above in ways that are different from those that have been carried out up to this point in time (Scribano & Roche Cárcel, 2020). Thus, within this volume, the various chapters engage with elements of the body and its emotions. The experiences encompassed in the chapters give an account of the conflicts that the migrating person faces while trying to be included in an educational system within a city, and while using languages that are different from those that they are familiar with. These experiences within educational systems allow schools and classrooms to be a space for both friendly meetings and conflicts for migrating people. These places serve as sites for identities to take shape and are a way of inhabiting the world in relation with others. This is the case of young people in migrating families in the United States, who face constant movement in search of favorable economic conditions for family work, dealing with language barriers and the loss of formal academic opportunities, as discussed in the chapter by Yenny Saldaña, Rebecca Campbell-Montalvo, Mariana Santiago, Ana Guevara, Liliana Mata, Eduardo Morales, Briana Salazar, Cristina Saldaña, and Adolfo Saldaña. Or the voices of adolescents who, in search of educational opportunities within the university, are displaced to urban enclaves and face the dilemma of identifying based on their Indigenous or Afro-diasporic roots, or attempting to leave them aside with the tension that this decision represents, a point which Maure Aguirre takes up in her chapter. Said roots are also expressed in Claudia Carrillo's chapter, in the games that the primary school children play in a school in Chile, and the dressing style that relates to their identity. These Afro-diasporic roots also serve to highlight their cultural particularities. This tension appears when migrating people need to re-learn how to name things, which implies a different way of being and of conceiving of the world. This is also the case of the Indigenous migrating people who leave their communities to look for sources of employment and development. In order to address this tension, they have to seek links of support not only across the land but also across time and generations, as described by Irasema Villanueva and María Elena Tovar in their chapter. Similarly, María Mercedes Eguiguren takes up the circumstances and predicaments that are woven between the desire for growth, the need of a better education, and the search for those in other spaces, places, and even different countries. Likewise, the need to be seen and recognized as people is also critical. This implies leaving behind relationships of domination and power (over migrating people), in the search for an understanding of the causes that led to that migration, which can stem from conditions of violence and insecurity, as Miguel Angel Martínez highlights in his chapter.

The diverse narratives that this volume encompasses emphasize that recognition of migrant people should begin with their value as people, based on those actions that express not only instrumental reasoning, but also show how their bodies live and inhabit different spaces, by way of their emotions and affections that, in turn, connect them with other people. It is necessary to reject the notion that the body is a territory or receptacle of violence (Segato, 2016), as is the case with migrating people, in which they suffer as much from physical violence as from cultural and structural violences that make dignified living conditions impossible. How, then, do we break this cycle of violence? How do we achieve a recognition of the migrating people that allows us to establish peaceful relationships, growth, and development within a community? How do we promote meeting spaces, both in daily life and within educational institutions, that promote this recognition of the body and the emotions of the people in migrating situations? For that, the sociology of bodies and emotions can be accompanied by proposals that emphasize cordial reasoning and an ethic of care, a proposal which we will address in the next section.

Care, Community, and Their Relation to Migrating People

For the Brazilian philosopher Leonardo Boff (2015), eating together means more than just consuming food to satisfy certain biological needs. In line with Boff, the act of sharing food with someone is part of what makes us human beings; it goes beyond producing and cooking food, it implies giving them a flavor in which both the spices that give aromas and seasoning to the food and the setting of the moment with the people with whom we share the food are also interwoven (Boff, 2015). Scribano (2009) also brings attention to the role of food, to exemplify how relationships between bodies and emotions are established. Scribano goes even deeper into how they frame meetings, parties, or important events. For Quiche thinker María Jacinta Xón Riquiac (2020), food represents an expression of her Indigenous identity and a meeting space in which stories and knowledges that are passed from generation to generation as a part of a tradition around the fire and the preparation of food are shared. Thus, not only is it a finished product, but also the process of and time dedicated to its preparation. Food also implies the conversation during this process, which frames a relationship with the cosmos, the universe, life, nature, memories of those who are not present, and the essence of the fire within the home. Nevertheless, food can also exemplify moments of exclusion and discrimination, as narrated by Anzaldúa in her childhood experience as a Chicana:

> ...eating from a bag in school, hiding our *'lonches'* potatoes with chorizo behind our hands, cupped like mugs, and eating them with our heads down so that the other children could not see. The evidence could be found folded within the tortilla. The white children laughed, calling us *'tortilleros'*, the Mexican children took that word as a stick that they could use to hit each other. My brothers, my sister and I began to bring sandwiches with white bread to school. After some time we stopped bringing food altogether.[7] (Anzaldúa, 2001, pp. 133–134, emphasis in original).

For Anzaldúa, this scene shows a constant fight for recognition and acknowledgement of the value of her Mexican roots against the rejection that she feels due to said roots, in spite of being part of the sixth generation of children of migrants in Texas (Anzaldúa, 2001, p. 129). She calls attention to how in this scene, food is a point of encounter with the past, her heritage as a Latina and Mexican present in the type of food that she brings to school, but it is also a moment of conflict given the reaction of rejection and discrimination on the part of her American companions whom she identifies as 'white children' (Anzaldúa, 2001, pp. 133–134). This is a narrative where emotions and affections are articulated through details such as the food, language, and the color of the skin. Then sharing a meal becomes a moment that recalls the reflections from De Sena and Scribano, but which also frames one of the activities of care that provoke us to look for different ways to relate with one another.

When speaking about migrating people and care, one tends to undermine care in those scenarios where migrant women carry out tasks related to childcare or elderly care, a perspective limiting the way in which care is understood in relation to the phenomenon of migration (Rosas, 2018). It is important to understand that the practice of care is not confined solely to women, but rather it encompasses the whole of society, since it is tied to ageing, labor policies, instability, reduction of public spending, and access to pensions and healthcare services, among other situations that may make people vulnerable (Vega, Martínez & Paredes, 2018). As a starting point, the reflection about care comes from an ethical perspective that looks to promote those abilities and attitudes that allow us to resolve situations of conflict in a non-violent way (Castillo-González, 2017). However, one of the greatest complications that arises from speaking about care within the context of migration is still the incipient terrain that has been centered on 'the analysis of a type of care that is sold in the labor market and that is salaried beyond its formality and remunerative level. The care practices that are not negotiated in the market and that are carried out without pay or underpaid have received less attention'[8] (Rosas, 2018, p. 299). Therefore, it is necessary to reconsider the relevance of care from other perspectives allowing us to prioritize embodied life, intersubjectivity, collaboration, and communal living (Vega, Martínez & Paredes, 2018).

Boff (2012) distinguishes between natural-objective care and conscious-ethical care. The first notion refers to the actions that individuals naturally take to care for their bodies, minds, health, lives, and the lives of the people they love. Under this type of care, they also consider other human beings' actions and the damage that they can cause. By conscious-ethical care, Boff refers to the natural care that is consciously assumed as an active ethical principle present in people's behavior and attitudes. In other words, this second notion of care represents a commitment to considering care as crucial to people's actions and their life projects (Boff, 2012). This type of care highlights a social perspective that endorses a concern for the other, and the search to establish 'structures of support and holding' (Boff, 2012, p. 23), prevention, and precaution. These structures could be both social and institutional, whose intention is to develop a sense of community. In this sense, in order to achieve the sought-after recognition of the value of care in the community, in line with Boff, the development of another type of rationality, a 'sensitive and cordial logic' (Boff, 2012, p. 29) is necessary; one which confronts the instrumental reasoning characteristic of contemporary societies. This cordial reasoning, whose main characteristic emerges from the heart, encompasses the passions and the affections of human beings, and 'it is structured around the *pathos* of concern, of the profound sentiment in the sense of the capacity for affecting and being affected'[9] (Boff, 2012, p. 49).

From this approach, Boff opens the possibility of considering the concept of care from the intersubjectivity that comes from shared experiences or encounters where the body and affections take on a central role, as a form of self-care and mutual care. This possibility signals another way-of-being-in-the-world-with-others where care helps us to recover the connection with other human beings, Nature and Life. This way-of-being-care acknowledges our bodies' presence and relevance and implies the relationship of these bodies in the particular spaces that they share with others. An example of this approach can be seen in *Brujas Migrantes* (Migrant Witches), a group of women located in Madrid who share their experiences of migration. They are migrating women of Abiayala who work mainly in domestic and care activities. What is interesting about *Brujas Migrantes* is that they identify as a community of self-caregivers. There they share dreams, disappointments, and frustrations; in other words, they share their lives (Moreira, Rodríguez & Malo, 2018). In the words of Ana, one of the *Brujas Migrantes* member:

> So in the coven we do that: we share, we laugh, we make jokes, we eat, and we listen to each other, because all of us have burdens and sometimes in activism, in spaces of support for local associations, that stays in the background, and we have brought it to the foreground as a group. In order to strengthen ourselves from within [the group] and therefore we can give [care and support] to the others. [...] There is something spiritual in what we do, not so much tied to religions but rather spirituality among our group. It is the creation of a circle of women. That gives us the strength to continue with our activism, because activism is difficult. The day-to-day, survival, uncertainty, fighting with this system that is weighing us down, people who are in a very disadvantaged situation, that put us in that situation[10] (Moreira, Rodríguez & Malo, 2018, p. 324).

In this same case, one can also appreciate the emphasis that De Sena and Scribano (2019) put on being aware of those activities that involve the body and which, perhaps, have not been granted enough importance. Those activities can signify a change in weaving other social fabrics and webs of support. *Brujas Migrantes* is also a group that puts into question the policies and social, institutional, and state practices where care has been commodified into the shape of a woman who cares for children, elderly adults, the sick. The *Brujas* collective questions the instrumental and market-based logic that sees care as a product to be bought and sold, and they highlight the need to reevaluate care as communal practices (Moreira, Rodríguez & Malo, 2018). Here we understand communal care as 'those activities directed toward conserving, continuing, or repairing our world, so that we might live in it in the best possible way; considering that that world includes our bodies, our individualities, and our surroundings'[11] (Rosas, 2018, p. 305).

Then, the next question is: how do we understand this approach of care that endorses a sensitive and cordial reasoning, alongside a sense of community with the relevance of bodies and emotions regarding migrating people? Following our discussion above and the narratives and analysis in the chapters in this volume, this is a question with no easy answers.

Addressing this question requires firstly that migrating people be recognized as a being able to speak beyond being subjected singularly to being a 'migrant.' The relevance of this approach comes from the recognition of the sense of dignity inherent in any person, and also from considering the value of diversity, and how this diversity is expressed through actions like food preparation and sharing, language, the way one moves, one's attire, and so on. This recognition begins with the act of listening to the other, with registering the needs that they might have. In the case of a migrating person, this entails listening to their stories to learn about what produced the migration journey and the needs that they might have. This exercise of listening will engender a sense of community and care.

The experiences narrated in this book show how some of the policies and actions meant to support migrating people were at some point designed without considering their experiences, challenges, emotions, and knowledges. Therefore, these policies and actions fail to recover the intersubjectivity from the perspective of the sociology of body and emotions, and their connections to care. This failure is present in some of the strategies developed to help and support migrating people, as they are not part of the process of defining their needs and then of finding out ways to address those needs. This strategy can be seen in the different ways in which the educational processes conceive of migrating people as quotas within a program of cultural diversity. If the focus is given to migrants as people (López Sáenz, 2019), then deriving a sense of care from bodies and emotions would imply considering other forms of support, as demonstrated by the *Brujas Migrantes*. There is a sense of solidarity and care that arises from sharing experiences, emotions, stories, memories, food, and a communal life. Thus, educational processes play an important role in engaging with migrating people and their intersubjectivity with other members of the society. How, then, could this approach to care be part of the educational processes within migration contexts? This is the question we address in next and final section of this chapter.

A Pedagogy Based on Bodies, Care, and Emotions

A 'pedagogy of cruelty' highlights the normalization of attitudes and actions that express cruelty and violence against other human beings (Segato, 2016). Even though this type of pedagogy mainly addresses feminicides and violence against women, it also applies to migrating people, migrating children, rivers, and territories, which are considered as 'objects' of use and for exchange (Abenshushan, et al. 2018). The main facet of this pedagogy of cruelty is that 'the cruelty is directly proportional to the isolation of citizens through their inability to be sensible'[12] (Segato, 2016, p. 21), where the body becomes the ultimate expression where violence and dominance is written, in both metaphorical and physical ways

(Lozano, 2018). This kind of relationship denies the relevance of bodies, emotions, and practices of care as we have discussed thus far. Abiayala has a diversity of experiences in matters of migration that encourages expressions of solidarity and brother- and sisterhood (Segna, 2020), but which also engenders expressions of racism, discrimination, precarization, and punishment (Gago, 2018).

Nonetheless, there are ways to reconstruct and deconstruct histories and identities through sharing some of the experiences of those migrating people (even if they are painful) with others (Espinosa-Dulanto, Calderon-Berumen & O'Donald, 2020). In this sense, Comins-Mingol (2017) proposes a 'pedagogy of care' whose objective 'is to reinforce the ability to care, develop a sincere concern for those who suffer, and recognize our competencies as agents of change through action'[13] (Comins-Mingol, 2017, p. 187). For this author, the pedagogy of care emphasizes a way-of-being-cared-for in two senses: first, as values that are instilled through the processes of teaching and that are related to solidarity, respect, recognition, listening, and empathy; and second, as the putting-into-practice of those values within educational environments. This approach implies reshaping of structures toward a more internal focus within the schools that allows for the practice of care with people. Thus, the pedagogy of care is linked with the development of the conscious-ethical care to which Boff refers and which underlines the commitment to create communities.

For Comins-Mingol (2017), the pedagogy of care can blend other important elements within education in order to find alternatives of discovery and development that allow for the transformation of one's reality and the breaking down of models of oppression and exploitation. In the case of migrating people, schools and other educational spaces where the community gathers can offer an opportunity for sharing those experiences in order to reconstruct and deconstruct the self (Espinosa-Dulanto, Calderon-Berumen & O'Donald, 2020). These kinds of spaces can promote social justice, respect, recognition, and empathy through specific activities and practices where migrating people take part (Nuño, 2020). It commonly requires the sensitivity and support from the teacher or the professor to enhance an environment where confidence and diversity can arise. Espinosa-Dulanto and Calderon-Berumen are interested in highlighting the difficulties that migrating people who share connections with Abiayala face within the educational context. O'Donald recounts her experiences with these minoritized communities while working as a Spanish teacher in Texas. Together, these scholars use narratives and testimonies to give students the opportunity to reflect on their identities as inhabitants of borderlands (Espinosa-Dulanto, Calderon-Berumen & O'Donald, 2020). In line with Gloria Anzaldúa's work (Anzaldúa & Keating, 2013), these authors transform their classroom into 'Nepantla spaces' (Espinosa-Dulanto, Calderon-Berumen & O'Donald, 2020, p. 18). Nepantla represents a space of transformation, re/construction and re/creation. 'It is a safe space to inter/connect with ourselves and with others' (Espinosa-Dulanto, Calderon-Berumen & O'Donald, 2020, p. 19) through poetry, narratives, and fictional texts that they create and share. In this process of encounter and creation, the teacher becomes part of the community and the journey. 'We write with our students, we become vulnerable while analyzing and processing the poetry and the writing process' (Espinosa-Dulanto, Calderon-Berumen & O'Donald, 2020, p. 26). It is a form of developing a sense of community in this Nepantla space.

This kind of practice breaks with the educational models of productivity and exploitation (Comins-Mingol, 2017). These practices also confront the regulation of emotions that promote particular stereotypes to reinforce specific relationships also attached to the models of productivity and exploitation mentioned above (Scribano & De Sena, 2020). Educational policies are part of the state's plans and strategies to regulate and manipulate the feelings, perceptions, and emotions of subjects. However, the school also offers the opportunity to socialize and develop sensitivities for imagining and creating other possible scenarios (Nuño, 2020). Within this distinct form of pedagogy, care is a crucial component for the discussion of education, as it highlights the fact that it is as much an end in itself as those curricular materials that should be included as a way to value activities of care, as a medium through which different relationships are built.

In the case of migrating people, the act of being constructed as 'foreigners' can push them toward engaging in activities withing the 'illegal' sector, but they can also organize themselves from a perspective of care in a communal sense. Such is the case of the experience of the Bolivian migration in Argentina as documented by Verónica Gago (2018). Gago analyzes how the Argentine textile economy has been powered by the labor of migrating people. Importantly, around the textile factories is woven a series of care services as an infrastructure that sustains people and builds up a community encompassing the multiple realities that they live: constant movement, searching for other means of employment, the need to acquire other knowledges in order to access other means of employment, the desire to exercise professions that are not recognized within the territory (as is the case with medicine), the lack of access to healthcare services for fear of being reported to the authorities, the piecing together of clandestine clinics where those still-necessary healthcare services are offered. This is possible because there is a sense of community that is founded on the recognition of migrants as people.

We also witness this communal care in classrooms and educational spaces, as Espinosa-Dulanto, Calderon-Berumen and O'Donald (2020) point out in mentioning the vulnerability shared among themselves as educators in sharing and listening to the narratives of their students (Espinosa-Dulanto, Calderon-Berumen & O'Donald, 2020). This necessary sensitivity on the part of educators is key in the reflection and analysis of Maure Aguirre's chapter in this volume, where she describes the concerns of the teacher in caring for the particular needs of her students, beyond the English language learning. Likewise, the shaping of communities of refuge and care can be established among the children even through simple expressions, such as the opportune warning of a possible voice of authority that disapproves of practices that the children consider important for themselves and their identities, as Claudia Carrillo describes in her chapter in this volume. The experience of the children recounted by Carrillo also shows how those children care for each other in the face of the teachers who have not shown that sensitivity discussed above, and that for the same reason they are not able to create an environment in which they feel safe and confident. That is, they fail to create that Nepantla space. At the same time, this experience shows how care is an experience that is constructed and that is shared communally, that is, the creation of those spaces of assurance and community comes about through relationships that allow people to recognize each other, to listen to each other, to protect each other, and to care for each other.

Thus, a pedagogy that accentuates the relevance of emotions, care, and expressions of the body is capacious in registering the existence of migrating people as people. Key is important to develop a sensitivity and empathy that does not reproduce models of exploitation and oppression of migrating people. In this sense, a pedagogy of care is aware of the need for care and support that migrating people require, which implies having room for meeting spaces where experiences, words, memories, ways of being and coexisting can be shared; in other words, ways of inhabiting and making communities. From the perspective of classrooms, one must seek to create spaces that allow for the creation of education through the solidarity that breaks with a logic of learning and memorization, and allows one to reconnect with the inquisitive spirit that is capable of observing those injustices and inequities that occur within current realities (Nuño 2020). This inquisitive spirit is crucial for an ethical reflection that seeks the development of the best possible society, that is one supported by recognition and empathy toward the other. In order to develop it, it is necessary that educational institutions promote spaces for meeting and care, like the Nepantla of Anzaldúa (Anzaldúa & Keating, 2013; Espinosa-Dulanto, Calderon-Berumen & O'Donald, 2020), where students are not seen as mere subjects for reproducing academic knowledge, but rather who are educated as empathetic and sensitive people, from the perspective of intersubjective relationships in which the expressions of their bodies and their emotions are valued. It also requires paying attention to how those care networks are woven in spaces that go beyond the academic setting, in spaces that foster meaningful encounters. If we reassume the importance of the body and the role of emotions outside of a logic of reproduction of the market and consumption, a pedagogy based on care can help with the development of a sense of community, of an *us*. There cannot be an end to the violence, discrimination, and exploitation of the other if they are not recognized as people (López Sáenz, 2019).

A pedagogy that is attentive to emotions, care, and bodies implies a path in constant movement, where the relationship with the other and the search for development of abilities that respond to that call for care are implicit. It is not a simple task; it requires a restructuring of educational institutions and practices that take into account the intersubjectivity that comes from the recognition of the person as a relevant element that defines their existence. What is required is a recognition of migrating people as part of a common world. Hence, the critical attention to considering, knowing, and recognizing the experiences that arise within the varied settings from within Abiayala. Through those settings, we propose a different notion of the body and of living.

Notes

1 Original in Spanish: 'Los seres humanos poseen diferentes dimensiones: biológica, social, cultural, económica, política, psicológica e ideológica. El cuerpo materializa estas dimensiones como una complejidad reflexiva y existencial en un proyecto integral de lo humano.'
2 Original in Spanish: 'Si tan solo al cruzar la frontera cambiara el color de la piel; no es donde naces, es del color que naces.'
3 Original in Spanish: 'Porque parece que basta con mirar. Mirar su cuerpo. Ese cuerpo que él "ve". Estas calificaciones que parten de la condición de inmigrante, del origen, el color, la labor que desempeñan, vienen a explicar un modo de ser y a señalar ese racismo que vuelve a definir características culturales o psicológicas.'
4 Original in Spanish: 'La realidad concreta, intensiva de la existencia humana, de la conciencia, el pensamiento y hasta de la libertad.'
5 Original in Spanish: 'Nuestro cuerpo es exterioridad ante todo: espacialidad sin discusión, coexistencia como destino y verdad.'
6 Original in Spanish: 'Territorios de creatividad, goce y autonomía de la vida.'
7 Original in Spanish: '…comer de la bolsa en la escuela, esconder nuestros "*lonches*" *papas con chorizo* tras las manos ahuecadas en forma de taza y tragarlos cabizbajos para que las otras criaturas no pudieran ver. El delito se encontraba doblado entre la tortilla. Las criaturas blancas se reían, llamándonos "*tortilleros*," las criaturas mexicanas tomaban esa palabra como un garrote con el que se podían pegar uno al otro. Mis hermanos, mi hermana y yo empezamos a traer sándwiches de pan blanco a la escuela. Después de un tiempo dejamos de llevar comida totalmente.'
8 Original in Spanish: 'El análisis de un tipo de cuidado que se vende en el mercado de trabajo y que es asalariado, más allá de su formalidad y nivel remunerativo. Menos atención han recibido los cuidados que no se negocian en el mercado y que son realizados de forma no-remunerada o sub- remunerada.'
9 Original in Spanish: 'Se estructura alrededor del *pathos* del afecto, del sentimiento profundo en el sentido de la capacidad para afectar y ser afectado.'

10 Original in Spanish: 'Entonces en el aquelarre hacemos eso: compartimos, reímos, hacemos bromas, comemos y nos escuchamos, porque todas tenemos cargas y a veces en el activismo, en espacios del asociacionismo, eso queda en segundo plano, y nosotras hemos puesto eso en primer plano como grupo. Para fortalecernos desde dentro y que de esa manera podamos dar a las demás. [...] Hay algo de espiritual en lo que hacemos, no tanto ligado a religiones, sino espiritualidad entre nosotras. Es la creación de un círculo de mujeres. Eso nos da fuerzas para continuar en el activismo, porque el activismo es duro. El día a día, la supervivencia, la precariedad, el luchar con este sistema que nos está cargando tanto a las personas que estamos en una situación más desfavorecida, que nos ponen en esa situación.'
11 Original in Spanish: 'Aquellas actividades dirigidas a conservar, continuar o reparar nuestro mundo, para que podamos vivir en él lo mejor posible; considerando que ese mundo incluye nuestros cuerpos, nuestras individualidades y nuestro entorno.'
12 Original in Spanish: 'La crueldad habitual es directamente proporcional al aislamiento de los ciudadanos mediante su desesnsitización.'
13 Original in Spanish: 'Es fortalecer la capacidad de cuidar, desarrollar una preocupación sincera por aquellos que sufren y reconocer nuestras competencias como agentes de cambio a través de la acción.'

References

Abenshushan, V. et. al. (2018). Disolutas (A Ante Cabe Con Contra) Las Pedagogías de la Crueldad [Dissolute (A Facing Might With Against) Pedagogies of Cruelty]. In G. Jauregui (Ed.). *Tsunami*. Mexico: Sexto Piso. pp. 13–24.

ACHS. (2020). *Yo te cuido, tú me cuidas* [I take care of you, you take care of me]. YouTube Video. Available at: https://youtu.be/Tc64m_Uc4Xk.

Agamben, G. (1998). *Homo Sacer: Sovereign Power and Bare Life*. United States: Stanford University Press.

Anzaldúa, G. & Keating, A. L. (Eds.). (2013). *This Bridge We Call Home: Radical Vision for Transformation*. New York: Routledge.

Anzaldúa, G., Castillo, A. & Alarcon, N. (2001). La prieta [The Dark Woman]. *Debate Feminista*, 24, 129–141.

Boff, L. (2012). *El cuidado necesario* [The necessary care]. Spain: Trotta.

Boff, L. (2015). *Derechos del corazón* [Rights from the heart]. Spain: Trotta.

Camarena, M. (2020). El poder de imaginar a los otros [The power of imagine others]. *Revista Latinoamericana de Estudios sobre Cuerpos, Emociones y Sociedad*, 34(12), 85–87.

Cantú-Sanchez, M., De León-Zepeda, C., & Cantú, N. E. (Eds.). (2020). *Teaching Gloria E. Anzaldua. Pedagogy and Practice for our Classrooms and Communities*. United States: The University of Arizona Press.

Castillo-González, M. C. (2017). La cultura de paz como meta, principio y cuidado [The culture of peace as an aim, principle and care]. In D. E. García-González. (Ed.). *Razones para la paz*. Mexico: Transcend/Tecnológico de Monterrey. pp. 33–59.

Cátedra Racismos y Migraciones Contemporáneas. (2020). Catedra Racismos y Migraciones Contemporáneas rechaza plan de retorno humanitario [The Research Seminar Contemporary Racisms and Migrations rejects the humanitarian return plan]. *Radio Universidad de Chile*. Available at: https://radio.uchile.cl/2018/11/09/catedra-de-racismos-y-migraciones-de-la-u-de-chile-rechaza-plan-de-retorno-humanitario/.

_____. (2020). *Contra el racismo mediático en tiempos de pandemia* [Against media racism in times of pandemic]. Universidad de Chile. Available at: https://www.uchile.cl/noticias/162424/declaracion-contra-el-racismo-mediatico-en-tiempos-de-pandemia.

CEPAL-UNESCO. (2020). *Informe Covid-19* [Brief Covid-19]. August 2020. Available at: file:///Users/L01136176/Downloads/374075spa.pdf.

Cepeda-Mayorga, I. (2019). Pautas corporales para una normalización de la violencia [Boddy patterns for normalizing violence]. In D. E. García-González & J. A. Camargo Castillo (Eds.), *Para pazado mañana, filosofía de anteayer*. Mexico: Bonilla Artiga Editores, pp. 207–223.

Cervio, A., Lisdero, P., & D'hers, V. (2020). "Cuerpos Precarios": Habitar, respirar y trabajar en el sur global. Una mirada desde la sociología de los cuerpos/emociones ["Precarious Bodies": Inhabit, breathe and work in the Global South. A look from the sociology of bodies/emotions]. *Empiria. Revista de metodología de ciencias sociales*, 0(47), 43–63.

Comins-Mingol, I. (2017). ¿Hacia qué modo-de-ser en el mundo? Por una pedagogía del cuidar [Towards what way-of-being in the world? For a pedagogy of caring]. *Documentación Social*, (187), 145–160.

De Sena, A. & Scribano, A. (2019). *Social Policies and Emotions*. Springer International Publishing. Kindle OS Edition.

Di Caudo, M. V. (2016). Interculturalidad y Universidad. Cuando lo distinto (no) cabe en el mismo molde [Interculturality and University. When the different (does not) fit in the same mold]. In M. V. Di Caudo, D. L. Erazo & M. C. Ospina (Coords.). *Interculturalidad y Educación desde el Sur*. Ecuador: Universidad Politécnica Salesiana. pp. 93–130.

Echenberg, M. (2015). Paz y literatura. Imaginarios para la construcción de paz [Peace and Literature. Imaginary for peace building]. In F. Montiel & D. E. García-González (Coords.). *Manual de construcción de paz*. Mexico: Transcend/Tecnologico de Monterrey. pp. 211–236.

Enríquez, G. (2019). La formación de capacidades en la modernidad a través de la familia y la escuela [The formation of capacities during Modernity through family and school]. *Revista Latinoamericana de Estudios sobre el Cuerpo, Emoociones y Sociedad*, (29), 12–22.

Espinosa-Dulanto, M., Calderon-Berumen, F. & O'Donald, K. (2020). Nepantla Connection. In M. Cantú-Sanchez, C. De León-Zepeda, & N.E. Cantú (Eds.), *Teaching Gloria E. Anzaldua. Pedagogy and Practice for our Classrooms and Communities*. United States: The University of Arizona Press, pp. 15–32.

Figari, C. & Scribano, A. (2009). *Hacia una sociología de los cuerpos y las emociones en América Latina* [Towards a Sociology of Bodies and Emotions in Latin America]. Buenos Aires: CLACSO, Ciccus.

Foucault, M. (2001). *Defender la sociedad. Curso en el Collége de France (1975-1976)* [Defending society. Course at the Collége de France (1975-1976)]. Buenos Aires: Fondo de Cultura Económica.

Fraser, N. & Honneth A. (2003). *Redistribution or Recognition: A Political-Philosophical Exchange*. London: Verso.

Gago, V. (2018). Neo-comunidad: circuitos clandestinos, explotación y resistencias [Neo-community: clandestine circuits, exploitation and resistance]. In C. Vega, R. Martínez. & M. Paredes (Eds.), *Experiencias y vínculos cooperativos en el sostenimiento de la vida en América Latina y el sur de Europa*. Spain: Traficante de sueños. pp. 97–114.

Gálvez, D. (2020). Racismo en la Frontera [Racism on the Border]. *CIPER*. Available at: https://www.ciperchile.cl/2020/09/12/racismo-en-la-frontera/.

Gandini, L. (2020). Caravanas migrantes: de respuestas institucionales diferenciadas a la reorientación de la política migratoria [Migrant caravans: differentiated institutional responses to the reorientation of migration policy]. *REMHU, Revista Interdisciplinaria*, 28(60), 51–69.

Garcés, M. (2013). *Un mundo común* [A common world]. Spain: Ediciones Bellatera.

Honneth, A. (1997). *La lucha por el reconocimiento* [The struggle for recognition]. Spain: Critica.

Ibañez, A. M., & Rozo, S. (2020). Forced Migration and the Spread of Infectious Diseases. *SSRN Electronic Journal*. http://doi.org/10.2139/ssrn.3600649.

Irobi, E. (2006). The Philosophy of the Sea. *Worlds & Knowledges Otherwise*, 1(3), 1–14.

Laurent-Perrault, E. (2020). Arturo Alfonso Schomburg, the Quintessential Maroon: Toward an African Diasporic Epistemology. *Small Axe: A Caribbean Journal of Criticism*, 24(1 (61)), 132–141. https://doi.org/10.1215/07990537-8190674

López-Araya, S. (2017). Huellas en un cuerpo: La Prieta de Gloria Anzaldúa [Footprints on a body: La Prieta of Gloria Anzaldua]. *Cuerpos y fronteras. Temas de nuestra América*, 33(61), 161–166.

López López, L. (2019). Refusing Making. *Journal of Curriculum and Pedagogy*, 161–174. https://doi.org/10.1080/15505170.2018.1541828.

López Sáenz, M. C. (2019). Razones del Feminismo Frente a la Arrogancia de la Razón Dominante [Reasons for feminism facing the arrogance of dominant reason]. *Investigaciones fenomenológicas*, (16), 233–257.

Lozano, B. (2018). No adónde va, sino de dónde viene [Not where it goes, but where it comes from]. In Jauregui, G. (Ed.), *Tsunami*. Mexico: Sexto Piso. pp. 101–117.

Moreira, A., Rodríguez, M. & Malo, M. (2018). Aquelarres de resistencia. Una conversa que busca una confluencia [Covenants of Resistance. A Conversation Seeking a Confluence]. In C. Vega, R. Martínez. & M. Paredes (Eds.), *Experiencias y vínculos cooperativos en el sostenimiento de la vida en América Latina y el sur de Europa*. Spain: Traficante de sueños. pp. 97–114.

Naciones Unidas. (2020) *Informe de políticas: La educación durante la COVID-19 y después de ella* [Policy brief: Education during COVID-19 and beyond]. August 2020. Available at: https://www.un.org/sites/un2.un.org/files/policy_brief_-_education_during_covid-19_and_beyond_spanish.pdf.

Nuño, A. (2020) Irreverent Pedagogies. In M. Cantú-Sanchez, C. De León-Zepeda, & N.E. Cantú (Eds.), *Teaching Gloria E. Anzaldua. Pedagogy and Practice for our Classrooms and Communities*. United States: The University of Arizona Press. pp. 59–74.

Organización Internacional para las Migraciones. (2021). *World Migration Report 2020*. Available at: https://worldmigrationreport.iom.int/wmr-2020-interactive/?lang=EN.

Pérez Rosales, V. (1923) *Ensayo sobre Chile* [Essay on Chile]. Editor General Rafael Sagredo Baeza. Santiago: Cámara de la Construcción.

Ramírez. M. T. (2017). El cuerpo por sí mismo. De la fenomenología del cuerpo a laontología del ser corporal [The Body by Itself. From the Phenomenology of the Body toan Ontology of the Embodied Self]. *Open Insight*, *VIII*(14), 49–68.

Rivera Cusicanqui, S. (2018). *Un mundo ch'ixi es posible. Ensayos desde un presente en crisis* [A Ch'ixi World is Possible. Essays from a Present in Crisis]. Buenos Aires: Tinta Limón.

Rosas, C. (2018). Mujeres migrantes en el cuidado comunitario. Organización, jerarquías y disputas al sur de Buenos Aires [Migrant women in community care. Organization, hierarchies and disputes in the South of Buenos Aires]. In C. Vega, R. Martínez, & M. Paredes (Eds.), *Experiencias y vínculos cooperativos en el sostenimiento de la vida en América Latina y el sur de Europa*. Spain: Traficante de sueños. pp. 299–321.

Salazar, S. (2019). Caravanas, migrantes y desplazados: experiencias y debates en torno a las formas contemporáneas de movilidad humana [Caravans, migrants and displaced persons: experiences and debates around contemporary forms of human mobility]. *Iberoforum. Revista de Ciencias Sociales de la Universidad Iberoamericana*, *XIV*(27).

Scribano, A. (2009). A modo de epílogo. ¿Por qué una mirada sociológica de los cuerpos y las emociones? [As an epilogue. Why a sociological look at the bodies and emotions?]. In A. Scribano, & C., Fígari (Comp.), *Cuerpo(s), Subjetividad(es) y Conflicto(s) Hacia una sociología de los cuerpos y las emociones desde Latinoamérica*. Buenos Aires: CLACSO-CICCUS. pp. 141–151.

_____. (2016). La Sociología de los Cuerpos y las Emociones en América Latina a través del GT26 de la Asociación Latinoamericana de Sociología ALAS [The Sociology of Bodies and Emotions in Latin America through the GT26 of the Latin American Sociology Association ALAS]. *Espacio Abierto. Cuaderno Venezolano de Sociología*, *25*(4), 159–168.

Scribano, A. & De Sena, A. (2020). The New Heroes: Applause and Sensibilities in the Era of the COVID-19. *Culture e Studi del Sociale*, *5*(1), 273–285.

Scribano, A. & Korstanje, M. (2020) *Imagining the Alterity: The Position of the Other in the Classic Sociology and Anthropology*. Nueva York: Nova Science Publishers.

Scribano, A., & Roche Cárcel, J. (2020). Cuerpos y emociones en riesgo en el Siglo XXI. Presentación [Bodies and Emotions at Risk in the 21st Century. Presentation]. *Empiria. Revista de metodología de ciencias sociales*, 47, 15–19. Available at: http://revistas.uned.es/index.php/empiria/article/view/27443/21414.

Segato, R. (2016). *La guerra contra las mujeres* [The war on women]. Spain: Traficantes de sueños.

Segna, J. (2020). *La situación de los migrantes en América Latina en el contexto del COVID-19* [The situation of migrants in Latin America in the context of COVID-19] PNUD, 19 May 2020. Available at: https://www.latinamerica.undp.org/content/rblac/es/home/blog/2020/la-situacion-de-los-migrantes-en-america-latina-en-el-contexto-d.html.

Taylor, Charles. (1993). *El multiculturalismo y la política de reconocimiento*. Mexico: Fondo de Cultura Economica.

Tijoux, M. E. (Ed.) (2016). *Racismo en Chile: la piel como marca de la inmigración* [Racism in Chile: the skin as mark of immigration. Santiago: Editorial Universitaria.

Tijoux, M. E. (2020). Racismo chileno en tiempos de pandemia [Chilean racism in times of pandemic]. *Le Monde Diplomatique*. June 2020. Available at: https://www.lemondediplomatique.cl/2020/06/racismo-chileno-en-tiempos-de-pandemia.html.

Tijoux, M. E. & Riveros, J. (2019). Cuerpos inmigrantes, cuerpos ideales. El racismo y la educación en la construcción de la identidad [Immigrant bodies, ideal body. Racism and education in the construction of identity]. *Estudios Pedagógicos*, 45(3), 397–405.

Tres, J. & Rodríguez, M. (2020). Migrantes y COVID-19: ¿Qué están haciendo los países de América Latina con más migrantes para apoyarlos durante la pandemia? [Migrants and COVID-19: What are Latin American countries doing with more migrants to support during the pandemic?]. *Banco Interamericano de Desarrollo. La maleta abierta*. Available at: https://blogs.iadb.org/migracion/es/migrantes-y-covid-19-que-estan-haciendo-los-paises-de-america-latina-con-mas-migrantes-para-apoyarlos-durante-la-pandemia/.

Vega, C., Martínez, R. & Paredes, M. (2018). Introducción. In Experiencias, ámbitos y vínculos cooperativos para el sostenimiento de la vida. [Experiences, areas and cooperative links for sustaining life]. In C. Vega, R. Martínez, & M. Paredes (Eds.), *Cuidado, comunidad y común. Experiencias cooperativas en el sostenimiento de la vida*. Spain: Traficante de sueños. pp. 15–49.

Xón Riquiac, M.J. (2020). Chi uwach loq'alaj q'ij saq. The Sacred Existing in Knowing/Learning from Space/Time. In L. López López, & G. Coello (Eds.), *Indigenous Futures and Learnings Taking Place*. New York: Routledge. pp. 56–77.

Zapata, C. (2005). Origen y función de los intelectuales indígenas [Origin and role of indigeneous intellectuals]. *Cuadernos Interculturales*, 3(4), 65–87.

Index

16th century 45, 98
19th century 37–38, 45, 98, 101–103
20th century 45, 79–84, 90, 98–106
21st century 36–52, 98, 107
Abiayala 41, 136–139, 143, 147–152
academics 104, 138–143, 151; challenges 126; development 18–22, 28, 121; gaps 17; opportunities 32, 88; skills 26; years 66, 73
accumulation: of injustices 104; of migratory experiences 99
adaptation 73, 90–91
adolescents 20, 42, 91, 117, 119, 124, 143
advancement 66, 70–72, 83, 89
Advancement Via Individual Determination, *see* AVID
aesthetics 11, 40, 42, 46–52
AFJROTC (Airforce Junior Reserve Officer's Training Corps) 72–74
African 6, 10–13, 23–24, 37, 49, 81
African American 60, 62, 72
aggression 123–131
agrarian conflicts 99, 104–105
agriculture 59, 100
Airforce Junior Reserve Officer's Training Corps, *see* AFJROTC
airlines 42
Amazon 25, 30
American culture 20
American Indian 60–62
ancestors 3, 13
ancestral festivals 23
ancestral knowledge 29, 42, 44
ancestral practices 13
ancestral traditions 40, 52
Andean city 81, 94
Andean history 83

Andean region 82
Andes 80, 82
antiblackness 9–10, 12, 22, 45
Anzaldúa, Gloria 139–140, 145, 149, 151
Argentina 141, 150
Asistencia Social y Capacitación para Hortalizas de la Subsecretaría de Asuntos Indígenas 99
assimilation 6, 38, 43–44, 50–51, 79, 81, 91
assymetry 128–129
asymmetrical behavior 101
asymmetrical power 41, 45
authentic narratives 63
autonomy 90, 106, 130–131, 142
AVID (Advancement Via Individual Determination) 70

Back-to-School Tailgate Party 62
barbarians 43
barbarism 37, 45
Barbie dolls 46–49
Beijing Agreement 112
Belém do Pará 111
beliefs 30, 40, 42, 52, 104, 119
belonging 25, 31, 41, 122, 126
belongings 120
Berlin 92
bilingual 17, 60, 68–69
bilingualism 59
biographies 80, 124, 128, 131
Black girl 1–13
Black people 9, 21, 27
Black presence 9
blackness 27
Boff, Leonardo 139, 144, 146, 149
Bolivia 43

Bolivians 150
borderlands 149
borders 3–6, 12, 36–37, 43, 68, 82, 98–100, 106–107, 109, 113, 137, 140
Boston 109
boundaries 70, 101, 137, 139
Brigadas Nacionales de Búsqueda de Personas Desaparecidas (National Brigades for the Search of Disappeared Persons) 117, 120
Brujas Migrantes (Migrant Witches) 147–148
bureaucratic 43

Calderón, [Felipe] 119
campesinos 103, 123, 126
Cañar 80
canons 18, 47–48
capitalism 50, 125, 136, 140, 142
Cariamanga 85
Caribbean 11, 24, 38
Catholics 103
CEDAW (Convention on the Elimination of All Forms of Discrimination against Women) 111–112
CEDH (State Human Rights Commission) 110
Central Americans 100, 102, 106
Central Independiente de Obreros Agrícolas y Campesinos, *see* CIOAC
Central University 86
Chamula 102
Chapultenango 107–113
Chenalhó 106
Chiapa de Corzo 108, 110
Chiapanecans 106
Chiapas 98–113, 118–120, 126
Chiapas State Environmental Prosecutor's Office, *see* PAECH
Chicago 107
Chicago School 82
Chichonal 107–110
children 12, 36–38, 41–51, 59–61, 64–65, 69, 73–75, 80, 86, 88, 90–92, 101–102, 105–110, 113, 117, 124, 136–137, 143–151
Chile 7, 11, 36–52, 143
Chilean identity 43–44
Chilean Ministry of National Education 51
Chimba, La 11, 37

Chocó 24–25, 31
Christian American family 20
Christian city 37
Christian obligation 101
Christianization 101
Chujes 100
Church 101, 103
CIOAC (Central Independiente de Obreros Agrícolas y Campesinos) 103
citizens 19, 25, 32–33, 38, 43, 84, 87, 110, 148
citizenship 43, 62
civilian population 120
civilization 30, 37, 84
civilizing view 43
clandestine clinics 150
clandestine graves 117
class, social 38, 79, 81–88, 119, 126
classes, school 20–21, 25–30, 46, 63, 67–70, 72–73
classification 37–39, 45
classism 44
classmates 23–24, 49, 70–72, 91
classrooms 9, 11, 46–49, 63, 113, 143, 149–151
CMDPDH (Mexican Commission for the Defense and Promotion of Human Rights) 118
CNDH (Comisión Nacional de Derechos Humanos) 118
Coalition for the Defense of the Migrant and the American Friends Service Committee 126
coexistence 40, 45, 52, 111, 123, 130, 141–142, 151
coffee production 98, 102–103
cognitive development 44
cognitive justice 40, 49–51
Cold War 87
Colegio de Bachilleres de Chiapas 112
Colegio de Naturales 43
collaboration 5, 121, 146
collective creation 6–13
collective cultural mechanisms 108
collective encounter 127
collective growth 114
collective labor 3
collective memory 40
collective objectives 126
collective practices 44, 104–105
collective self 7

collectives 3, 7, 117–125, 129, 131, 147; *see also* Brujas Migrantes
Colombia 3, 7, 17–33, 43, 46–47
Colombian Ministry of Culture 32
Colombian Ministry of Education 17
colonial apparatus 5–9, 41, 137
colonial capitalism 50
colonial context 43
colonial cultural patterns 5–9, 17, 105
colonial name 3, 5
colonial period 38, 100, 103
colonial settlement 81
coloniality 4, 37
colonization 101
colonizing discourses 17
colonizing perspectives 23, 32
colonizing practices 21
colony 99, 101
Comisión Mexicana de Defensa y Promoción de los Derechos Humanos, *see* CMDPDH
Comisión Nacional de Derechos Humanos, *see* CNDH
communal mandate 105
communality 121–131
Coneval, *see* National Council for the Evaluation of Social Development Policy
Confederación de Trabajadores de México, *see* CTM
construction of meaning 124
construction of mobility 93
consumerism 141
consumerist society 128
Convention on the Elimination of All Forms of Discrimination against Women, *see* CEDAW
cosmovisions 40, 45, 52
countryside 38, 82, 84, 126
crime 98, 113, 118–120, 123, 128–130
criminality 124
criminals 120–124, 129, 136
crisis 87–92, 107, 126, 136
Critical Race Theory 63
CTM (Confederación de Trabajadores de México) 103
Cuenca 80, 84
curricular materials 44, 150
curricular unit 21, 25, 29
curriculum 20–21, 33, 38, 67, 73, 112
customary law 102
customs 30, 43, 103–106, 112–113

dances 10, 44, 73, 142
death 12, 40, 89, 123, 125
dehumanization 22, 45
democracy 12, 17, 25, 31, 33, 45, 50, 125–126, 128, 131
democratic logic 39
democratic transitions 124
denaturalization 127
deportation 43, 68, 109, 136, 138
descent 11, 18, 49
dialects 60
diaspora 4, 8–10, 24, 61, 107
dignity 4, 7, 13, 110, 112, 126, 136, 138, 148
disasters 99, 108, 117
discipline 36, 45–46, 51
discrimination 19–32, 59–74, 91, 102, 108–112, 137–140, 142, 145, 149, 152
displaced people 118–129
dispossession 23, 104, 123, 126, 141
diversity 20–25, 29–31, 45, 98, 139, 143, 148–149
dominance 8, 31, 148
domination 9, 28–30, 41, 79, 101, 103, 128, 139–144
Dominican Republic 43

Earth 6–7, 40–41, 50–52, 122–125
ecology 50
ecology of knowledge 37, 40
economy 24, 98, 100, 102–103, 123, 150
ecosystems 41, 50
Ecuador 3, 7, 10, 79–94
El Naranjo, *see* Naranjo, El
elite bilingualism 59
elites 37, 81–87, 117
emigration 79, 86, 90–94
empowerment 49, 112–113
English language 8, 17, 20, 151
enslaved peoples 23–24
enslavement 136
environmental regulations 110
equality 13, 21–22, 98, 104, 112
equity 21–22, 25, 31–33, 50, 72, 98, 112
ethnicity 22, 27, 29, 60, 63, 71, 110
Eurocentrism 37, 41, 49–50
Europe 9, 50, 81, 88
European expansion 98
European perspectives 3, 6, 40, 45, 48, 83

existentialism 3, 40
exploitation 5, 23, 100, 113, 124, 136, 140–141, 149–152
expulsion 141
EZLN (Zapatista Army of Liberation), see Zapatista movement

Facebook 3, 111
fairness 22, 25, 29, 31, 33, 139
farmworkers 59–61, 66, 71–75
Federal Environmental Prosecutor's Office (Profepa) 110
Florida 10, 59–75
Florida Department of Education 59–62
folkloric clothing 73
food 6, 8, 24, 26, 63–64, 72–73, 105, 107, 120, 142, 144–145, 148
foreign languages 17, 33, 59, 130
foreigners 42, 139, 150
Francisco León 107–108
freedom 12–13, 41, 101, 141

gender 11, 21, 26, 101, 105–106, 119, 128, 139
gender awareness 113
gender equity 106, 112
gender-based violence 111
General Law of Victims 119
General Secretariat of the State Government 110
global dynamics 36
globalization 30, 83, 98–100, 114, 131
government 17–19, 21, 32–33, 79, 83, 87, 99, 101, 104–106, 110, 119, 124–125
grandchildren 12, 107
Guadalajara 108
Guatemala 7, 12, 100
Guatemalans 98, 102
Guayaquil 80, 84
Guerrero 61, 68, 118–120, 126
Gunas 5–7

Haiti 42–43, 46–47
Haitians 7, 42
health 110–111, 120, 136
healthcare 11–12, 18, 32, 117, 138, 146, 150
hegemonic
hegemony 22, 41, 44, 47–51, 117, 120
heritage 11, 43, 145

hierarchy 18, 20, 22, 37, 51, 84–85, 93
Hispanic male-chauvinist paradigm 101
Hispanics 69, 71
historical memory, see memory
historization 127
Hmong 72–73
homogenization 44–45, 51
hostilities 125
Huitiupán 102–103
human rights 98, 110–113, 118–121, 124–126, 128, 131
human rights violations 117, 127, 129
human trafficking 98, 113
Humanitarian Return Plan 42
humanitarianism 124, 136
hydroelectric projects 100–104

ideology 36, 39, 79, 141
idividualization 123–124
IDMC (International Displacement Monitoring Centre) 118
illegality 44
imaginaries 84, 87, 93
imaginations 7, 10, 82
IMER (Instituto Mexicano del Exterior) 109
immigrant experience 91, 140
immigrants 9, 11, 38, 42, 69, 89, 136
immigration 37–38, 42, 63, 68, 94
imperialism 7–8, 17
imprisonment 45, 104
inclusivity 7, 22, 33
India 98
Indians 13, 60–62
Indigeneity 60
Indigenous Consultation Agreement 169
Indigenous languages 30, 60, 69, 100
Indigenous people 5, 7, 12, 41, 48, 100, 102, 105, 113, 126
Indigenous University 109
INEGI (National Institute of Statistics and Geography) 101
inequalities 8, 12, 36, 42, 63, 80, 83–84, 93, 124–125, 137–138
inequities 18, 151
inferiority18, 23, 31, 37, 45, 137
infrastructure 101, 105–106, 150
injustices 8, 36, 50, 61, 63, 73–74, 104, 122, 138, 151
Institute of Mexicans Abroad 109

institutional framework 38
Instituto Mexicano del Exterior, *see* IMER
Instituto Nacional para la Evaluación de la Educación 101
integration 43, 83, 104, 127, 130
interculturality 21–22, 25
International Displacement Monitoring Centre, *see* IDMC
International Organization for Migration, *see* IOM
intersectionality 128
intersubjectivity 141–142, 146, 148, 152
IOM (International Organization for Migration) 136
isolation 81, 100, 148
Italy 80
Itzantún 103–104

Jaltecos 100
journalism 86
justice 40, 49, 50–51, 104, 124, 127, 131, 139, 149

Kakchiqueles 100
Kanjobales 100
kindergarten 66–67
knowledges 6, 31, 137, 145, 148, 150

La Chimba, *see* Chimba, La
labor-income gap 101
Lacandones 100
language ideologies 60
language proficiency 29
LatCrit 63
Latinization 60
Law on Violence against Women 112
legal codes 104
legal system 43
legality 44
Leticia 25
LGTBI community 31
liberation 104–105
linguistic groups 104
linguistic resources 73
literacy 6, 101, 107–109
Los Altos 102–104, 112
Los Angeles 107

machismo 103
Madrid 90–93, 147

male-chauvinist paradigm 101
Mames 100
Mapocho river 11, 37
Mapuche 43
marginalization 21, 31, 33, 37, 99–102, 111, 117, 130
Massachusetts 109
Mayans 100, 102
Medellín 17–24
mejorar 83
memory 19, 111, 117, 124, 129
Mequé 109
mestizos 18, 23, 79, 81, 102–103, 110–111
Mexican Americans 61
Mexican Commission for the Defense and Promotion of Human Rights, *see* CMDPDH
Mexicans 61, 71, 98, 109
Miami 82, 107
Michigan 10, 64–67
Michoacán 118, 120, 126
middle class, *see* class, social
Migrant Advocates 60, 64
Migrant Education Program 59–62
Migrant Witches, *see* Brujas Migrantes
migrating person 139, 142–143, 148
migration studies 82
migratory chains 81
military 17, 43, 51, 74
millenary Nasa sense-thoughts 40
Ministry of the Interior and Public Security of Chile 42
missionaries 104
mobile selves 82
mobilization 104, 113, 128
Mochós 100
modernity 37, 83–84, 101
modernization 79, 102
monoculture 20, 37, 50
monolingualism 18, 60, 62, 104, 108
Mother Earth, *see* Earth
multiculturalism 18, 32, 72

NAFTA (North American Free Trade Agreement) 98
Náhuatl 60, 68–69
Naranjo, El 108–109
narratives 63, 88–89, 103, 108, 118, 123–124, 144, 147, 149–150
Nasa 40
National Bilingual Plan 17

National Brigades for the Search of Disappeared Persons, *see* Brigadas Nacionales de Búsqueda de Personas Desaparecidas
National Council for the Evaluation of Social Development Policy (*Coneval*) 100, 109
National Guard 129
National Human Rights Commission, *see* CNDH
national identity 43–44, 79
National Institute for Educational Evaluation, *see* Instituto Nacional para la Evaluación de la Educación
National Institute of Statistics and Geography, *see* INEGI
national projects 43, 83, 104
nationalism 13, 44
nation-states 41–42, 50, 79, 82–83
natural disasters, *see* disasters
Nature 40, 52, 125, 145–146
Needs and Objectives for Migrant Advancement and Development, *see* NOMAD
neocolonial system 5, 117
neoliberalism 83, 88–90, 93, 98, 123
Nepantla spaces 149–151
New Jersey 82
new others 42–43
New York 107
NOMAD (Needs and Objectives for Migrant Advancement and Development) program 66
non-profit organization 62
normalization 36, 44–45, 119, 126, 138, 140–141, 148
normative [linguistic] codes 18
normative education 11
normative standardizations 121
North American Free Trade Agreement, *see* NAFTA
North Carolina 65, 67
Nuevo Carmen Tonapac 108, 110
Nuevo Guayabal 112

Oaxaca 118, 120, 126
Oaxacans 106
obligation 101
Ocosingo 106
Ohio 67
Okeechobee 65
oppression 18, 23, 61, 63, 73, 149, 151

organized crime, *see* crime
organized violence 117
otherness 36–38
Oxchuc 106

Pachamama 41, 50
PAECH (Chiapas State Environmental Prosecutor's Office) 110
paisa 23
partnerships 74
patriotic rituals 44
patriotic symbols 43
peasant movement 104
pedagogical intervention 21–22
pedagogical unit 25–26
pedagogy 9–10, 17–19, 33, 39–41, 128, 139, 148
pedagogy of care 139, 148–152
Pedagogy of Mother Earth 41
performances 46–47, 62
periphery 84–85
persecution 104, 118–125, 129–130
Peru 11–12, 43, 83
Peruvians 38, 82
phenotypes 32, 42
philosophy 3, 8, 10, 20, 139
pluriversity 40
poetry 3–4, 12, 150
police 129
policy 5, 60, 75, 109
political membership 126
politics 105, 123–125, 128, 136
polleros 106
polygamy 102
popular knowledge 44
postcolonial context 83
postcolonial State 83
poverty 89, 98–101, 109–113
powerlessness 126–128
precarization 117, 137–138, 149
pre-Hispanic economies 101
prestige 84–88
privatization 123
privilege 17–18, 26–32, 38, 60, 85–86, 131
Profepa, *see* Federal Environmental Prosecutor's Office
professionalization 81, 89
progress 27, 37, 100, 112, 121, 128, 137
proselytism 104
protection 5, 7, 41, 111, 117, 119–122, 127, 130

Protestants 103–104
public schools 36, 38, 50, 70
public space 85
pueblear 4, 11, 13–14
punishment 39, 45, 136–137, 149

Quechua 37
Querétaro 61
Quibdó 23–25
Quiche 145
quinceañeras 74
Quito 80, 84, 86–90

race 22, 26–27, 63, 72, 82, 119, 126, 128, 137, 140
racialization 42, 49, 62, 91
racism 8–9, 12, 22–23, 45–47, 60, 91, 119, 136–140, 149
rationality 13, 118, 123, 130, 146
regimes 44, 80, 83, 120, 131
Regional Conference on the Protection of Displaced Persons and Refugees 119
regulations 110
relationality 4, 6, 40
religion 43, 147
relocation 107–110
remittances 98, 107, 113
resistance 8, 12, 25, 45–51, 73–74, 118, 120–123, 126, 129
restoration 8, 120, 131
reverse racism 60
rights, *see* human rights
risk 13, 90, 94, 112–113, 120, 122–125, 127, 129, 131, 137
Riviera Maya 108
Romania 88
rural areas 18, 24–25, 61, 79
rural economy 102
rural migration 7
rural population 7, 62, 81, 85, 99, 105

safety 24, 41, 113, 127
San Cristóbal de las Casas 104, 106, 109
San Francisco 107
San Luis Potosí 61
Santiago de Chile 36–38, 47–49
scholarships 18–23, 87, 109, 112
Science, Technology, Engineering, and Math, *see* STEM
segregation 9, 37

self-transformation 84, 90–91
sexuality 22
Sierra Region 106
Simojovel 102–104
Sinaloa 120
skin color 23, 27, 31–32, 37, 42, 46–49, 70, 140, 145
skin tone, *see* skin color
Social Assistance and Training Program for Vegetable Gardens of the Undersecretary of Indigenous Affairs, *see* Asistencia Social y Capacitación para Hortalizas de la Subsecretaría de Asuntos Indígenas
social class, *see* class, social
social fabric 124, 147
social mobility 60, 79–93
social networks 107, 109, 111–113
social status 18, 27
socialization 4, 24, 41, 45
sociology 82, 141–142, 144, 148
Soconusco 102
solidarity 106, 108, 117, 124, 129–130, 148–151
South Carolina 109
sovereignty 43
Soviet Union 87
Spain 80, 90, 92
Spanish empire 101
Spanish fluency 74
standardization 47, 51, 121, 123
State Human Rights Commission, *see* CEDH
State Police 129
state violence 121, 130
STEM (Science, Technology, Engineering, and Math) 70
stereotypes 30–31, 46, 127, 137, 150
stigmatization 119
studies abroad 87–88
subalternity 82, 85
subjectivation 124
subjectivity 20–22, 27, 39, 82–83, 90–94, 128, 142
subjugation 101, 124
Subtractionist policies 59
superiority 27, 31–32, 37, 137
surveillance 119
survival 8, 10, 43, 50, 120–121, 131, 147

Tamaulipas 118, 120
technocratic pedagogy 39
Tecpatán 108
Tejanos 61
Tenorio Caicedo, Jenny 3–4
territorial belonging 126
territorial dislocation 129
territorial hierarchies 93
territorial limits 82
territoriality 40–41, 81
testimonies 10, 27, 86–89, 106, 117–131, 149
testimonios 59–75
Tojolabales 100
totaliterarian education 123
tradition 13, 20, 31, 37, 40, 45, 50, 52, 72–74, 79, 82, 87, 108–109, 112, 120, 136, 145
traditional modes of education 128, 131
trans-territoriality, *see* territoriality
transformation 9, 19–33, 43, 83–86, 90–91, 98–114, 122, 127–128, 141, 149–150
translanguaging 73
transmigration 98–99, 108
transnational connections 81, 87
transnational migrations 80
transnational space 89, 93
transnational studies 82
travel 11–12, 23, 28, 42, 66, 68–69, 87–88, 92, 106, 109
Tseltal 5, 99–113
Tsotsiles 5, 99–113
Tuxtla Gutiérrez 108

UNICEF [United Nations International Children's Emergency Fund] 42, 101
United Nations Secretary General on Internally Displaced Persons 120

United States 21, 32, 68–69, 98–99, 102, 105–109, 113, 143
university 24, 29, 32, 84–89, 106–107, 109–110, 143
urban remodeling 37
urbanization 79, 93

values 43, 149; 'civilized' 126; cosmopolitan 87; Indigenous 74; totaliterarian 123
Van Buren Migrant Program, *see* NOMAD
Venezuela 7, 43
Veracruz 118, 120
verbal journeys 63
vernacular 45
viceroyalty 101
victimization 124–125
Vicuña Mackenna, Benjamín 37
violence 12, 25, 45, 102–103, 106, 111–112, 117–131, 137–144, 148, 152
visibilization 127
vulnerability 125, 128, 138, 150

Western perspectives 47, 50–51, 81, 83, 118, 130, 137, 139
WhatsApp 111
women's liberation 104

xenoantagonism 13, 138
xenophobia 44, 119
Xón Riquiac, María Jacinta 145

Zapatista movement 103–105, 113
Zomés 109
Zoques 99–113

Printed in the United States
by Baker & Taylor Publisher Services